EILEEN GRAY

ARCHITECT | DESIGNER

EILEEN GRAY

ARCHITECT|DESIGNER

A BIOGRAPHY

PETER ADAM

Thames and Hudson

Project Director: Andreas Landshoff
Editor: Phyllis Freeman
Designer: Katy Homans with Bethany Johns
Photo Research: Barbara Lyons

CONTENTS

Pour créer, il faut d'abord remettre tout en question.

To create, one must first question everything.—Eileen Gray

The future projects light, the past only shadows.—Eileen Gray

Les poètes eux-mêmes ne pourraient écrire leur propre vie. Il y a trop de mystères, trop de vrais mensonges, trop d'enchevêtrement. Les dates se chevauchent, les années s'embrouillent.

Even poets cannot write their own life story. There are too many mysteries, too many true lies, too many entanglements. Dates become confused, years blur into one another.
                                        —Cocteau, *Opium*

Errata

Page 58   Delete "Possibly by Sugawara" at the end of the caption

Page 62   The last line of the caption should read:
           "Frame possibly by Sugawara"

Page 283   The photograph is reproduced upside down

Page 285   The first line of the caption should read:
           "The black-tiled sunbed with a small metal table
           which has a built-in hotplate at the center."

Page 373   The missing caption should read:
           "Exhibition at the Monika Kinley Gallery in London in
           1979 with Eileen's cork screen, an occasional table,
           a rug, and gouaches"

INTRODUCTION

I met Eileen Gray for the first time in 1960. She was eighty-two years old. This woman who is now regarded as a pioneer of modern design, and in the twenties and thirties was celebrated in architectural circles, was then totally forgotten. No magazine, no book spoke about her work; no one bought her furniture. Honed down by illness and age, she led the life of a recluse, a situation which suited her temperament. The only person sharing her solitary life was her faithful housekeeper, Louise Dany, who had joined Eileen in 1927 at the age of nineteen.

On November 8, 1972, at the famous Paris auction house of the Hôtel Drouot, where a sale was scheduled of Art Deco furniture belonging to the late dress designer and art collector Jacques Doucet, one curious item was listed in the catalogue: "GRAY (Eileen). Le Destin. 4-panel screen in lacquer decorated with figures in green and silver on a red background." When this lacquer screen fetched the stupendous price of over thirty-six thousand dollars, newspapers for the first time in thirty-five years carried the name of Eileen Gray—in *Le Figaro*, in *Le Monde*, in the London *Times* and the *Herald Tribune*. Collectors and a few art historians took notice. People started to look for her furniture as they did for Jacques-Emile Ruhlmann's or Jean Dunand's. The search for the mysterious Eileen Gray began. Here and there a few of her pieces had surfaced and were eagerly bought up by collectors, among them Yves Saint Laurent; Eileen Gray was suddenly fashionable again. Not that it made any difference to her. "C'est absurde," she used to say, and she continued to take her meals alone as she had done for the last thirty years of her life. Her only contacts with the outside world were two or three friends, who formed a kind of lifeline; people to whom she could unburden herself of the daily problems of a life made increasingly difficult by illness and old age.

In the last six years of her life there were exhibitions of her work in Paris, London, Los Angeles, Brussels, Vienna, and New York. But Eileen would not attend any of the official openings. When she was to be awarded honorary titles in London and her native Ireland, she would send friends to represent her at the ceremonies.

On November 5, 1976, she was buried at a quiet ceremony, without music or eulogies. Her ashes were laid to rest in the presence of three friends. I know this would have suited her very well.

Shortly before her death she burned almost all the letters and photographs that concerned her personal life. The discretion she had manifested all her life prevented her from leaving any traces, except in her work. It was there that she wanted her passions and preoccupations to be read. She demanded no posthumous renown. If she received it nevertheless, it was due to the strength of her work and the originality of the ideas it expressed. The absence of almost any information about her life has made her into a kind of cult figure, a role she never intended to play and one she would have wholeheartedly rejected.

Eileen Gray would not have approved of this book. She was never tempted to write her own biography; she shied away from any personal revelations. She might have accepted a few words about her work, although she would have thought them "unnecessary." That I, despite all this, have decided to write this book is not to betray a trust and a warm friendship, but to dispel much of the rumor, the numerous errors and speculations which have grown up around her name. It is also to make some order in the notes and letters she left to me and to recall the conversations and the many happy hours we spent together in Paris, London, and the south of France. She would have scolded me for making this public, but she would not have prevented me from doing so.

To try to recount Eileen's life is not an easy task. Most of the protagonists have disappeared and can no longer be questioned. When she was born, Queen Victoria was still on the throne, and when she died, almost a hundred years old, men had flown to the moon. All we can do is to piece together a few memories, to reanimate the souvenir of a life, which by all accounts, and in the truest sense of the word, was extraordinary.

The major source for this book was Eileen Gray herself. When we gathered her belongings after her death, I found scraps of papers, photographs, some torn-out pages of an old address book, the sales ledger of her shop, some work notes, quite a few architectural drawings, and much of the remnant paraphernalia of her personal life. All the words in quotation marks—if not otherwise attributed—are her own. They are based on surviving letters and personal conversations. My own notes about our many meetings were meant entirely for my own use; I never intended to publish them. She was for me foremost a friend, not a public person. Much of our conversation dealt with the present and the many banal happenings of daily life, such as replacing a blown fuse, not with her thoughts on the Bauhaus. Questions I now would have liked to have asked were never put to her. In any case, being more interested in other people's lives than in her own, she was never easily questioned. She was a reluctant and not always reliable witness. She did not like to look into the past (which in any case was blurred) and least of all into her own.

Acquaintances had only vague recollections of her. She had outlived most people's memories. Many details were filled in by Louise Dany. But the most formidable help came from her niece, Prunella Clough, Eileen's only true and lasting friend. A distinguished artist herself, she was able to share many of Eileen's preoccupations, thoughts, and worries. To both Louise and Prunella, I am bound in friendship and gratitude.

Some information was taken from the biographies and autobiographies of Eileen Gray's contemporaries during her early years in Paris.

I have purposely refrained from probing too deeply into the private lives of those who were at times her most intimate friends. In most lives there are areas which people like to keep to themselves and which have little bearing on their work. The right to privacy applies to the artist too.

I would like to thank my friend and publisher Andreas Landshoff, who suggested the book to me and never lost faith in the whole precarious endeavor, and Paul Gottlieb, president of Harry N. Abrams, who had the courage to bring it out. And my editor, Phyllis Freeman, who, totally unfrazzled, curbed the many excesses of my language and who always knew where Apollinaire was at a certain time and when a subjunctive is not a subjunctive. I would also like to thank Jan Vandenweghe for having made available his study of Eileen Gray's houses, which has been a valuable source of information.

Robin Symes and Christo Michaelides generously provided photographs of their collection. Further material was provided by Philippe Garner of Sotheby's London.

As for P. and F., I have no other way to show my affection and gratitude than to dedicate the book to them.

EARLY YOUTH

Eileen's parents:
James Maclaren Smith
and Eveleen Pounden
Gray

Eileen's family:
standing, her sister
Ethel, her father, her
brother James;
seated, her brother
Lonsdale, Eileen on
her mother's lap, and
her sister Thora

Eileen Gray was born in Ireland August 9, 1878, in the
family home, Brownswood. The elegant manor house stood
on a picturesque site on the banks of the River Slaney first
occupied by a castle. Brownswood was two miles from
Enniscorthy—in County Wexford, in the southeastern part of
Ireland—a rather obscure Norman town known for its cattle
market. From the thirteenth to the seventeenth century,
Brownswood Castle had belonged to the Brown family. In
March 1650, the Puritan governor of Wexford, Colonel
Cooke, captured the castle and, according to history,
massacred all its occupants. Today one wing of the ruined
castle can still be seen. Eileen's grandfather Captain
Jeremiah Lonsdale Pounden, a doctor, bought Brownswood
estate, with its manor house, at the beginning of the last
century for fifty-five hundred pounds (about twenty-five
thousand dollars).

Eileen's forebears on her mother's side were very
distinguished. Their peerage went back to the fifteenth
century, when the first Lord Gray was master of the
household of King James II. One of her great uncles was
postmaster general of Scotland. Her grandmother Lady Jane
Stewart, daughter of the tenth Earl of Moray, had married
Captain Pounden, and May 3, 1841, their only daughter,
Eveleen, was born.

Eveleen was certainly not a conventional child. Strong-
minded and independent, she ran off to Italy at twenty-one
with a good-looking thirty-year-old painter. James Maclaren
Smith, "from good middle-class stock," the son of Richard
Smith of Hazelgreen, was certainly not welcome as the
husband of the only daughter of this stern aristocratic
family. But they were married in 1863. In 1864, their first
son, James Maclaren Stuart, was born; two years later a girl,
Ethel Eveleen. Four years passed before they had another
child: in 1870, Lonsdale was born, followed in 1875 by
Thora Zelma Grace. And on August 9, 1878, their last
child, Kathleen Eileen Moray, was born. (In most
publications Eileen's birth date is erroneously given as 1879.
In later years Eileen herself was always very casual about

such matters. Once asked on television if she was ninety-six or ninety-seven, she simply replied: "Is there a difference?")

Eileen spent much of her childhood between London, where her parents had a townhouse in Kensington, and the old Brownswood House. She did not remember much of her grandparents; her grandmother was often ill, and another day the servants would whisper, "Her ladyship is better today."

For a while Eileen's parents kept the outward signs of respectability. She remembered them sitting silently at either end of the long dining-room table. But then her father went back to Italy, and except for a few visits, remained there for the rest of his life. So for Eileen, parental authority was represented by her mother, a woman of dominating nature and mild eccentricity. She had a rather solemn face, as if she rarely smiled; a woman whose pride was hurt through the loss of the love of her husband.

Eileen always respected her mother, but her love was for her father, with whom she often traveled and whose life must have seemed to her one of adventure and independence. If her mother instilled in Eileen good manners and a feeling for social propriety, her father taught her the love of freedom. He was tall and good-looking, with a fine nose and dark curly hair and mustache—and something of a dandy, fully aware of his powerful charm for women. Among Victorian artists, he was a minor figure who painted mostly landscapes and portraits in the Italian manner. Eileen inherited from him not only her beautiful eyes and fine nose, but also her love for art.

Growing up in a large ancient house as the youngest of five children, most of them many years older, Eileen felt lonely and unloved. Despite considerable wealth and many servants, life was far from comfortable at Brownswood. In the cold wet weather the children had to put on coats to cross the icy halls and staircases, and "even the nursery seemed never to warm up."

While Eileen's brothers and sisters drove around in a little horsedrawn cart, she would escape the nursery and go down to the beautiful River Slaney at the bottom of the grounds, or roam along the surrounding hills. In the ruins of the castle lived an old man "full of strange stories." Eileen used to go and visit him and sometimes managed to bring him some supper. On those lonely outings, withdrawing from the world of the grown-ups, she had the first inkling that life for a person of her temperament and disposition might never be

easy. She was an extremely frightened child; even toward the
end of her life, she wrote, "I have instinctive fears, fears of
ghosts, of people. This fright never left me and I have often
tried in vain to conquer it." Sometimes, the big dark house
creaking around her, she got up from her bed and quietly
put two chairs in front of her mother's door. There she slept
until dawn, when the servants found the half-frozen child.

But when the sun rose, much of her fear disappeared and
she became quite daring. She got hold of an old invalid
chair, and dragged it up the hill to race down at breakneck
speed. If fear was one side of her character, daring and
courage, often coupled with the joy of speed, was another.

Eileen longed for friendship, but lacked the skill of
enticing, managing, and conducting it. She remembered
being left behind when the others went to a ball, or being
scolded for not using a thimble. With a bit of jealousy, she
recalled watching her sister Thora being ball girl to a tennis
team of four men and receiving a beautiful silk scarf. The
shadow of her lonely childhood never left Eileen completely,
and for a long time she suffered the repercussions of a
stifling and unhappy youth.

Eileen's education, like that of most girls of her
background, was mostly private and at best sporadic.

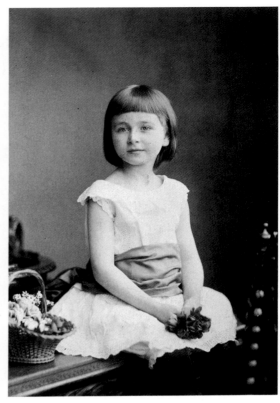

Eileen with her parents

Eileen at five

Various governesses were hired according to their manners or their compatibility with the household rather than for their intellectual ability. Eileen often regretted her lack of formal education, but she had the wit and curiosity to educate herself. She had, of course, the usual exposure to literature—nanny novels, as they were often referred to—some French and German, a bit of drawing and music. A most welcome break from these rather monotonous lessons were the trips to Germany or Italy to visit her father. Sometimes she was sent for a short while to a private school abroad. Before the First World War, the English upper classes looked to German culture and enlightenment for inspiration. It was customary to send one's children to Germany or Austria to immerse them in art and music. Eileen had a stint in a school in Dresden to perfect her understanding of music and the German language. She remembers being taken to Vienna and seeing her first opera—Wagner—hardly suitable for a child of eight. No wonder that she thought more of Vienna's castle than its opera house.

When Eileen was ten, her older sister Ethel married Henry Tufnell Campbell, the son of Lord Lindsay. Henry

was a snob, and Eileen, who never got on with Ethel,
disliked him intensely. Any manifestation of wealth or
importance was anathema to her; she considered any
ostentation vulgar. It was on Henry's instigation that the
children's name was changed. He persuaded his mother-in-
law to claim her title—Baroness Gray in the peerage of
Scotland, which she had inherited on the death of her uncle
in 1893. Eileen's father, James Maclaren Smith, received
Royal Licence to change his name to Smith-Gray and
thereafter the children were known by the name of Gray.

From early childhood on, Eileen hated the complacency
and arrogance of her class. Their pride and self-confidence
clashed with Eileen's inborn feeling of compassion and social
justice. She hardly ever made use of her title, "the
honorable," considering it suitable only really for operettas
and highly inappropriate for an architect talking to
workmen.

But worse was to come. In 1895, the beautiful old Irish
manor house was changed on Henry's initiative into what the
local press described as "a magnificent specimen of
Elizabethan architecture, with a charming parterre laid out
in faultless style; the entrance lodge, which has recently

Brownswood as it looked when Eileen was born

The house after "conversion" to nineteenth-century Tudor style

been completed, is quite a gem." Eileen hated all its pretentiousness. She kept a photograph of the beloved old house, which simply remained for her "the house," where she had lived through so many things, seen so much repressed hostility and so little tenderness. It was the destruction of her childhood home, more than anything else, that finally drove her away from her family. It had become a dead house, full of mannered, self-protective people. The old sepia-tinted photograph was all that remained with her of "the house" of her childhood.

By the middle of the 1890s, Eileen had grown into a tall striking young lady, her long auburn hair piled high on her head or hidden under a spectacular hat, giving her an air of sophistication that far exceeded her age. Most photographs reveal her feline quality and display a serenity only rarely interrupted by the blur of a smile.

The last year of the century was clouded by political events. The daily news of the Boer War preoccupied most families. Eileen's brother Lonsdale was sent to South Africa, and early in 1900 the family received the news that he had died there after drinking poisoned water. In the same year

Above: Eileen and
Thora in the French
Alps sporting—in the
snow—most
unsuitable straw
boaters; at left,
Lonsdale

Opposite, top, far
left: Eileen at about
eighteen

Opposite, top, near
left: Eileen at
Brownswood

Opposite, bottom:
James and Eileen
playing croquet

Eileen's father died, and she was much grieved. For the last
time she traveled with her family to Switzerland to bury him
at Territet, where he had lived the last few years of his life.

Most young women at that time chose marriage as the
best means to get away from their mothers and achieve some
independence, but Eileen's desire to be free was too strong to
be satisfied by the mere exchange of one kind of dependence
for another. Indeed, her passion for independence prevented
her all her life from marrying or forming any other durable
relationship. She had several affairs with men and women,
yet she never felt deeply enough to want to share a house
with any of them. Of course, for a woman of her looks and
background there were ample suitors. But Eileen, with a
certain sense of daring which was nurtured more by
stubbornness than courage, decided soon to escape the
regularity and banality of her existence and the atmosphere
of static respectability that characterized her upbringing. As
the first step in that direction, she asked her mother to allow
her to go to art school in London.

STUDENT YEARS

**Students at the Slade
School of Fine Arts,
about 1905**

**Women students at
the Slade doing
portrait studies,
spring term, 1904**

The art school a well-bred young woman would attend at the
turn of the century was the Slade School of Fine Arts,
named after a wealthy art lover, Felix Slade. It had opened
in 1871 in Gower Street, as part of the University of London
complex in the area later known as Bloomsbury. It was the
most respectable art school for ladies and gentlemen alike.
The study of art was considered a suitable pastime for ladies
from the upper and upper-middle classes, before marriage,
and in fact, the Slade had become a kind of finishing school
for girls of good families. The administration of the school
was careful to guard against any untoward influences; the
calendar for 1871 is reassuring: "It will be easy to keep
ladies' classes quite distinct from others, should it be
desirable to maintain such a separation; in any case, there
will be separate classes reserved for the exclusive use of
ladies."

By the time Eileen entered the school, in 1901, it was no
longer practical to separate the sexes and, except for the life
classes, ladies and gentlemen shared studios, but it was
strictly forbidden to talk to the models. Eileen was not, as
has often been stated, one of the first women students: she
was one of one hundred sixty-eight women; there were only
sixty men. As one can imagine, the lunch breaks, which were
largely used for "cupid hunting," became quite a worry to
the Slade authorities.

Her teachers were a distinguished trio: Henry Tonks, P.
Wilson Steer, and Frederick Brown. Frederick Brown was a
grim figure who resembled a stiff-backed army colonel more
than an artist. Paris-trained, he insisted that a drawing that
is not structural has no purpose and that the best source for
such a drawing is the study of old masters. Eileen paid seven
guineas (then about thirty-five dollars) a term to attend his
classes. Henry Tonks was younger, a fierce tall man who
used to reduce the women to tears when he became angry.
Wilson Steer was a celebrated artist who had also studied in
Paris. He was supposed to have been a terrible teacher, and
all Eileen could recall was that he would sit for hours
wearing a large overcoat in fear of the cold and the drafts.

Eileen was not impressed by the academic training of any of her teachers, who had been brought up mostly on Ruskin and the Pre-Raphaelites. Nor did she care much for the old gray atmosphere of the school, stifled by academic tradition. The dark, gloomy corridors that led to the cold studios were hung with religious paintings by former students. So one can understand that her attendance began to slacken during the two years she was enrolled there. While she first went every day, during the last term her name appears only three times a week on the daily register.

Like all students, Eileen had to attend classes in drawing from the antique. These classes were held in a huge room, where students copied plaster casts of classical sculptures, surrounded by prize works by painters like William Orpen. Eileen must have been quite good at copying because she was allowed also to paint from life, a privilege given only to proficient students, although, to be sure, the ladies' life class was at a safe distance from that for the men and only marginally tidier. (The men occupied the semibasement, whose walls were decorated with the paint scrapings of previous generations.) Students were also encouraged to copy in the National Gallery or the British Museum or even the Tate Gallery, which the Prince of Wales had officially opened three years earlier.

Visits to the museums were a must, not only for art students, but for anybody in good society, although museums now opened on Sundays, known as People's Days. One could regularly see tribes of young women demurely following a lady guide through the Elgin Marbles. Eileen watched them, distant and amused, while she explored the museums on her own. One of her favorites was the South Kensington Museum, not far from her home, which by official order of the queen, became known as the Victoria and Albert Museum in 1899. It was there that she first became interested in furniture and saw lacquer screens.

Of course, Eileen still lived at home in South Kensington, but she felt free. London was both alarming and exciting, offering the remote possibility of an adventure or an escape. In the beginning, both were only contemplated, but eventually they were taken up. Walking to school, she could observe people from all levels and occupations of life and her curiosity was sharpened. There were people on horses in the parks, and street vendors among the many music halls of the Soho district. But most of London was depressing and dismal; the long winter, with its fog and smoke-laden air, never seemed to end.

London for a woman of Eileen's upbringing consisted mostly of Chelsea and Belgravia and St. James's Park, Regent's Park, and Bloomsbury. Beyond that lay the unknown. People of different backgrounds did not mix—not even in parks. Hyde Park at the south end was aristocratic, its penny chairs thronged with the smart world, while the north side was frequented by the "populace." Eileen's favorite part was the so-called Reformers' Tree, where political firebrands, preachers, and cranks of all sorts held court. She did much walking, and sometimes took a bus rather than the traditional hansom. Omnibuses, still mostly horsedrawn, became quite popular, especially in the summer when one could sit on the open platform on the top. Of course, it was still considered bold for a young lady to venture into this hitherto exclusively male preserve. But Eileen was now more than ever determined not to be limited by conventions. She explored London, usually spending her lunchtimes in the little streets of Soho, which was then the center of the artists' world.

Her newly won freedom also meant new friends. Yet in 1900 life as a student was by no means so free as it is today; few men students mingled with the women students outside of class. But despite Eileen's shyness, which was often mistaken for an attitude of superiority, she managed to make a few friends—most of them fellow Slade students. There were the young painters Gerald Kelly and Wyndham Lewis; a young explorer, Henry Savage Landor; and two women, Kathleen Bruce and Jessie Gavin. In the years to come, all of them would meet in Paris.

TO PARIS

In 1900 Eileen had gone to Paris for the first time with her mother, a visit which had an immediate and profound influence on her life. During the first years of the century, the modern world materialized, and the place where it was most felt was Paris. The Baedeker of 1900 notes that the best time "to visit Paris is from April to June, when the elegant world goes to the sea to escape the heat. Their return does not happen before the end of October." Baedeker also advises that "in the theatre gentlemen are expected to keep their hats on until the curtain is raised."

Eileen was impressed with the generosity of the street plan of Paris, with the width of the leafy boulevards, the elegance of the shops, and the goings-on in the street, where electricity was replacing gas lamps. Everything seemed so much livelier and more carefree than in London. Everywhere there were theaters, concert halls, and variety palaces like La Scala and The Eldorado, with stars like Yvette Guilbert and Polaire. On the walls were posters of Sarah Bernhardt and the dancer Loïe Fuller, whose life in a few years' time would be linked with Eileen's.

The streets were quite crowded and the hansoms drawn by horses would soon be outnumbered by electric cars or those run on gasoline. A short portion of the Métro had been completed, but a lady would not travel on it. A fiacre was two francs (about forty cents) an hour, or one could venture on a bus drawn by three horses, which crossed the Pont Neuf and drove up the boulevard Saint-Michel. Eileen felt sorry for these poor creatures and walked rather than add to their burden. All her life she had an almost obsessive relationship with animals. She regularly looked after stray dogs or cats, and abhorred the idea of people hunting down animals. In her garden she displayed prominently the sign "Refuge d'oiseaux," and became enraged when the French, who are notable bird shooters, did not respect the sign.

Eileen and her mother had gone to Paris to see the great Universal Exhibition, which lasted for several months and covered vast areas with the Grand and Petit Palais as its center. Most countries had their own exhibition halls;

England offered a pastiche of an Elizabethan manor by Sir
Edwin Lutyens. Eileen had only begun to study art seriously
and the works of Charles Rennie Mackintosh, who had
designed the Glasgow School of Art three years earlier, were
things she knew only from hearsay. But in Paris she saw
designs by René Lalique, Eugène Grasset, and Emile Gallé,
which the three leading department stores, Le Bon Marché,
Le Louvre, and Le Printemps, had put on display.

Right from the first visit, the idea of returning to Paris
and perhaps studying there, occurred to her, and back at the
Slade, she forged a plan with her friends Kathleen Bruce and
Jessie Gavin to go there. It took persistence to persuade her
mother to give her permission, but in 1902 it was granted.

We owe much of the description of Eileen's first Paris years to Kathleen Bruce, a sculptor, later Lady Scott, the wife of Captain Robert Falcon Scott, the explorer. In 1949 she published her memoirs, *Self-Portrait of an Artist*, in which she described her early days in Paris with two friends. For reasons known only to herself, she called Eileen and Jessie Hermione and Joselyn.

> Off and away to Paris! I had two friends who thought that to go to Paris and to be an artist was a fine idea. They were both very pretty; Joselyn [Jessie] was tall and dark with dark eyes which seemed, with a sympathetic mockery, to take stock of all the meanest things in the basement of one's mind. She came, so it appeared, from a well-to-do middle-class home in the Midlands. The other lass [Eileen] was completely unlike Joselyn, and to me more lovable, though rather remote. She was fair, with wide-set, pale blue eyes, tall and of grand proportion, well-born and quaintly and beautifully dressed. But for a rather vague look and an absent-minded manner, she would have been wonderful. I thought she was wonderful and when, one night she told me that she lived her whole life in terror because there was madness in her family, I thought her not only wonderful to look at, but also the most romantic figure I had ever seen.

There was quite a lot of eccentricity in the Gray family that in those days might have been considered madness, but there was no serious psychological disorder. Eileen was indeed "the most romantic figure" to look at. Tall and always thin, she had a natural sense of style and a great liking for well-made and often expensive clothes. Having her own personal style, she never had to worry about a particular fashion. Immaculately dressed, she looked best in a well-tailored suit with a feminine silk shirt. She wore little jewelry, usually only a brooch and one ring on her beautifully manicured hands. She had a great weakness for handmade shoes and owned an enormous quantity of them. In the early years, she also had a great liking for hats, which gave her an aspect of aloof elegance. Her face was beautiful, with flawless complexion and clear blue eyes, always quizzically alert, watchful of the world. There was in her looks something of an underlying sadness, but she had a natural charm and girlish laughter that, if she wanted, could be very infectious.

Despite Haussmann's efforts to make Paris into a modern city, it was still, when Eileen arrived, an agglomeration of small villages. There were the elegant residential area around Saint-Germain, and the cheap quarters of Montmartre and

Montparnasse, where artists lived. Eileen and her two friends took lodgings in a "squalid" little pension, at 7 rue Barras, a small street not far from Montparnasse. The famous Café du Dôme was still a scruffy little place, the Coupole a workers' café, and the Sélect and Rotonde did not yet exist.

In those years many people looked to Paris as a refuge. After his release from Reading Gaol, Oscar Wilde had lived in a small hotel on the Left Bank. A twenty-one-year-old Irish writer, James Joyce, had settled briefly not far from where Eileen lived. From America came Leo Stein, soon to be followed by his sister, Gertrude. A young Polish writer, whom Eileen was to admire, had also arrived: Guglielmo-Alberto Kostrowitzky, known as Apollinaire.

The three women enrolled at the Ecole Colarossi, on the rue de la Grande Chaumière, an art school popular among foreign students. Since most students there came from abroad, many from America, contact with the French was minimal. In addition to the standard classes in drawing, painting, watercolor, and sculpture, there were special courses in costume and what was known as "decorative composition." Eileen attended drawing courses primarily. The classes stretched over the whole day, often starting at eight o'clock in the morning, but Eileen admitted she did not often attend the early ones. Soon the three women decided to change to the Académie Julian, on the rue de Dragon. Over its entrance door were written Ingres's words, "Cherchez le caractère dans la nature" and "Le dessin est la probité de l'Art." It had been founded in 1868 by a former prizefighter and artists' model, Rodolphe Julian, who was said to have known little about painting. The painter William Rothenstein described the place as "a congerie of studios crowded with students, the walls thick with palette scrapings, hot, airless and extremely noisy." The classes were crowded, and it was not always easy to find room for one's easel. But after the austerity of the Slade School, the atmosphere of the Académie Julian was bustling and exhilarating. There was very little discipline, and the classes were sometimes so noisy that one had trouble working. Most of the instructors had been trained at the official Ecole des Beaux-Arts.

Paris offered a whole new world of galleries and museums. Small galleries run by private dealers were still a rarity, one of the few exceptions being Vollard, who showed Cézanne on the rue Laffitte. His small premises always smelled of spices because Vollard, having come from the

island of Réunion, in the Indian Ocean, used to serve curries in the basement. Every spring, the huge exhibition in the Salon showed as many as five thousand works of art, and society flocked to the place de Breteuil, behind Les Invalides, to see art and to be seen doing so. In 1903 a new Salon was opened in the basement of the Petit Palais. It was the first Salon d'Automne. Its president was the architect Frantz Jourdain. It included nearly a thousand exhibits, among them examples from the decorative arts. This event was enthusiastically greeted by the leading critics of the day, Louis Vauxcelles and Claude Roger-Marx. In time, both of them were to become admirers of Eileen Gray's work. From then on the openings of the Salon d'Automne and the Salon des Indépendants were the two main social events in the art world, and there Eileen saw her first original Van Goghs, Gauguins, Seurats, Bonnards. In that year, 1902, there was a memorial exhibition of Henri de Toulouse-Lautrec, who had died the previous year in the arms of his mother.

At the Académie Julian the students talked about the group of penniless painters who regularly assembled on the rue Ravignan in Montmartre, in the building known as the Bateau-Lavoir. There was a young Dutchman, Kees van Dongen, Maurice Utrillo, and a strange melancholic Italian, Amedeo Modigliani. Eileen's interest was awakened, but the idea of seeking out any of these young and still unknown fellow artists could not have occurred to the three women. Outside art school, few people took notice of the new painters. Eileen remembered that most people were "hypnotized by Whistler," who died in London in 1903.

The Académie Julian held several *concours* each year in the form of exhibitions. The students were supposed to submit their work for judging in five categories: studio portraits, full-length figure of a woman, full-length figure of a man, torso of a woman, torso of a man. The dullness of these categories might explain somewhat Eileen's lack of interest in her studies. In 1903, in the English magazine *The Studio*, Clive Holland described the workings of French art schools:

> The life of the schools is intensely interesting, often amusing, and sometimes even tragic. The stronger natures among the girl art students will probably decide upon attending one of the mixed classes, and there they will work shoulder to shoulder with their brother art students, drawing from the costume or the living model. . . . At Colarossi's one morning there were five girls and half-a-score of men working at time sketches of a Spaniard in matador costume. . . .

Eileen must have belonged to the "stronger natures." She did enroll in the mixed classes.

Kathleen Bruce tells us:

> On the first day, passing an open door of one of the studios, I saw Hermione [Eileen] standing at the back of the room near the door. Hermione was standing composedly with her head critically on one side. At the end of the studio passed one by one, a string of nudes, male models. Each jumped for a moment onto the model throne, took a pose and jumped down. The model for the week was chosen.

And while Miss Bruce turned away feeling sick, not understanding how the lovely Hermione could stand there so calmly appraising, Eileen seemed totally undisturbed by the scene.

She was a great believer in decorum, but she despised familiarities. Conventional in her way of dealing with people, she was far from conventional and totally unshockable in sexual matters. She belonged to that enlightened generation of women who had fought very early for so-called sexual liberation, but would shy away from any personal revelations.

Only one of Eileen's student works has survived. A rather traditional life class drawing of a young woman that shows some skillful handling of the material, without being in any way distinguishable from any other student work. She may have destroyed the rest of her sketches, or they may have been lost during the Second World War along with her other art work. She had very little regard for the past and looked at her work as a painter with great critical modesty. "Painting is a life-long business," she had written later. But until the end of her life, she continued to draw or paint with sometimes remarkably beautiful results.

At the turn of the century, for an unmarried woman to go to Paris to study art was enterprising but not all that unusual. Clive Holland explains why "Paris has for many years been the Mecca of art students of both sexes. . . . English schools of painting . . . do not appear to encourage individuality, and more particularly the individuality of women," but he assures his readers that "the life they [these "lady art students"] lead there differs from that led by their male companions, both as regards its freedom and its strenuousness. . . ." Eileen and her friends, who were soon known as "les trois jolies anglaises," seem to have behaved exactly as described by Holland: "If she [the lady art student] be very independent she will eschew the *pension*,

Student work by
Eileen, age twenty-
two, about 1900

run on more or less dull or English lines, in favour of an
appartement au deuxième or *au troisième* . . . according to
her worldly wealth or lack of it. The lady art student who
lives *au première* is a *rara avis.* . . ." Kathleen, Jessie, and
Eileen did indeed take apartments. Kathleen and Jessie took
a studio together, while Eileen rented a place on the fifth
floor on the rue Bara. Life was cheap in those days; the rent
for a small furnished flat in the Saint-Germain area was one
hundred fifty to two hundred francs (thirty to forty dollars)
a month. Like all furnished flats, Eileen's was spartan in
decoration, very different from the bourgeois flats, which
were usually heavily decorated with eighteenth-century
furniture or its nineteenth-century imitations, the walls
covered in silk and velvet. There was almost no heating in

**Collage by Eileen,
age ninety-two, about
1970**

anyone's home, and very few people had a telephone. But the
modern world kept advancing: The first wireless message
crossed the Atlantic. Georges Méliès set up the first film
studio and was making *A Trip to the Moon*, and Freud
published his *Interpretation of Dreams*. But these events,
which would soon change the lives of many people, had little
bearing on the life of a young art student.

The indefatigable Holland informs us: The lady art
student "lives a solitary existence, varied only by the daily
visit to the school or *atelier* . . . the incursions of artist
friends (if she be emancipated these will be of both sexes);
the occasional visit to a place of amusement, when an escort
is available. . . ." Some of this is certainly applied to Eileen's
life, and her mother, who came to visit her from time to

time, thought it terribly proper, so ordinary it looked. "How pretty some of these little *appartements* are, and how interesting!" Holland remarks. "Few women are really untidy by natural inclination, and a girl's studio in Paris is usually a perfection of tidiness, compared with those of most men. . . . When she has been in the Quarter some little time she will probably have emancipated herself so far that she will even institute little functions in the form of studio teas or musical evenings. . . . How gay some of these little parties are! There is true Bohemian *camaraderie* about them. . . ." Bohemian camaraderie there might have been, but one can hardly imagine a woman of Eileen's temperament giving little studio teas or musical evenings. Instead, Eileen was having a good time. Paris meant the ultimate escape from the family from which she felt alienated; the cutting of roots. It enabled her to exorcise some of the memories of her past, although she never totally succeeded. Paris for her meant a new identity, a new freedom. And she made good use of it.

The romantic affection between Jessie and Eileen had grown into something more serious, as a rather prim and self-righteous Kathleen hints in her book: "I was never at all at ease with them, but it was many years before I discovered why. One evening a tall, thin, shy, nice-looking youth in corduroys and a Norfolk jacket came in. This was Joselyn [Jessie], with a wig and a slightly blackened moustache. 'We'll go to places and play chess in a café, I can take you to places where you can't go without a man.'"

This more or less innocent game of male disguises had been going on for a while and Eileen often recalled laughingly that once when she and Jessie entered a bar, the band struck up the Spanish national anthem because Jessie in her male attire looked so Spanish. This unorthodox behavior was not the only reason that Kathleen fell out with Eileen. Kathleen was very much in love with her cousin Henry, who had also arrived in Paris. Henry, who was half-Greek, half-Scottish, was a musician. He was "terribly good-looking" and well read and soon became enamored of Eileen. He took her out, often all night. Eileen remembers sitting in his studio talking until morning about Nietzsche, who was all the vogue among students. Henry gave her a little Greek torso she kept all her life.

But Henry was not the only admirer of this beautiful quiet girl with a dignified, aloof manner. There were the friends from the Slade who had come to Paris. One of them was Gerald Kelly. He was considered a brilliant young

painter. He had arrived the same year as Eileen, armed with
introductions. He stayed in the comfortable Hôtel de
l'Univers et Portugal. Later he took a studio on the rue
Campagne-Première, off the boulevard Montparnasse. Clive
Bell and Vanessa Stephen, whom Bell married, knew Kelly
well. Bell described him as a man of wit, culture, and ideas.
He was a scholar able to convince himself by elaborate
argument that so-and-so was an artist. His knowledge of art
was encyclopedic. He was invited to see Monet at Giverny,
and soon he met Rodin, Maillol, and Degas, whom he called
"a funny little irritable man." Kelly was a successful painter,
in 1904 exhibiting at the Salons in the same room as
Boldini, Mucha, Sickert, and Alma-Tadema. To Eileen he
seemed someone quite extraordinary, and she took to this
talkative Irishman; he was good company.

Kelly began to paint Eileen's portrait. The poet Aleister
Crowley, who stayed with Kelly in his studio, described in

his *Confessions* how Kelly in his paintings, "aiming at the
low tone of Whistler and Velasquez, would ultimately use
paint the colour of mud for the highlight of a blonde. He
once picked out an old canvas to paint over and had gone
some distance before he discovered that it was his favourite
portrait of the Hon. Eileen Grey [*sic*]."

Aleister Crowley was one of the strangest friends of this
period Eileen met through Kelly. Crowley had come to Paris
in October 1902, after two years of traveling through
Mexico, Hawaii, and India. He was not yet famous, but had
made a small reputation for himself with some poems he

had published. Eileen remembered that he had a great feeling for luxury and was given to wearing silk shirts and a floppy bow tie around his neck and rings of semiprecious stones on his fingers. He had begun to dabble in the supernatural and later called himself the Great Beast, Prince Chiva Khan. Occultism was fashionable especially in intellectual circles, sometimes helped along with hashish or a whiff of opium. Amateur magic thrived among painters and writers. Eileen's sessions with Crowley were far less exotic than this, and by her account, rather boring: "I don't know how I put up with this nonsense, but he was very lonely." As usual, her natural kindness got the better of her. In 1905, Crowley, under the pseudonym H. D. Carr, published a slim volume of poems, *Rosa Mundi and Other Love Songs with an original composition by Rodin*, issued in rose wrappers, printed by the small publishing house of Philippe Renouard on the rue des Saints-Pères. There among the poems dedicated to and praising Xantippe, Mary, Norah, Flavia, Annie, Bruenhilde, Dora, and Fatima is one poem called "Eileen." It celebrates the shy and unapproachable goddess of Scotland's lochs, culminating in the verse:

> The frosty fingers of the wind; the eyes
> Of melancholy wind; The voice serene
> Of the love-moved wind: The exalting secrecies
> Of the subtle wind: Lament O harmonies
> Of the most musical wind! Eileen!

Eileen remembers spending many evenings in Kelly's studio listening to him describe a meeting with Rodin, or the art dealer Paul Durand-Ruel, Eleonora Duse or Maillol, or waiting with Crowley for something "magic" to happen. Of course, she was too shy to ask Kelly ever to take her along to meet his friends and too polite to break off those endless sessions with Crowley.

Eileen was a good listener; she had a natural curiosity and was always keen to explore new things without ever losing her critical capacity. She was not easily impressed by anything parading under the label "avant-garde." Only when it came to technical inventions would she concede a true step forward.

Another friend who had come to Paris at this time was Wyndham Lewis, who had been at the Slade from 1898 to 1901. They found themselves together again at the Académie Julian. Behind Lewis's shyness and striking good looks was a formidable personality, hesitating between a career as a writer or that of a painter. Like most expatriates, he had taken lodgings around Montparnasse. Kathleen Bruce had found him a studio right next to hers at 22 rue Delambre. He and Eileen would talk about Turgenev and Baudelaire and Huysmans. But he was not a dependable friend; he would often disappear, not to be seen for weeks. Like most male students, he preferred the lighter company of French models or midinettes to that of well-brought-up English girls. The memoirs of Wyndham Lewis and of his fellow artist Augustus John are full of bragging adventures, of roaming around in cabarets or cafés, where a respectable woman would not go. But sometimes they would take Eileen along, for, as Crowley complained in his autobiography, they had to deal with the "affectation of the woman art student to claim to be treated exactly as if they were men in every respect." They would go to the Café de Versailles or a little place called Le Chat Blanc, on the rue d'Odessa. Gerald Kelly took Eileen to the house of the famous writer Marcel Schwob, who lived with Marguerite Moreno, an actress from the Comédie Française. André-Meyer-Marcel Schwob kept regular open house; his salon was a meeting place for many writers. A translator of *Hamlet*, he spoke English fluently. There Eileen met Paul Léautaud, a young writer who was a friend of Gide, Proust, and Valéry and had just published his first novel, *Le Petit Ami*. Antoine Albalat described him in his memoirs, *Trente ans de Quartier Latin*, as the "alarming and spicy Léautaud, happy misanthrope, loving animals too much to love people. He hates clichés, mocks stupidity and pedantry. He mistrusts inherited ideas, he respects nothing. When he speaks, everything—his voice, his gestures, his nostrils—vibrates with frankness and conviction." It is not surprising that Eileen was taken with this thirty-two-year-old with the pale face and beautiful deep voice. This was someone who seemed not to want to conform, who lived outside society, surrounded only by dogs and cats that he picked up in the streets, a man apparently quite free from religion, mystique, or morals. He was intelligent and lucid. Eileen invited him to come and visit her on the rue Bara. We can only gather what happened from Léautaud's extensive diaries. (He was an avid diary writer, filling thirteen volumes that spanned his entire life.) Eileen must have made quite an impression on him. "J'aime les âmes un peu en marge" ("I like marginal souls"), he had said. Eileen appears seven times in his diaries as "la jolie anglaise de la rue Bara."

Eileen and Léautaud had met in 1904. According to his
account, she had asked him to come and see her "at eleven
o'clock at night to speak about love." The amorous
expectations of the suitor were disappointed. When he
arrived, he discovered that Eileen was not alone. She was
with Jessie, a fact that would not have deterred the notorious
libertine. According to his account it was his timidity that
spoiled the evening. In 1926, twenty-two years after the
incident, he noted, "While making order in my
correspondence, I rediscovered the letters of my English
painter of the rue Bara who was so pretty, what a fool I was,
and that must be the name she had given me. All I needed

to do was to utter one word, make one gesture, and I would have had the prettiest mistress, who asked for nothing better. And a rich one into the bargain. Imbecile, imbecile that I was."

What really happened seemed to emerge from a note from 1912: "They closed the door in my face without putting the light on in the hall." Léautaud in his inordinate vanity had certainly knocked at the wrong door, but Eileen was a good sport not easily shocked or put out by such amorous behavior; she continued to borrow books from him, and he kept on trying to see her. Eileen soon had forgotten the whole affair, and for Léautaud she remained one of "the missed chances of my life"—a role that suited her fine.

Eileen also met a young English doctor who wished to make a name for himself as a novelist, William Somerset Maugham. Maugham has described the café Le Chat Blanc in his novel *The Magician*, published in 1908. The main character was none other than Aleister Crowley. There was also in the novel a young lady who had come to Paris from London to study art, but the similarities to Eileen are purely coincidental.

Although friendship and companionship among the Bohèmes was free and easy, Eileen's natural shyness, her reclusive upbringing, and her halting French all prevented her from meeting many people. Clive Bell wrote, about 1904: "I am puzzled by the persistence with which French-speaking English and American artists of the quarter for the most part keep to themselves. Very few had French friends, or took part in the intellectual life of Paris." This was certainly also true of Eileen. "We were so hedged in, it seems unbelievable that all this artistic life went on under our noses and we knew nothing about it." She stuck mostly to her own kind, spending much time with some cousins or Jessie, who had married René Raoul Duval, a well-to-do restaurateur. She changed her name to Jacqueline ("Jackie" or "Jack" to most of her friends). Her generous friendship with Eileen lasted most of their lives.

Jackie loved nightclubs and the two girls, sometimes with an escort or alone, Jackie in her brilliant male disguise, went out dancing all night and ended up in the morning having breakfast in Les Halles. Jackie was socially enterprising. She had some friends who knew literary celebrities such as Anatole France, Henri de Regnier, and Paul Adam. Sometimes she would take Eileen along to those gatherings, and Eileen met a number of the leading writers and poets but she never sought to pursue closer acquaintance (though Anatole France signed her copy of *Les Dieux ont soif*).

Eileen also went once or twice to the Closerie des Lilas, which was not the smart restaurant it is nowadays, but a small, unpretentious place where writers met under the huge chestnut tree. She noticed a writer there she much admired and whose novels she bought in serialized form in magazines, under the name of Colette Willy. But Eileen would not dare to approach the illustrious circle.

Of course events in the city were widely discussed among the English. In 1905 the first "Fauves" exhibition aroused much talk among students. Eileen remembers going to see the play *Ubu Roi*, by Alfred Jarry, which A.-M. Lugné-Poe had first put on in 1896 in the Théâtre de l'Oeuvre. It shocked so many people because of its language that it split Paris into Ubuists and anti-Ubuists. Eileen became an Ubuist but never dared to tell her family or cousins who had also come to Paris that she had actually seen the play.

The idea of traveling was always exhilarating to Eileen. During her holidays she had of course gone home to visit her family. She had also, like most well-off art students, attended a summer class for artists in Normandy. Eileen remembered the happy summer spent in Caudebec-en-Caux, where she took art lessons from Francis Hodgkin, the New Zealand painter who taught there.

Around 1904, after Jackie and René Raoul Duval's child had died in its infancy, René suggested that the two of them go with Eileen to Tunisia. Traveling to North Africa meant travel beyond familiar borders and the experience of a new and foreign culture. Eileen never forgot her first encounter with the desert. The Raoul Duvals had rented an Arab house in the old town of Biskra and, thoughtfully, taken a cook along. Biskra was where Oscar Wilde and Lord Alfred Douglas had stayed at the Royal Hotel. Eileen and her friends remained there for four weeks, making many camel rides into the desert, accompanied by an Arab guide and an interpreter. André Gide in his diaries wrote of the charm and seduction of Biskra, which he had visited in 1895, and all her life Eileen kept an early edition of his *L'Immoraliste*, which described the enchantments this place offered for the senses. Like Gide, she was moved by "the immense solitude which the desert provoked."

Twice they got lost and had to spend the night in the desert. Another time they stayed a few nights at the beautiful oasis of Kairouan, where few tourists went, and saw native dances and ate Arab food. Jackie and Eileen smoked kef, a sensation that Eileen enjoyed so much that she would have a slight smile in the sixties and seventies whenever someone told her about smoking marijuana. A heavy smoker, she never tried hashish again, but as a souvenir of those happy hours under the faultless night sky, she always kept some scented cigarettes in a little wooden case, and when she felt happy, she would offer one to her guests.

But the trip was not altogether pleasant. The Raoul Duvals were very possessive and as often in life, Eileen felt "strapped in." She always hated even the mildest constraint—unless it was self-imposed. So she was quite glad to be back in Paris, in her own little flat.

In 1904, Eileen also went to Spain for the first time. Soon afterward, she caught typhoid fever from eating oysters, which nearly cost her her life. Her alarmed mother rushed to Paris and when Eileen was better, took her to Hyères in the south of France to convalesce.

Hyères, with its elegant stucco houses and rather grand *allées* with shady palm trees, was the oldest of the winter seaside resorts on the Côte d'Azur. It was much visited by the English. Outside, the landscape of Provence with its surrounding hills was still totally unspoiled. There was the pungent smell of rosemary and the sweet scent of the oleander and the noise of crickets.

During this trip Eileen developed a lifelong passion for the Mediterranean landscape. She spent many years of her life living in this blessed stretch of land from the promontory of Saint-Tropez to the Italian border. She built three houses there and decorated three flats. Until the last year of her life—when she was almost a hundred years old—she twice a year made the train journey from Paris to Saint-Raphaël: once to see the spring flowers and then to see the wine harvest brought in. "I cannot return to Paris yet, I have just planted two little cypresses which need watering for eight days," she wrote in a letter. "Now that I have replanted the vines, I think I might be able to overlook some of the monstrosities which are growing up around me and starting to block my view of the sea."

Eileen had a strong relationship with nature—not in the sentimental, pretty sense, but recognizing it as a strong life-giving power: "Let us not forget the vivid forces nature can give us," she wrote when she was well past middle age. "We are born surrounded with buildings and have broken the tie

**Eileen with Henry
Savage Landor in
Italy**

which allows us to communicate with those things which make our strength, like leaves in a vase."

And she always loved the sea. She talked about the "special grandeur" of it, the strengthening virtue which lies in the monotony of the ever-repeating waves, and she quoted a line from the poet Henri Michaux, "L'océan est la répétition d'un peu d'eau, répétition considérable."

Soon after Eileen, her health regained, returned to Paris, Crowley became engaged to Kelly's sister Rose and took away the diamond brooch he had given to Eileen. Not that it made much difference to her. As often later in life, she was quickly bored by any clique or group whose ritual behavior she saw through with her usual intelligence and inborn censoriousness. Kelly later became president of the Royal Academy in London, and Eileen simply used to refer to him as "a man I used to know in my student days in Paris." Crowley continued to send her all his books, but she tore out the dedications.

A more serious suitor, and one much favored by her family, was Henry Savage Landor, a fellow student at the Académie Julian. Not an especially attractive man, with an unusually high forehead, he came from a grand and wealthy family; his grandfather was Walter Savage Landor, a distinguished writer and scholar.

Henry Landor was an explorer and, by the time he met Eileen, had traveled widely. He was the first white man to reach the source of the Brahmaputra River in Tibet, in 1897, and in 1899 held the world record for mountain climbing, having reached twenty-three thousand four hundred feet on Mount Lumpa in Nepal. Eileen, mistrustful as usual, never quite believed his stories but she was fascinated enough to agree to meet his parents. The Landors lived mostly in Italy and owned a vast house, the Villa Gherdisca, near Florence. Eileen was photographed sitting at an elegant table on a terrace next to him. She is wearing the most fetching hat with a long veil and is trying to muster a smile. After the family received her at the end of a long room, "like on a state visit," she decided that this match, however desired by both families, was not for her. Her other admirers, Geoffrey Brailsford and Everard Colthrope, who later became a famous Orientalist and had himself photographed for her in Tokyo, did not fare much better, despite the netsukes he showered her with. Nor did a Mr. Lestrop, whom her mother thought "suitable to marry," or the writer Stephen Haweis, a fellow student who emigrated to Dominica and kept writing to her all his life, sending her "unasked for" photographs "looking like a very, very old chimpanzee." "No sense of *pudeur*," she commented, furious.

Of course young women of wealthy families were groomed to move in the right circles. They were prepared to make good wives. To take up an independent life was considered improper, to say the least. The desire to be left alone was eccentric. Eileen was not afraid to be considered either. She had no intention of changing her personality or modifying it in order to conform to the standard pattern her family expected of her. She was never openly rebellious, but she lived her life according to her standards, not those of a class. Her solitary childhood had taught her to be resourceful, and she was well prepared to fight those who were determined to destroy her longing for freedom.

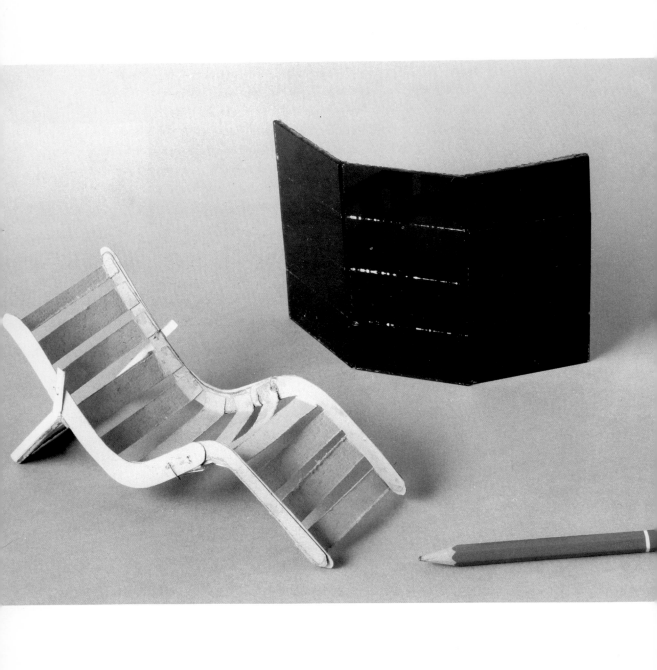

LIFE AS A PROFESSIONAL

Eileen became increasingly bored with drawing; she always thought that she was not very proficient at it. Her instinct told her that she needed to try her hand at something more practical. Being self-taught as a designer and architect, she was never quite able to see things directly from drawings. (Later, she made small models of chairs and houses instead of drafting plans.) So it was almost the logical step for her to design screens or panels for decorating walls.

The world of decorators and designers at the beginning of this century was not so organized as it became a few years later, but interest in the decorative arts spread fast. In 1901, in Paris, the Société Nationale des Artistes Décorateurs was founded. It included such well-established designer-decorators as Hector Guimard, architect of the entrances of the Métro, Eugène Gaillard, Eugène Grasset, and the sculptor (and actress) Sarah Bernhardt. Around them was a group of mostly young men: Pierre Chareau, Francis Jourdain, Maurice Dufrêne, Paul Follot, and others. One of the aims of this society was to free its members from the exhibitions of the painting world, which had hitherto provided their only forum, and to enable them to organize their own shows. "The exclusive presentation of painting, sculpture, graphics and architecture cannot nowadays give a true and complete picture of the aesthetics of an era," Frantz Jourdain (father of Francis) recalled in his history of the Salon d'Automne, published in 1928. "We resolved consequently to return the decorative arts, treated as a Cinderella, to the important place they occupied in the past."

From 1906 onward, the Société des Artistes Décorateurs showed their work in an annual exhibition in the Pavillon Marsan. It was an event that everyone interested in design or decoration attended, and Eileen became a regular visitor. At first, the exhibitions showed only individual pieces of furniture. But in 1923 they started to show whole room settings specially executed by one designer.

In England, the first of the ground-breaking *Studio* magazine competitions was held in 1902, singling out graphic and decorative art works of distinction. Josef

Hoffmann and Koloman Moser visited Charles Rennie Mackintosh in Glasgow after seeing his work at the Vienna Secession Exhibition of 1900. When they returned to Vienna, they founded the Wiener Werkstätte (1903).

Eileen had a keen interest in the decorative arts and began to follow newspaper reports on the major exhibitions in France and outside. Throughout her life Eileen freely absorbed influences from other designers. Her preference for simpler lines was certainly related to the thought of the Arts and Crafts Movement of her native country. In contrast to the rich excesses of the French and Belgian Art Nouveau, it was a precursor of De Stijl and Russian Constructivism, two movements Eileen came to value. The influence of the Vienna school through the paintings of Gustav Klimt and the architecture of Otto Wagner is also visible in her early work. Her later concern with fusing architecture and furniture also found inspiration in Hoffmann's Palais Stoclet in Brussels and the work of Antoni Gaudí in Barcelona and Henry van der Velde in Belgium. All of them saw architecture and furniture design as a whole.

A few years later, in 1907, Hermann Muthesius and a group of fellow architects founded the Deutsche Werkbund in Berlin. The Werkbund's first Paris exhibition was in 1910, by which time Eileen was well into design and was much impressed by their work. Their well-made furniture and their extensive use of wood was a revelation to most French designers. Their simplicity, which stood in direct opposition to the elaborateness of French taste, mostly still mired in the imitation of earlier periods, certainly appealed to her.

In *Art et Décoration*, the famous critic M.-P. Verneuil summed up the French reaction, displaying a rather chauvinistic attitude to the foreign contributions:

> This exhibit commands respect, a formidable accomplishment showing the result of research into the design of their country. . . . We approve without reserve the desire of these German artists to create a modern style which is in harmony with modern life and the daily needs in their country . . . to create a national style. . . . The Bavarians are certainly nearer to us than the Prussians but they are German nevertheless, and our Latin taste will never receive any inspiration from German taste. . . . The heaviness, the brutality in their contrasts, the ostentatiousness so contrary to our taste, which calls for ease, measure, grace, harmony. . . . We can learn from them but they cannot inspire us. Yet one must praise the admirable organization of these artists, having mounted a show which is more than just an exhibition. It is lasting and definitive, an intelligent collaboration between

merchants and artists who do not—as in our country—work in isolation from each other. . . . It is the result of hard labor and beautiful artistic effort. It is here that we see the beginning of an effort by artists to become conscious of their social role and their rights.

Verneuil might not have appreciated the austerity and the rigor of the designs by Bruno Paul, Paul Wenz, and Richard Riemerschmid but he rightly observed a unity of conception in the Werkbund in all aspects of design, from furniture and lamps to materials—something lacking in France. While these designers had absorbed the influences of Holland, England, and France, the French remained totally rooted in their past. It was this that Eileen wholeheartedly rejected and that made her turn increasingly to design in other countries.

After spending three years in Paris, Eileen returned in 1905 to England because of her mother's ill health. She remained there for almost two years. Sporadically she looked in at the Slade and continued to draw, but now she seriously wanted a change.

One day in London, in Dean Street, she happened to stumble upon a lacquer repair shop run by a Mr. D. Charles, who, with two workmen, repaired antique lacquer screens. She had seen some old Chinese and Japanese screens and was greatly attracted by the elegance of the material and the smoothness of the texture. She walked into Charles's shop and inquired if she could work there for a while. Charles, certainly surprised at this enterprising student, was very friendly and invited her to study the materials. He used mostly colored European varnishes to repair the screens but he had also some real lacquer from China. Of course there was no question of a beginner like Eileen doing any real lacquer work, but she watched the men and helped for a few weeks, rubbing down the many coats of lacquer required.

When she returned to Paris at the end of 1906, she took with her samples of the materials and the names of some people who worked in the field. For the next twenty-five years, Eileen kept in contact with Charles. She would sometimes ask him for samples or advice.

Either through Charles directly, or through one of his contacts, Eileen met the man who was responsible for teaching her the art of lacquer. The name of her mentor was Sugawara—or, as the French spell it, Sougawara—a penniless Japanese student in his twenties. A native of Jahoji, a small village in the north of Japan famous for its lacquer

Sugawara making wooden sculptures in the studio on the rue Guénégaud; photograph by Eileen

work, Sugawara had come to Paris to restore the lacquer pieces Japan had sent to the Universal Exhibition of 1900. He liked Paris so much that he remained there. When Eileen met him, he was living with some friends. Eileen asked him to teach her the ancient craft of lacquer. Eventually she mastered the medium to a perfection that assures her a place as one of the great lacquer artists in history. For a while Eileen remained in contact with him, but when she changed from lacquer to more modern materials, their lives separated. Sugawara remained in France until his death in 1970, leading an obscure existence despite his importance to the practice of lacquer work. Andrée Dorac Gerbaud, in her book *L'Art du Laque*, states that "the art of lacquer in France owes him a lot, yet no work of his survives."

Paris was rapidly changing; the yellow fiacres with their coachmen in shiny white top hats began to disappear. Electric lights were no longer a rarity. In 1905 the first automobile show was held at the Grand Palais. Eileen was certainly moving with her times. She had taken her own apartment on the rue des Saints-Pères and got her driver's license. By 1907 Eileen had decided to make Paris her

Early small round table, with a hexagonal base, in brown lacquer

permanent home, and she was looking for a larger place. She heard about an apartment in one of those dignified houses on the rue Bonaparte, number 21, a stone's throw from the quays of the Seine and the little square of Saint-Germain-des-Prés. The apartment was on the second floor of the old *hôtel particulier* of the Marquis de Cyr, a classical eighteenth-century building of elegant proportions. Reached by a wide sweeping staircase, the apartment had windows looking on to a cobblestoned inner courtyard, flanked by two impressive pillars adorned with urns and separated from the street by a high wall. Eileen's apartment was formidable, consisting of an entrance hall, a big salon, a dining room, two bedrooms, and a kitchen. The rent was three thousand francs a year (six hundred dollars in 1907), which was certainly not cheap, and she wrote to her mother asking if she could increase her allowance so that she could take this place "to live and work in." Permission was granted. Eileen, overjoyed, moved in. She had taken the first step on the road to a profession.

Eileen in Byron look, about 1910

She obtained the owner's agreement to get rid of two gilded mirrors that hung in the study and the dining room, and she engaged an English architect to remove a balcony in front of a glassed-in gallery. Her study was painted blue— "A particular color in accordance with the taste of Mademoiselle Gray," as the landlord's inventory laconically stated. She also totally modernized the bathroom. Three years later she bought the flat and remained in it for seventy years.

During all those years—from the time Eileen was twenty-nine until her death at ninety-eight—it would see only a few changes. It is amazing that this woman who decorated other people's homes and built houses did relatively little to her own place. The salon, with its three tall French windows, was mostly painted white, and although she loathed the plaster moldings on the ceilings (which she used to call by their French nickname, "pâtisseries"), as a tenant, she was not allowed to remove them, and later she never bothered. At some time she painted her bedroom all black, with a thick blue line to separate the walls from the black ceiling. The same black was used in the kitchen. But later the flat was again all white. In the twenties, when she began to make metal furniture, the salon contained a sofa in chrome, covered in bright blue wool. There was a round table with a white glass top, "which got broken when someone sat on it," and two unusual and comfortable armchairs, which became known as Bibendum chairs.

She had made a little note for a decorative scheme she must have liked, since she kept the little torn-out page: "Chambre: all from silver paper with the ceiling a brilliant black circle inside a brilliant white circle. Furniture made from étain [pewter], grey curtains." This stunning color scheme was probably never executed. Eileen always rejected the pretty, the merely decorative. The impression one gained from all her interiors was that of simple practical comfort, of common sense with a strong personal taste. Nowhere a feeling of clutter or overdecoration. None of her own rooms was ever a shopwindow for a designer; they were simply places to live and work in. She quite liked a kind of shock effect; she painted an antique chair a plain gray and covered it in rough gray linen; or she put a primitive African stool next to an elegant table. But all this came effortlessly, without much thinking. She had a certain sense of luxury, but it was the luxury of materials: a rare silk or a precious wood.

Once settled in her apartment, she began to work with Sugawara to learn the art of lacquer making seriously. It is a very demanding process, requiring both patience and hard work. Lacquer is the resin from the *Rhus verniciflua* or *Rhus succedanea* trees, which grow in the Far East. Once its impurities have settled out, it will dry to a hard shiny substance.

In a little notebook, Eileen made notes of her tryouts and failures: how to use coromandel, or *sabi*, a powdered stone she imported from Japan, which again was mixed with lacquer. In her neat handwriting she recorded how to whiten wood and how to make a mold in plaster of Paris. One chapter dealt with the best ways to achieve rugged surfaces and how to use charcoal. Her craftsmanlike approach to everything she undertook speaks from every line she wrote down. Patiently she learned the whole process; sometimes when she had applied the lacquer too thickly, it would ripple, and she had to start all over again. She was certainly not a patient person at all; on the contrary, her impatience and the anger it could produce were feared among the people she worked with. But she had a kind of obstinacy which would not allow her to give up once she started on something until she had achieved a result that satisfied her always critical mind and eye.

After filling page after page of her notebook with the different ways of obtaining a certain texture or color, she started by making small lacquer objects and panels in relief. "They were an attempt to simplify the figurative with almost geometrical designs and to replace those ghastly drapes and curves of Tiffany and Art Nouveau," she explained. Gradually she achieved pieces of great subtlety and richness. She avoided the often shiny vulgarity of commercial lacquer pieces, and tried to perfect the austerity that had initially attracted her to the material.

At first Eileen used Chinese lacquer, which she imported from Charles in London. But gradually, through the influence of Sugawara, she changed to Japanese lacquer. According to her, there was not much difference between the two: "The Chinese lacquer had more oil in it and was less resistant than the Japanese one, which was harder." She used to grind down powdered felt, mixing it to a fine paste with lacquer, to fill the joints. Then with rice gum she would glue silk or a very fine fabric all over the surface to smooth the grain, leaving just a slight trace of it.

Lacquer has to dry in a humid atmosphere so Eileen put her work into the bathroom at the far end of her flat and kept the taps running all night. Her flat was filled with the smell and dust of the process and everywhere there were little samples waiting to dry.

Eileen did some pieces in the traditional black color, but she preferred to experiment by adding natural dye to lacquer, thereby achieving extraordinary tonalities: a reddish brown, a brilliant red, and most of all a blue which she was the first to achieve. Sometimes she added silver or gold leaf or inlaid mother-of-pearl, covering the whole with a fine coat of lacquer, "like thin honey."

She often despaired at the endless painstaking work: "Lacquer takes so long, twenty coats, sometimes forty coats, and the other side of the wood has to be lacquered too, otherwise it will warp." Like most people working with

**Above: Black lacquer
bowl**

**Right: Lacquer plate
with silver inlay.
Eileen made several
sets of plates with
silver inlay in red or
brown lacquer**

lacquer, Eileen caught the lacquer disease, a rash that affected her hands and forearms and would not heal easily. She was rather surprised when it appeared. She had heard about it and loved the stories of the newborn children of Japanese lacquerists who have some leaves of the lacquer tree put in their first bath to make them immune. As she persisted in working with the material, she became quite immune to it and never made much of this illness. She was brought up never to have any self-pity and, despite numerous illnesses and partial blindness in later years, would never waste much time talking about them.

Sugawara and Eileen worked together for four years. They must have been quite successful because soon after she had moved into the rue Bonaparte, she was in need of a cabinetmaker to supply her with the wooden pieces for panels and screens. She discovered a young carpenter on her street, tried him out, and put him under contract. This process of discovering workmen and training them continued throughout her professional life. She always enjoyed the contact with craftsmen. Some worked directly under her guidance and exclusively for her, others she called upon only for a particular task. Her address book was always filled with the names of little workshops for leather, ivory, chrome, cork, or whatever material she needed. It also lists quite a few names of lacquer suppliers, some of them from Japan. Through Sugawara she met other lacquer people in Paris: Inagaki, Ousouda.

Most furniture designers of that period did not start as craftsmen, they were painters or architects, but many employed the finest workmen to realize their ideas. Similarly, Eileen was dependent on artisans, and she would patiently hover over them during the execution of her designs. The close collaboration with workmen trained her eye and helped her to eliminate superficial decorations, of which the period was fond. Her early designs were not totally free from such touches as silk tassels in lieu of handles, but she soon found more practical solutions. Of course, Eileen's increasing preference for simpler lines was not only an aesthetic one, it also had a sound reason. The application of lacquer demanded less elaborate surfaces.

Soon the flat in the rue Bonaparte became too cramped to live and work in. She found a place for Sugawara not far away, on the top floor of a building on the rue Guénégaud, a little street leading to the Seine. It was there where most of the lacquer work was done.

Eileen's lacquer tools
and materials:
powdered pigments,
palette knives,
incising implements,
spatulas, stone
weight, brushes, and
unfinished panels and
containers

Small brown lacquer
panel depicting a man
with a dagger
menacing another, as
a figure at top left
looks on; about
1913. Possibly by
Sugawara

The most famous lacquer artist of the twenties was a
Swiss, Jean Dunand. Dunand le Dinandier (brassworker), as
he became known, started life as a sculptor and
metalworker, using mostly brass. After Eileen had joined the
Société des Artistes Décorateurs, she had met Dunand, who
in 1908 had become the secretary of this organization. At
that time he did not yet work in lacquer but was searching
for different ways to decorate his hammered metal pieces.
Eileen recalled that he was very methodical, making all sorts
of experiments: "How to do this and that." One day he came
to see her in the rue Bonaparte because, he claimed, he was
"terribly interested in what she did." He asked if he could

**Above: Lotus table
with dark-green
lacquer, ivory, and
amber rings; designed
for Jacques Doucet
about 1913**

**Right: Siren chair in
black lacquer
ornamented with a
carved siren and sea
horse; designed
before 1913**

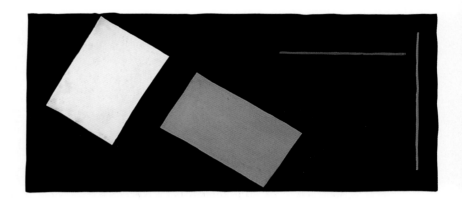

borrow Sugawara to teach him the art of lacquer, and he bought from her an unfinished screen to practice on. Eileen must have quite liked her visitor to part with one of her unfinished pieces of lacquer and to allow him to "do with it whatever he wanted," and in 1912, Jean Dunand became Sugawara's second student. Dunand noted studiously, like a French schoolboy, their first lesson, May 16, 1912; the second lesson, May 21. Diligently he wrote down the tools and the advice his young teacher gave him. In the meantime, Sugawara continued to work with Eileen Gray, reporting regularly about Dunand's progress.

One day Eileen went to see Dunand in his workshop, but she did not like much of what she saw. She displayed her usual censoriousness, calling it "almost imitations of old things." Of course Dunand was not yet the lacquer artist he would become. Later, in contrast to Eileen's solitary working methods, Dunand employed up to a hundred people in his studio, sometimes lacquering for other designers and making larger and larger screens. He was finally commissioned to do lacquer work on the ocean liners *Normandie* and *Atlantique*. He exhibited his first lacquer screens in the Salon des Artistes Décorateurs in 1921, eight years after Eileen had exhibited her first lacquer screen at the same place.

But now lacquer was not the only material she worked in. Trying to apply her knowledge of painting and drawing to another flat surface that could be "used," she began to design rugs. Many artists began to translate their skill into rug design. The most famous designer was Bruno da Silva Bruhns, a painter and decorator who had started his own workshop in a small village in the Aisne. Like Eileen, he later worked for the dress designer Jacques Doucet and the Maharaja of Indore. Eileen always admired the work of Bruhns, who had learned his trade by buying Oriental carpets and taking them apart. Later Colette, André Gide, Mistinguett, and many society people bought his carpets.

Around 1907 a young cellist from the Royal College of Music, Evelyn Wyld, had come to Paris. Their older sisters being close friends, Evelyn and Eileen had known each other from childhood. Evelyn was accompanied by Kate Weatherby. Kate came from a wealthy brewer's family. She was very athletic and loved riding. A strong character, she was independent and emancipated. Like Eileen, who was a year older, she had come to Paris to escape from the restraints of her family. Evelyn Wyld was also strong-willed, a trait she probably inherited from her two aunts, Henrietta

Small lacquer panel depicting a woman in a Japanese landscape, in a black lacquer frame with a rose; about 1913. Possibly by Sugawara

(Etta) and Eva Burdon-Muller, who were both active in the suffragette movement. Etta was the editor of the *Women's Penny Paper*. Eileen, Kate, and Evelyn soon became friends and remained friends for the rest of their lives; their friendship survived many shocks and disagreements. Eileen had just begun to work in lacquer, and the three were contemplating what to do in Paris and how Evelyn could make a career. Kate was a great initiator of projects; "a breath of fresh air," as Eileen used to describe her. It was Kate who pushed Evelyn to try her hand at making rugs, as she later nagged Eileen to design furniture. Kate had also a certain decorative flair; she would paint a room with four shades of white. Eileen and Evelyn traveled to North Africa. They spent some time working with Arab women in Morocco in order to learn weaving and dyeing wool with natural colors. As with her lessons in lacquer work, Eileen now took a special notebook to write down her experiences with wool: how to achieve a certain dye or to weave a certain texture.

In 1909, Evelyn returned to England to learn about weaving and rug knotting, while Eileen started to make designs for rugs. From England, Evelyn brought back looms and wool and a teacher from the National School of Weavers.

Eileen was once more on the lookout for a place, this time to set up a workshop for carpet making. She found three rooms in a dark and narrow little street in Saint-Germain, on the top floor of 17 rue Visconti, the building from which Balzac, early in the last century, ran a printshop. It was a delightful place with a small garden at the back and enough space to install a couple of looms. Eileen and Evelyn set up a partnership for carpet making with the understanding that one would design the patterns, the other look after the execution of them. It was Eileen's first step into the world of abstract art. In most of her lacquer work of this period she was trying to free herself from the influence of the organic forms of Art Nouveau, but in her carpet designs she went further, into out-and-out geometrical patterning.

By 1910, the year the Seine burst its banks, the water flowing down most of the little streets around Saint-Germain, Eileen had a little empire going in this area. There were a carpenter and a *polisseuse* working on the rue Bonaparte; on the rue Guénégaud, Sugawara was making lacquer; and on the rue Visconti, Evelyn, a much tougher and more dominating personality than Eileen ever was, took on a couple of French women to teach them weaving. It soon turned out that carpets were much easier to sell and certainly much cheaper to make than the costly and time-consuming lacquer work. But her production capacity being so small, Eileen had to wait another ten years before the carpet side of her enterprise really started to pay its way.

Of course Eileen had not totally given up her social life. She had stopped seeing her old friends from the Slade School, but through her lacquer work she continued to meet new people. One of her acquaintances and a lifelong admirer of her work was Maurice Martin du Gard, editor of *Les Ecrits Nouveaux*, a friend of Proust and Gide. He was a collector of modern furniture and bought pieces by Pierre-Emile Legrain and other fashionable designers. Another acquaintance was the important art critic Claude Roger-Marx. Eileen also kept up her friendship with the Raoul Duvals, who had a lively social life. A young ex-banker from Germany, Daniel Henry Kahnweiler, had opened a gallery in 1907 on the rue Vignon and Eileen attended its opening. Jacques Rouché, later to become a client, had opened his new experimental Théâtre des Arts. Colette had finally decided to

Eileen, her sister Ethel, and a friend in a family car

drop the name of her husband, Willy, and began to publish under her own. Like many people, Eileen laughed heartily about the scandal at the Moulin Rouge, where Colette appeared in a play, *Madame la Marquise de Mornay*. She was partnered by the author, the Marquise de Belboeuf, alias Mathilde de Mornay, who preferred to be known as Uncle Max. (Most people knew her as "Missy.") When the two ladies kissed passionately at the end of a sketch, the Marquis, who was in the audience, called the police and closed the theater down. Eileen also went to the Ballets-Russes, which Diaghilev had brought to Paris in 1909. Its designers, especially Léon Bakst, strongly influenced fashion and decoration, with their splashes of color and Oriental patterns, and also left a mark on Eileen's designs.

There were other events which Eileen followed with interest and which would also have some bearing on her future career. When in 1909, Filippo Tommaso Marinetti published his *Futurist Manifesto*, Eileen immediately bought a copy. In Chicago, Frank Lloyd Wright had designed his Robie House, introducing a new idea of organic architecture. In Berlin, at the AEG factory, Peter Behrens showed the possibilities of more functional design. Eileen, having still not learned the art of socializing, could at least concentrate

on perfecting her education and follow the new inventions in
art and technology. Like so many other people at this time,
she was fascinated by cars and airplanes, and she bought her
first car, a Chenard Walker. In 1908 the fashionable Motor
Show exhibited in one corner a collection of airplanes. This
was known as the "air locomotion show." From then on it
became an annual event that Eileen did not want to miss.
Almost daily, ever since Clément Ader had built his flying
machine, there were reports of people in all sorts of machines
trying to take off into the sky.

In England, Eileen had been introduced to the world of
aviators through a friend of her mother's, C. S. Rolls of the
Rolls-Royce family, a well-known racing driver and
balloonist. Eileen had her "baptême de l'air," as she called
it, when she went up with him in a balloon. Racing drivers
used to surround themselves with pretty women of high
society, and Eileen used both these attributes to learn about

the new inventions, which became a lifelong passion. In
1908, Henry Farman, an art student turned racing driver
(and the son of the Paris correspondent of *The Standard*),
captured headlines when in Issy-les-Moulineaux, outside of
Paris, a biplane he piloted made the first circular flight.
Soon after, Eileen made his acquaintance. It has erroneously
been reported that she flew with him in a plane, but
certainly she dreamt of going up in one.

It has also been reported that she flew the Channel with
Hubert Latham. Unfortunately, the story is also not true. In
1909, Latham—or, as the French called him, "Lattam"—a
young French aviator of English extraction, was trying out
his monoplane—an Antoinette—at Mourmelon-le-Grand on
the Châlons plains. The sports and society columns were full
of reports of this good-looking, chain-smoking young man,
educated at Oxford, speaking English with a stilted accent,
who liked the company of smart women. Eileen had met
Latham at a social gathering when he was trying to cross
the Channel in a balloon, and one day, when it was
announced that he would try to win the ten-thousand-pound
(fifty-thousand-dollar) prize offered by the *Daily Mail* for
crossing the Channel, René Raoul Duval called Eileen early
in the morning and invited her to come and watch him take
off. They drove to Sangatte, near Calais. "It was a vile
summer's day," she recalled. By the time they reached the
coast, a number of newspapermen had gathered and also
quite a few elegant men and women from Paris society.
Latham's engineer/inventor, the burly red-bearded Léon
Levavasseur, tried to keep the curious crowd at bay. The
terrible weather persisted, and at night they finally gave up.
Three weeks later, July 19, 1909, he tried again. Eileen was
on the boat that accompanied the flight. She saw him ditch,
twelve miles out to sea. She always remembered the sight of
Latham floating in the water in his tweeds. He tried once
more, only to be fished out within reach of the white cliffs of
Dover. Eileen was amused by his famous *sang-froid*—he was
supposed to have shot a duck from his plane—and the story
about his getting five thousand dollars from an American
millionaire for flying low over his house. In Paris, Eileen
sometimes had dinner with Latham, but soon afterward he
was killed, ironically, by a wounded buffalo while out
hunting.

Though she did not fly with Latham, she certainly flew
with Chéron in 1913 near Marseilles and, later, in the
twenties, was one of the first passengers to fly on the airmail

Chana Orloff in a sketch by Amedeo Modigliani

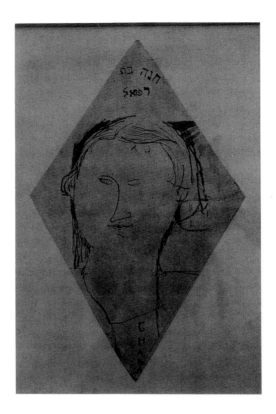

plane from Mexico City to Acapulco. The thrill of these flights always remained with her, and her fascination with the new flying machines was reflected in some of her later designs, especially in a couple of lamps.

By 1912 or 1913 Eileen was no longer unknown. Her lacquer work began to sell and was even exhibited. The smart Paris world began to take notice of this English artist. But Eileen still had very little talent for forming friendships. She remembered talking sometimes to Foujita "because he was so solitary." But she met the vivacious Russian sculptor Chana Orloff, a friend of Max Jacob, Cendrars, and Marie Laurencin. Chana Orloff was born in a small Ukrainian village in 1888. In 1905 her family had emigrated to Palestine, and in 1910 she decided to go to Paris to study at the Ecole des Arts Décoratifs, where she began to do wood carving. She was a great friend of Modigliani, who sketched her on an envelope while both were sitting in a café. "Chana, daughter of Raphael," the painter wrote in Hebrew letters on the drawing. Chana and Eileen saw each other often, but Eileen used to complain that Chana never took her along to meet her famous friends, who regularly gathered at La Plume on the boulevard Saint-Michel: "I think she was a bit jealous." One day, when Chana did ask her to have dinner with some friends, Eileen was too shy to go—to her

Loïe Fuller, The Dancer, a bronze lamp by Raoul-François Larche, about 1900. Collection The Museum of Modern Art, New York. Gift of Anthony Russo

later regret. At the dinner was Guillaume Apollinaire. As so often, her shyness was the reason for much loneliness. The friendship with Chana Orloff lasted to the 1920s, when Eileen exhibited Orloff's work in her gallery, Jean Désert.

Another friendship dates from these prewar years: that with Gaby Bloch. Gabrielle Bloch was the companion-cum-manager of the famous American dancer Marie Louise Fuller, known as Loïe Fuller, who in 1892 had arrived in Paris, bringing with her her famous twirling dance. She wore a wide robe and arranged the lights in a way which caught the material reflected in a mirror. She became the craze of Paris, and artists and society flocked to the Folies-Bergère to see her dance. Rodin put her on the same level as Isadora Duncan. Painters painted her, and she was finally immortalized in a famous Art Nouveau lamp designed around 1900 by Raoul-François Larche. Eileen described her as a small and rather plump American.

Loïe Fuller was interested in anything that came from Japan, and for a while she toured Europe with a company of Japanese dancers and actors who appeared in Japanese dress. Eileen had met Loïe Fuller through friends, and their mutual interest in Japanese culture drew them together. Gabrielle Bloch, the daughter of a wealthy banker, had seen Loïe Fuller for the first time when she was fourteen years old. Immediately she became so infatuated that she wrote pages and pages of emotion-filled poetry. Loïe Fuller

remembered in her autobiography, *Fifteen Years of a Dancer's Life*, which was published in 1913: "For eight years Gab and I have lived together on terms of the greatest intimacy." We owe the American dancer this description of Gaby: "[She] is deeply serious. She has long, black eyes which seem to slumber perpetually. . . . so calm, so silent, so undemonstrative . . . nothing can induce Gab to meet people. Gab has an iron will. . . ." This formidable lady "at sixteen was studying the literature of ancient India," and at eighteen published her mother's manuscript about India. Isadora Duncan also described Gabrielle Bloch in her autobiography, *My Life*. Traveling with Loïe Fuller to Berlin and Leipzig, Isadora saw "in the midst of these nereids, nymphs, iridescent apparitions [which always surrounded Fuller], there was a strange figure in a black tailor-made. She was shy, reticent, with finely moulded yet strong face, black hair brushed straight back from her forehead, with sad, intelligent eyes. She invariably held her hands in the pockets of her suit." Eileen was attracted by this strong woman only a year older than herself. Gaby Bloch's reserve struck a chord Eileen knew well, and her life became intertwined with Gaby's for the next fifteen years.

In 1912, Eileen, her sister Thora, Gaby Bloch, and another friend, Florence Gardiner, went to America together. It was Eileen's first Atlantic crossing. She loved New York. Walking over the Brooklyn Bridge, she could not get enough

Eileen about 1913

of the exhilarating view of the skyscrapers of Lower Manhattan. They took a train all across the United States, stopping in the Rocky Mountains and visiting the Grand Canyon, which Eileen photographed. They ended up in California. "Dead tired, they traveled all the way up to Seattle and then back to San Francisco until they couldn't see another city."

Eileen needed to be alone to digest the many impressions which had inundated her over those last few weeks. She left her three traveling companions and took a rest in Monterey, on the beautiful and rugged coast of California, where later Gaby joined her. When she returned to Paris, "everything seemed to be so small." But Eileen did not have much time to contemplate; her new friends drew her into a whirlpool of activities. Gaby had a liking for luxury. At the elegant restaurant Prunier, a special table was always set aside for them with a bottle of Tokay wine. For a while Eileen enjoyed the lively and gay life of her friends, reminiscent of the years when she roamed the night spots of Paris with Jackie Raoul Duval.

During the last years before the First World War, Paris was gripped by an almost frantic desire for pleasure. The couturier Paul Poiret and his wife, Denise, gave "fêtes de Bacchus," receiving *le tout Paris* wearing wigs of golden wire with grapes. After working with Jacques Doucet, Poiret had opened his own couture house. He tried his hand at many things. He dressed Sarah Bernhardt in her famous trouser suit for *L'Aiglon* and created furniture, materials, and scents. Everybody seemed to be looking for new sensations in fashion, design, and art. And never before had the three worlds so completely seemed to overlap and feed on each other. Poiret had opened his new house, decorated by Louis Süe, with a ball for the Ballets-Russes, which in 1913 presented the Paris audience with a new ballet by Stravinsky, *Le Sacre du Printemps*, that literally unseated the audience. Every new art form was eagerly lapped up by a wealthy society, and Paris became once more a Mecca for artists.

The rooms of Cubist work at the Salon des Indépendants and the Salon d'Automne of 1911 attracted wide attention, and two years later Apollinaire published *Les Peintres cubistes*. Montparnasse had dethroned Montmartre as the center of the artists' world. At the Dôme and the Rotonde one could see Modigliani selling a drawing for a drink or Picasso chatting with Juan Gris and Léger. There were Chagall and Archipenko, Zadkine and the young Max Ernst; there were the Delaunays and Diego Rivera with his Russian wife. More artists arrived from all over the world: Mondrian from Holland, Tatlin from Russia, bringing with him news about a Cubo-Futurist movement formed by artists and poets. In 1914 Marcel Duchamp made his first readymades. There was an active interchange between Paris and Berlin, and the new names were now Kandinsky and *Der Sturm*. The influence of the Russian ballet, Cubist painting, the discovery of Tutankhamen's tomb with the ensuing Egyptian influence did not bypass Eileen. She absorbed many of the new ideas in her work, which had taken off with great speed. Her lacquer work, especially her screens, was suddenly in demand. Sugawara and she often worked day and night on large lacquer panels. To her great surprise Eileen turned from an earnest student into a professional designer whose work was being taken seriously and even creating some public attention. The transition seemed to have been smooth; she scarcely seemed to have noticed it. Her great modesty would never, even in later life, allow her to spend much time reflecting on how and why things happened.

AN ARTIST IN LACQUER

Some of Us Paint Miniatures, Weave Strange Tissues, or "Do Things With a Pen," But Miss Eileen Gray Chooses Lacquer As a Medium of Expression

What is the mystery which impels? What desire sways these strange figures? This door when completed—the illustration represents only a part of the design—will be more than usually interesting. Miss Gray who is a successful artist in "oils," fascinated by the difficulties of lacquer, now gives it her undivided attention

(Centre, above) This beautiful screen of blue lacquer is very simple but most effective in design. By what process of rubbing, by what mixture of resin and colour, by what subtle feeling for decorative line her effects are produced, only Miss Gray knows, but the results are here for all to wonder at; for all to covet

Influenced by the modernists is Miss Gray's art, so they say. But is it not rather that she stands alone, unique, the champion of a singularly direct free method of expression, and for this she has chosen the strange medium of lacquer. This design for a table-top, which dimly suggests the zodiac, is palely illumined by a silver planet

(Left) There is something Japanese in the spirit of this sand-grey table-top, where white fishes dart about a black pool, in which float strange grey leaf forms. Best adapted to lacquer are flat surfaces carefully covered with cloth or silk before the resinous gum is applied, thus rendering the grain of the wood for ever invisible

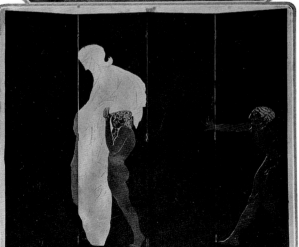

SOME of us paint miniatures. Some of us, as Kipling puts it, "do things with a pen." Some of us weave strange tissues on hand-looms. Suspecting ourselves of histrionic ability we aspire to the stage, or cherish secret hopes of one day figuring in politics. But not one of us—is there, indeed, one other?—has chosen, as has Miss Eileen Gray, lacquer as a medium of expression.

For years a successful artist in oils, it was in search of a new medium that Miss Gray opened, as it were, a lacquered gate and entered a new field. Her first production was a lacquered screen, and then, fascinated by the difficulties of the work, she made another; afterwards designing tables, chairs, and other objects which she executed in lacquer.

Artists saw her work and pronounced it good. Collectors saw it and added specimens of Miss Gray's lacquer to their collections. No less a person of taste than Doucet purchased the screen shown in the centre below. Very striking in colour is this screen, which is done in brilliant red lacquer. The nude figures are rendered in dark blue with just a suggestion of silver in the outline, which throws the figures slightly in relief, and the draped, mysterious figure is done in silver.

By what process of rubbing, by what mixture of resin and colour, by what subtle feeling for decorative line Miss Gray produces her effects, only Miss Gray knows; but the results are here for us all to wonder at, for us all to covet.

The difficulties of the work are great. Best adapted to lacquer are flat surfaces, which are carefully covered with cloth or silk before the resinous gum is applied, thus rendering the grain of the wood for ever invisible. Then—but it is forbidden to write of the manner in which colour is mixed with the gum, which, by a process of rubbing and drying—and lacquer perversely dries best in a damp atmosphere—results in the mirror-like, flinty surface we know so well.

Miss Gray is an artist of rather an extraordinary sort, expressing herself sometimes with a terseness which is almost Japanese, as in the sand-grey table-top reproduced in the centre of this page, where white fishes dart about a black pool in which float strange grey leaf-forms. Again, as in the design for a door shown at the left above, she stirs the imagination. This door when completed—the illustration represents only a part of the design—will be more than usually interesting.

All the shades of blue, made brilliant by much polishing, appear in the curious design for a table-top reproduced at the right above. This design, which dimly suggests the zodiac, is palely illuminated by a silver planet. Of blue lacquer again is the screen, still in an unfinished state, shown in the centre above, where dark blue mountains rear themselves against a paler blue heaven, across which streams a milky way of silver stars.

A. S.

(Left) A person of no less taste than Doucet purchased this screen. It is very striking in colour, being of brilliant red lacquer, with nude figures of dark blue, and just a suggestion of silver in the outline which throws them slightly into relief. The draped mysterious figure is done in silver

THE LACQUER CULT

It would be wrong to imagine that Eileen, despite her various workshops and activities, was engaged in large-scale production of screens and furniture. Being a slow and painstaking worker, she turned out only a few pieces. Most of the early ones were too expensive for a wide public and were ultimately sold at cost price or even at a loss. But gradually her name became more known: "Some people suddenly became interested in my work, there was so little stuff around—most people still imitated the old furniture, and so I got more work."

Her first large four-panel screen, in Chinese lacquer, was made for her friend Florence Gardiner. Called *La Voie Lactée* (The Milky Way), it showed a nude figure striding over a mountain, the hair turning into the Milky Way. The design was formed of mother-of-pearl against a background that was almost midnight blue. Eileen laid the mother-of-pearl in before the lacquer was completely dry, and the two substances dried together. But she was not happy with the color, "which still had a greenish tone." Unfortunately this important first work seems to have been lost. According to Eileen's recollections, "The screen was shipped to England and later ended up in Canada or Australia." Two pictures of it survive: it was reproduced in the Dutch magazine *Wendingen* in 1924 and in an article in English *Vogue* in August 1917, entitled "An Artist in Lacquer." (The fashion editor of *Vogue*, Madge Garland, who knew Eileen through her family, went to Paris to see her work and arranged for the article.) According to the accompanying description: "This beautiful screen of blue lacquer is very simple but most effective in design. By what process of rubbing, by what mixture of resin and colour, by what subtle feeling for decorative line her effects are produced, only Miss Gray knows, but the results are here for all to wonder at." The article goes on to say: "fascinated by the difficulties of the work, she made another [screen]; afterwards designing tables, chairs, and other objects which she executed in lacquer."

Some of the other pieces reproduced in *Vogue* also date

from the early years: a rectangular tabletop suggesting some
zodiac signs with a floating silver planet in the middle, a
round sand-gray table with white fish in a black pool in
which floated gray leaf forms. One of the panels seems to
have been influenced by the works of Gustav Klimt, who had
painted the walls of the much talked-about Palais Stoclet
designed by Josef Hoffmann in Brussels.

Three years later English *Harper's Bazaar*, under the
sensationalist title "Lacquer Walls and Furniture Displace
Old Gods in Paris and London," reported: "There is in Paris
today an artist whose work in lacquer is exciting much
interest among those mondaines who must always be the
first to sanction the new, in people, art or drama. When Miss
Gray exhibited her first work in this difficult medium, the
smart world of Paris first stared, then talked and then
accepted it avidly. It was new, distinctly novel and oh so very
expensive. Overnight, as it were, lacquer became the rage."
This rather simplistic account of Eileen's career does not
quite correspond to the reality. Her rise was not quite so
meteoric.

In 1913, Eileen was invited to exhibit some of her work
at the VIII Salon de la Société des Artistes Décorateurs. She
showed some of her lacquer panels, one of them called *Om
Mani Padme Hum* (the title of this panel was the six sounds
of the sacred Buddhist prayer meaning "Hail the jewel in the
Lotus, hail"). There was also a panel for a library in silver
and yellow lacquer and a frieze. It was the first time her
designs were seen by the general public. It also established
her as a professional designer alongside the best in French
design. Jacques-Emile Ruhlmann showed his furniture for
the first time in the same Salon, which enabled him quickly

**Six-part screen in
dark brown lacquer
with tan incisions**

to establish himself as one of the most sought-after designers
of expensive furniture. Another artist who exhibited his
furniture for the first time there was Robert Mallet-Stevens,
who showed a music room and an entrance hall. Eileen also
displayed a blue and red lacquer panel she had made about
1912 entitled *Le Magicien de la Nuit*. It was reproduced in
March 1913 in the magazine *Art et Décoration*, which
reported: "Miss Gray uses that admirable material lacquer
and creates with it interesting and unusual mantelpieces,
friezes, and library panels. Seeing her entries, one regrets
that this beautiful technique is not more favored by our
decorators."

Among the "smart set" who came to see her work were
three influential people who eventually became her clients:
the Vicomte Charles de Noailles, the famous couturier
Jacques Doucet, and the writer Elisabeth de Gramont,
otherwise known as the Duchesse de Clermont-Tonnerre. The

Duchesse was a famous society hostess, a friend of Gertrude Stein and Natalie Barney. Proust modeled the Duchesse de Guermantes after her. Because of her left-wing leanings, she was sometimes known as the "Red Duchess." Most people knew her as "Lily." Eileen always referred to her as "L'Orage" ("The Storm"), a pun on *tonnerre* ("thunder") and a reflection of the passionate intensity with which she took up everything new. Elisabeth de Gramont was a great admirer of Eileen's work, and she was the first person in France to write an article about her (in *Feuillets d'Art*, 1922).

Eileen's first important client was Jacques Doucet, the king of French fashion, of whose creations Proust's heroines dreamed. But Doucet was not only Paris's most famous and most prestigious couturier, he was also a passionate collector of paintings, furniture, and rare books. He would enter history as one of the great collectors. To have such a discerning amateur as a patron was certainly a great accolade. Here was a man who had the reputation of always wanting to own the most rare and the most beautiful objects. Doucet had seen Eileen's blue and red lacquer panel, *Le Magicien*, at the 1913 Salon and immediately asked to meet the artist. A few days later he arrived at the rue

Lacquer panel for a
door, reproduced at
upper left in *Vogue*,
depicting two women
against an abstract
background, with an
unfinished frame in
silver lacquer

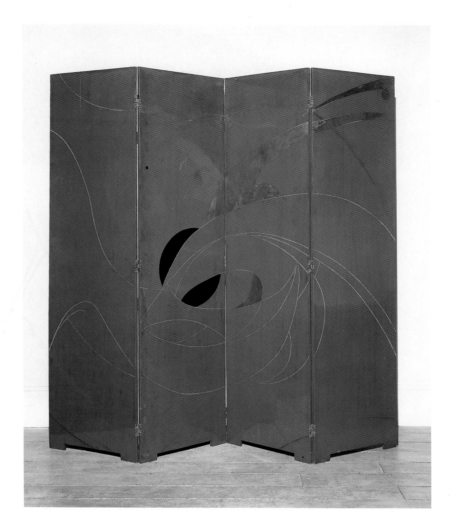

Le Destin, a four-panel screen designed in 1913. On the front, two youths, one carrying a shrouded old man; on the back, an abstract design of swirling lines

Bonaparte, where, Eileen remembered, she was "just putting
the finishing touches to the large four-panel screen" later
known as *Le Destin*. It depicted an allegorical scene of one
small figure looking at another carrying a large, heavy
figure. Eileen had been struck by a drawing of a madman
she had seen at the famous La Salpetrière hospital in Paris.
She copied the main motif and "added another figure to it,"
using pewter against a deep red background.

She was continuously experimenting to achieve different
shades and colors. Repeatedly she had written to London to
her first mentor, Charles, to inquire about her favorite color,
blue, and was told by him and several other lacquer artists
that it could not be achieved in lacquer; green always crept
in and dominated. With her usual stubbornness she
continued to work on it. In 1913, Charles warned her to use
Prussian blue from a tube instead of a powder.
Experimenting further, Eileen remembers having got hold of
"a new chemical substance" that finally gave her the desired
blue. Eileen was delighted; she had won against all odds.
Again and again she would use this dark blue, which

Opposite: Two-tier round table (*guéridon*), with legs of silver lacquer sculptured in an African-inspired style; on the top a red and silver *bilboquet* (cup and ball) design, which Eileen claimed its purchaser, Jacques Doucet, had added later

Right: Detail of leg of *bilboquet* table

obviously had enchanted Doucet when he had seen *Le Magicien*. According to Eileen, he purchased *Le Destin* for fifteen hundred francs (about three hundred dollars).

In 1912, after the death of the woman he loved, Doucet had sold his entire collection of eighteenth-century furniture, objects, paintings, and drawings—including work by Chardin, Boucher, and Watteau. Before the sale *le tout Paris* went to his sumptuous *hôtel particulier* on the rue Spontini to inspect his treasures. While he was off playing golf, the sale fetched the incredible sum of thirteen million francs (two and a half million dollars). He gave up the rue Spontini home, but it was not only the painful memory of a great love that had prompted this radical step, it was also the recognition that he wanted to live among things of his time.

He asked Paul Iribe to design a new apartment at 46 avenue du Bois. Iribe, a friend of Paul Poiret, by now the other great dress designer of the day, had begun as a painter and was primarily known as an illustrator for magazines like *Le Témoin* and *L'Assiette au Beurre*. His illustrations for the Poiret couture house were sent out to fashionable clients. Later Iribe founded his own decorating shop, where he sold his furniture, wallpapers, and fabrics. For the task of decorating Doucet's apartment, he engaged a young assistant, Pierre-Emile Legrain. Iribe asked Eileen to design some furniture for Doucet, and thus Eileen met Legrain. Legrain had great admiration for Eileen's work, and he often recommended her to other clients, such as Madame Tachard, Maurice Martin du Gard, the Vicomte de Noailles, and others. She liked Legrain, and she shared with him a love of African art, which had become all the rage in Paris. Until the end of her life she kept a little African figure with eyes inlaid in mother-of-pearl, which she had mounted on a lacquer base, and an African mask, which she had painted gray.

Elisabeth de Gramont, in the first volume of her memoirs, *Au Temps des Equipages*, described Doucet as someone "who dressed the ladies when there were still ladies without ever mentioning the word money, and he spent his money nobly. He surrounded himself with pictures, furniture, books, manuscripts. He moved toward modern art with a rare assurance and collected new things with discerning taste. He collected the lacquer work of Eileen Grey [*sic*] and the new writing of Aragon."

Among the lacquer work Eileen did for Doucet were some of her most important early pieces: the Lotus table with four

tassels, each ending in a ball of amber (a material of which
Eileen was very fond), and a small round black-topped table
with an inlaid *bilboquet* (cup and ball) design in silver and
red on the top, which Eileen always claimed was not done by
her but added later to her table. A small bright red table
with two drawers and an "enormous wardrobe which would
open up like a *boutique*, to keep all his many small precious
objects in," done in red and blue lacquer, are both
apparently now lost.

Only a few photographs survive of Doucet's apartment,
hailed as a "temple of Modern Art" by the magazine *Fémina*
in January 1925, which described it and reproduced
photographs of some of its rooms. One entered it through a

Doucet's studio on the rue Saint-James (using furniture moved from his avenue du Bois apartment). The *bilboquet* table by Eileen, the sofa by Marcel Coard, rugs by Jean Lurçat; on the wall, Rousseau's *Snake Charmer*

door with crystal by Lalique. Eileen's table shared a prime position with a sofa by Marcel Coard, a chest by Paul Iribe, and carpets by the still-unknown Jean Lurçat. A recent biography of Jacques Doucet (*Mystère et Splendeurs de Jacques Doucet 1853–1929*, by François Chapon) contributes further details of this famous apartment: "the dining room which was conceived by Poiret, has lamps from the Atelier Martine in the form of fruit baskets filled with fruit and flowers made from crystal . . . lacquer panels painted by Fauconnet . . . armchairs designed by Iribe . . . masses of cushions scattered over the mosaic floor . . . in the center, the table shining like an immobile wave, reflecting an enormous crystal fish. This table is oval, very simple, but made from precious wood." Eileen shared with her client a strong liking for precious materials. The many artists who worked for Doucet were all encouraged to use nothing but the most precious woods, ebony and zebra wood, and the most precious techniques, lacquer especially.

Doucet's great collection of original manuscripts, rare books, and graphics became the basis for the famous

Bibliothèque Littéraire Jacques Doucet in Paris. At his death it contained over 100,000 books, 10,000 prints, 2,000 manuscripts and volumes of original documents, and 150,000 photographs. His collection of modern paintings was legendary; he owned Picasso's *Demoiselles d'Avignon* and *The Snake Charmer* by the Douanier Rousseau. After the war he employed two young and still-obscure men, André Breton and his friend Louis Aragon, to build up his formidable collection of contemporary art. When Doucet wanted to have his collection of modern paintings put into new frames, he called on the finest designers to make them. Etienne Cournault, a *peintre-verrier* (stained-glass artist), was asked to create a frame for a Braque. Legrain framed five Picassos. Iribe made a brown lacquer frame for a Manet. Rose Adler made a metal and gold-leather frame for a watercolor by Picabia. Eileen was asked to make lacquer frames for his Van Goghs, a task she found "boring." She could be very obstinate and her relationships with clients were never of the best, or at least tended not to endure. She had nothing against the charming and affable Doucet, a slightly fragile figure who usually wore a velvet jacket, his face half hidden behind a white beard. But she considered him a snob, and when he saw that some door panels she had designed for him were reproduced in a magazine, he canceled the order. "He did not want anything other people had seen before." Another time, "he whisked away things before I even had time to have a photograph taken."

Eileen always refused to sign her work; even her drawings do not bear her signature—a mixture of pride and modesty. The *Le Destin* screen sold to Doucet is one of the rare pieces bearing her name. This unusual concession was certainly made at the client's insistence.

Doucet was known to be very demanding. Artists had to work to his orders. André Masson was asked to add a bird to one of his paintings before Doucet bought it, and Max Ernst had to remove two of the five vases in a picture of his. It was Doucet's idea to add silk tassels to the Lotus table and Eileen only reluctantly obliged. "If I had a pair of scissors, I would cut off those horrible tassels," she said when she saw the table again in an exhibition fifty years after she had made it. She always resented interference. It was this, more than anything else, that prompted her in later life to speak disparagingly of Doucet. He had to take the blame for all the world of "mondanité" which she abhorred. She rather uncharitably said in a magazine interview (in *Connaissance des Arts*, 1973) that Doucet's taste was common, "le goût d'un couturier." She objected to Doucet's first flat, which to her "was still only a cluttered, slightly modernized version of the old traditional eighteenth-century interior." She kept her distance; for her he remained always "Monsieur Doucet" and not "Monsieur Jacques," as he was known among his clients.

Her unkind words were directed more against the world Doucet represented, the superficial, momentarily chic world of a society Eileen had little in common with. She could hardly have resented the grand old man himself, who was one of the first to buy her furniture and to draw attention to her work. Paul Valéry wrote, "Nobody better than Doucet knew how to foresee the variations of taste and, coming to the help of budding talent, sustained the most powerful experiments in all fields of art and literature." It is not true, as has often been said, that Doucet discovered Eileen Gray, but the purchase of her work by a distinguished collector certainly helped to launch her career.

Doucet had a good eye for design and prided himself on being a great discoverer of talent. During the war, in 1917, he persuaded the wounded Pierre-Emile Legrain to try his hand at bookbinding, and Legrain became famous for it. At the 1919 Salon des Indépendants, Doucet discovered the Hungarian Gustav Miklos and commissioned him to design objects and carpets for him. In 1923, he found Rose Adler studying bookbinding at the Ecole d'Art Décoratif with André Langrand and entrusted her with the design of a table. At the 1925 Exhibition of Arts Décoratifs he was one of the first to buy a rug by a young designer, Jean Lurçat, at Marie Cuttoli's stand. From 1926 to 1929, Doucet was preoccupied with creating a "studio moderne" to hold his new furniture and modern paintings. He asked the architect Paul Ruaud to construct an annex in the courtyard of the house belonging to his wife. This remarkable temple of what later would be called "Art Deco" exists no longer. Only a few photographs survive. Doucet supervised the building, which consisted of an entrance and a staircase made by Joseph Csaky in glass and metal. Iribe had gone to America to design some film sets, so Legrain looked after the furnishings of the studio and the so-called Oriental cabinet, a room with a mosaic floor and walls covered in cowhide with gold studs. With his own furniture and that he had chosen from other designers, Legrain certainly had created an interior of rare taste. He himself designed many pieces, made from African wood. The room had a luminous ceiling

**Doucet's Oriental
cabinet with Eileen's
Lotus table display-
ing a collection of
antique bronzes**

by Monlaert. There was a huge glass door by René Lalique,
mounted on steel. Other designers who created pieces for
Doucet's studio were André Groult, Marcel Coard, and Rose
Adler. There were carpets by Lurçat, Miklos, and Louis
Marcoussis.

Doucet had taken only a small part of his collection of
Art Deco furniture to the studio: a *canapé gondole* by
Coard, some of the stools by Legrain, and Eileen Gray's
Lotus table and her little *bilboquet* table. The studio
contained what Doucet considered the quintessentials of
modern art and design.

In 1929, a short time after completion of the studio,
Legrain died and so did Doucet.

In 1930 a long article appeared in *L'Illustration*, with
several photographs of Doucet's studio, showing Eileen's
tassel table in the center of the Oriental cabinet surrounded
by figures by Brancusi and paintings by de Chirico and Max

Ernst. The accompanying article, by André Joubin, mentions the furniture of Adler, Groult, Coard, and Legrain. Eileen's name does not figure anywhere.

Few of Doucet's friends ever saw this studio, which, in the history of interior design, has taken on an almost mystical reputation, greatly enhanced by the widely reported sale of much of its furniture in 1972—the sale that also drew the attention of collectors to Eileen Gray.

Doucet's first purchase of a screen in 1913 had not only enhanced her professional standing, it had also introduced new clients and friends. Eileen at least felt some satisfaction at having achieved something worthwhile that responded to her inbuilt desire to invent and to experiment with new materials.

For a while, Eileen saw quite a lot of Loïe Fuller and Gaby Bloch, but then as usual she grew tired of any cliquish behavior and withdrew. "I just had to go and concentrate on work. I left for Sarajevo a few weeks before the assassination [June 28, 1914] of Archduke Ferdinand, heir to the Austrian throne," she remembered. However conventional or even old-fashioned she was in some ways, she was modern in her desire to move and constantly to seize new ground. "The struggle for liberty is nothing but the constant appropriation of liberty," a passage she had noted in a letter from Ibsen to Georg Brandes; "as long as it is striven after, it goes [on] expanding." In any case, the First World War brought many important changes to everybody's life; Eileen's was no exception.

THE GREAT WAR

July 23, 1914, Austria declared war on Serbia. August 14,
the Germans declared war on Russia. Gertrude Stein wrote:
"In the Spring and early Summer of 1914, a whole life was
over." Eileen was thirty-five years old when the Great War
started and her family urged her to return home
immediately. But home was now Paris; also, she was working
on several pieces for Doucet. However, with the realities of
war and its ensuing austerity, there was soon little need for
expensively designed interiors.

Paris before the war had been a thoroughly cosmopolitan
city. Now people had to prove their allegiance. Everybody
had to be extremely patriotic and join in the general hatred
of the German aggressor. The rue Richard-Wagner was
renamed to erase its Teutonic taint, and eau de Cologne
became known as eau de Louvain.

Right from the start, the toll of human life was terrible.
Ambulance driving became the fashion among foreign
writers and artists. E. E. Cummings, Ernest Hemingway,
and John Dos Passos came from the United States to drive
ambulances. Women followed suit. Gertrude Stein and Alice
B. Toklas dragged out their old Ford (called Lady Godiva),
and Loïe Fuller and Gaby Bloch also drove a kind of
ambulance. Another convoy included Misia Sert, Paul Iribe,
and Jean Cocteau. And Eileen, Evelyn Wyld, and Kate
Weatherby joined in. This was one way to display one's
loyalty to the host country. It was just as well for a foreigner
like Eileen to do this overtly, because the suspicion of
anything non-French developed into real spy mania, as
Eileen would soon experience herself. Anonymous letters
poured into the local police station denouncing foreigners.
"You cannot imagine how every foreigner is suspect here,"
Juan Gris wrote to his dealer, Kahnweiler, "no matter what
his nationality may be." Kahnweiler, who had been born in
Germany, was in Italy when war broke out. He went at once
to Switzerland to avoid internment as an enemy alien; the
government confiscated his collection, and it was sold at
public auction in Paris after the war.

René Raoul Duval worked as an interpreter at English

General Headquarters in France and arranged for Eileen and her friends to serve as relief workers for Madame Archdeacon, a trained nurse who ran a hospital that had opened on the Champs-Elysées. The women had to fetch the wounded soldiers arriving in trains from the front at the station of Aubervillier-la-Courneuve and transport them to various makeshift hospitals, supervised by the Duchesse de Clermont-Tonnerre. Each convoy was a terrible sight; the smell of blood and gangrene and the suffering of the young men were hard to bear. The women worked day and night, replacing each other after twelve hours to get a bit of sleep. Eileen remembered Evelyn bossing her around, ordering her to scrub the floors of a mansion requisitioned for the wounded. One night Eileen's car was stopped by military police on the lookout for two spies. Eileen had to wait for hours despite the suffering soldiers in the back of her car, and finally she threw a fit of anger. Only then was she allowed to deliver the soldiers to the hospital.

By 1915 Evelyn Wyld had returned to England to set up an emergency fund, collecting money for French troops. She drove trucks full of goods back to France, distributing them among the soldiers. Kate Weatherby got involved in some plans for French farmers and had moved to the south of France. Eileen suddenly felt very alone in Paris; she also felt that her services were no longer needed. There were plenty of women driving ambulances. Her mother, with her son about to be called up, begged her to return to England, and at the end of 1915, Eileen decided to leave France. She took Sugawara along. They tried to pack her car with the maximum number of tools and some unfinished pieces of furniture, which would allow them to go on working. She locked up the rue Bonaparte and the rue Guénégaud. Eileen, Sugawara, and a driver set off on the long and tiring journey on the crowded French country roads.

When they finally arrived in London, she rented a place in Cheyne Walk—a kind of disused toolshop, with a spare room in the back for Sugawara to sleep in. Eileen of course had to stay at her mother's townhouse in Kensington. It is not difficult to imagine what it must have meant, after her years of total freedom, to live with her mother again. Fortunately, her mother spent much of the time in their country house at Enniscorthy, in Ireland.

Having only a few friends left in England, Eileen spent as much time as possible in her little workroom. She desperately tried to get some clients for her furniture.

Despite the extraordinary praise in the *Vogue* article in 1917, she could not sell a single piece. Eileen found that English taste was a far cry from the luxurious sophistication of her French clients. It still favored the plainer and more matter-of-fact woodwork that was produced by the Omega Workshop of Roger Fry and others of the Bloomsbury set. Nobody wanted her furniture. All she managed to sell was a "silly table with legs like a stork." It was hardly the time to sell expensive furniture. The Germans attempted to starve Britain with a submarine blockade, and there were shortages of many kinds of food. There were blackouts and constant Zeppelin raids. Everybody tried to manage as well as possible. Christie's held art sales for the Red Cross, and income tax was raised a few shillings to help the war effort.

There was personal hardship too. She had accompanied her mother and two sisters to Tilbury to say good-bye to her brother James, who was called to arms. He died in 1919, as a result of the injuries he received during the war.

Eileen felt miserable and desperately lonely. She missed the few friends she had in Paris and, most of all, her workers and the lively atmosphere of her workrooms in Paris. By 1917 she decided that she had to go back to France. She drove to Enniscorthy to say good-bye to her mother, and then she and Sugawara began the long and difficult journey to France.

Paris was experiencing one of its coldest winters. The streets were covered with snow; there was almost no wood or coal. But Eileen felt she was home again. She reopened her workrooms. Paris, after London, seemed teeming with life. The ballet *Parade*, with decor by Picasso and choreography by Massine, opened at the Théâtre du Châtelet, and Apollinaire had written a new play, *Les Mamelles de Tirésias*. At the end of the next year, on November 11, 1918, the Armistice was signed. For the first time Paris saw the place de la Concorde floodlit by hundreds of wall projectors which the French army had put there.

In 1919, Eileen's mother died. Eileen went back to Ireland for the funeral. She saw "the house" for the last time. The strange relationship with her mother had come to an end. It was the last duty of a daughter who was rebellious and had pushed against the limits of what the conventions would allow, but who also had a great desire to conform. Not being a fighter, she had often done what was expected of her. Her mother would have claimed to know all the important things about her daughter. In fact she knew very little about Eileen and understood even less.

ENTERING THE TWENTIES: RUE DE LOTA

In truth the Paris Eileen had returned to was totally different from the Paris she had known before. The war was over, but it had taken a terrific toll, especially among the young, and many of these were artists. Apollinaire had died. Braque had been wounded, Picasso and Matisse had left Paris. People's minds were occupied with the loss of human life. There was no money for luxury, but after the austerity of the war years, people wanted to forget and all around there was a feeling of optimism.

Restaurants and theaters opened their doors again, and newspapers and magazines began to appear on the kiosks. French intellectuals began again to indulge in one of their favorite pastimes: they talked about literature. In December 1919 the Prix Goncourt went to Marcel Proust for his *A l'Ombre des Jeunes Filles en Fleur*. There were also many new faces, especially from America and England. Soon Paris was again in fashion and for people with pounds and dollars to spend, life was again cheap. In 1920 there were eight hundred thousand English and five hundred thousand American visitors. In the next few years the city would fill up with foreigners, among them women of singular originality and talent: Sylvia Beach, Kay Boyle, Janet Flanner, Nancy Cunard. A woman with a profession was no longer a rarity. The women who had heroically looked after the wounded and taken the place of their men would not now easily give up their newly found privileges and responsibilities. A social revolution took place that would help Eileen's career in the next few years. By 1920, Paris felt as it had always felt, or so it seemed. At the Théâtre des Champs-Elysées, Jean Cocteau presented a show with music by Francis Poulenc, Georges Auric, Erik Satie, and Darius Milhaud; and Max Jacob was run over by a car trying to get to the première of the Ballets-Russes, and ended in the hospital instead. Those with money dressed again, and when the King and Queen of England paid a state visit, Lord Derby, the British ambassador, gave a grandiose reception for *le tout Paris*. It was the beginning of a period of luxury and richness. Not for everybody, of course, but for the middle classes, life took an unexpected upswing. The boulevard Montparnasse had lost all its village character and its cafés, especially the Dôme and the Sélect, became a sort of Babel for artists. Soon the first *boîtes* opened. The Bal Nègre and La Jungle, with their jazz music, were a far cry from the café-theaters and music halls of the prewar years. There was a whole new vocabulary with phrases like "la surprise party" or "le nervous breakdown." In 1918, Le Corbusier had published with Amédée Ozenfant the Purist manifesto *Après le Cubisme (After Cubism)*, which helped to popularize the word "Cubist," first used in connection with the Salon of 1908. It now entered the vocabulary of society gatherings and, according to the writer Maurice Sachs, was used for the most extraordinary occasions. "He is a bit Cubist"—describing a young man with slight sexual deviation. One blamed Cubism for the illegitimate child of a girl from a good family, and someone who was a follower of Trotsky was greeted as "encore un Cubiste" ("another Cubist").

Eileen was no longer the aloof girl of her early years. She was a woman in her forties who had known recognition. She would go to openings of art exhibitions, see the first Chaplin films or Robert Wiene's *The Cabinet of Dr. Caligari*, and laugh at some Dada events with the rest of Paris. Many years later, when told about Christo's efforts to wrap up the coasts, she remembered that Picabia had asked to paint the cliffs of Dieppe blue "because nature was no longer beautiful enough."

There were changes everywhere. Paris had a new airport at Orly with hangars designed by Eugène Freyssinet. It was not only the big towns that changed; tiny fishing ports on the Riviera began to eclipse the traditional summer resorts of French society, Trouville and Deauville, and people began to talk about Saint-Tropez and Saint-Maxime.

With increasing prosperity came the desire to change lifestyles. Those who could afford it changed their houses and flats. People who had lived for centuries with the same furniture began to employ decorators, and bedrooms changed into Egyptian boudoirs. With their ottomans, hanging lamps, and brocade, the apartments of the rich resembled European versions of *The Thousand and One Nights*.

The new style was born which later took on the name Art Deco, an expression Eileen loathed. It was not, as is often assumed, a counterreaction against Art Nouveau but grew out of various tendencies: a feeling for luxurious material, the Orientalism fired by the Ballets-Russes, the Africanism and the Cubism of the modern painters, and the need for simpler furniture made for smaller rooms. But whatever the reason, it was certainly the style adopted by those who thought themselves the tastemakers of French society. The activity of decorating was discovered in a big way; it became fashion, as fleeting as the fashion of a dress, and practiced by very much the same people who crowded into the *haute couture* houses.

Many of these trendsetters called on renowned designers to decorate their flats. The *couturière* Madeleine Vionnet and the milliner Madame Agnès asked Jean Dunand to fill their houses with his lacquered furniture. The dress designer Jeanne Lanvin's salon was decorated by Albert Rateau. "Modern luxury is insatiable," wrote the Duchesse de Clermont-Tonnerre. "The Madame Suzannes . . . and among royalty let us mention Paul Poiret and Jacques Doucet." It was no wonder that people remembered the woman who, before the war, had designed for Jacques Doucet. In 1919 Eileen began to make sketches for an apartment on the rue de Lota in the sixteenth arrondissement for Madame Mathieu-Lévy, the wealthy owner of a famous modiste salon, Suzanne Talbot. The millinery shop had been started by Madame Jeanne Tachard. In 1917 she sold the business to her chief saleslady, Madame Mathieu-Lévy. Pierre Legrain decorated Madame Tachard's Paris apartment and her house in Saint-Cloud. He also installed Pierre Meyer in a *hôtel particulier* on the avenue Montaigne. Both became clients of Eileen Gray. Madame Tachard, a close friend of Doucet and Legrain and a woman of refined and discerning taste, had seen Eileen's work, and it was she who recommended her to Madame Mathieu-Lévy.

A few days after Madame Mathieu-Lévy had come to see Eileen on the rue Bonaparte, Eileen went to see her apartment on the rue de Lota. Eileen objected immediately to the "disgraceful" moldings on the ceiling and walls, which must have surprised the new client, since she had just seen the very same moldings in her designer's own apartment. As it turned out, Madame Mathieu-Lévy wanted a radically new look for her flat and gladly accepted all the suggestions of her decorator. It was Eileen's most ambitious and extensive commission so far, and she threw herself into the task with great verve. She was no longer limited to designing individual pieces, but was finally able to create an entire environment, with lamps, carpets, and wall coverings—the

Entrance hall of the rue de Lota apartment. Eileen used four hundred fifty small lacquered brick panels; she also designed the parchment ceiling light and the rug

first step in a development that would eventually lead her away from mere decoration to architecture. The work on the rue de Lota took over four years; in 1922 Eileen was still doing some big lacquer screens, and the hall of the apartment was not finished until 1924. Madame Mathieu-Lévy, a small vivacious woman in her thirties, was very demanding and wanted more and more pieces of furniture. At one time she asked Eileen to do some bar stools; Eileen considered them "something too silly," and refused. Madame Mathieu-Lévy's taste was for the luxurious and rather rich interior, much in vogue in those days. But Eileen managed eventually to create an environment which was luxurious in the extreme and yet of such great simplicity that it stood out radically from the interiors of other decorators.

If Doucet's first flat with its mixture of furniture from different designers still gives the impression of a cluttered traditional interior, Madame Mathieu-Lévy's flat shows a rare homogeneity. It was the result of one person's taste and style.

More than ten years before Pierre Chareau designed the complete interior for La Maison de Verre (1932), Eileen created a total new look for an apartment. In the furniture one recognizes a radical change from the pieces she had designed for Jacques Doucet, although the same refinement prevailed. The furniture was starker, more sculptural than anything she had done before. The influence of Cubism on the decorative arts had been strong ever since André Mare had presented his Maison Cubiste in the Salon d'Automne of 1912. During the next years designers like Robert Mallet-Stevens, Djo Bourgeois, and Chareau replaced the flowering lines of Art Nouveau by more angular shapes. Furniture began to take on the forms of cubes, spheres, and circles. The influence of Cubism did not bypass Eileen. And nowhere was this more visible than in the brick screens she devised for the rue de Lota.

In the entrance hall they were made of small lacquer panels in mat gray, gold, and silver. These coverings involved an enormous amount of lacquer work, and Sugawara took on three more assistants. But he still could not cope. Eileen approached other lacquer artists in Paris, such as Inagaki, to help her.

Over the years, Inagaki would often help her out when Sugawara was too busy. He lacquered a large table for her and made some lacquer panels and a mirror. He also made several ivory handles. There were other people interested in her work, and it was necessary to take a larger *atelier* on the rue Guénégaud. It was on the second floor and had three rooms. In one she set up her own work table and a large plan chest for her designs. In the second one Sugawara worked, and at the back was a large room for the lacquer workers, who at that time included three assistants and one *polisseuse*.

To decorate an entire flat and cover all the walls was indeed a mammoth task. The screen that covered the hall consisted of four hundred fifty thin lacquer pieces textured with *sabi*. Except for one screen that hid the servants' entrance and could be moved, most of the screens were fixed to the wall. At the end of the narrow hall was a sumptuous lacquer door in black and gold which led into the salon. The walls of the entire salon were paneled screens in a geometrical design; a small screen stood at the side.

For the salon Madame Mathieu-Lévy asked her to design "something extravagant" and Eileen, thinking of the languorous attitude the dancer Ida Rubenstein struck in the

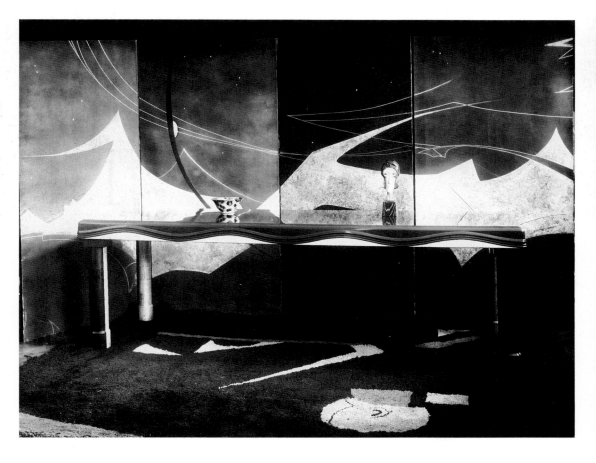

Salon of the rue de
Lota apartment
Above: The Pirogue
sofa at right. The
large lacquer panels,
the ostrich egg ceiling
light, and the lacquer
base of the Egyptian
statuette were also
designed by Eileen

Opposite: The black
lacquer wall panels
were streaked with
overtones of silver,
slightly tarnished in
places. A wooden
head by Sugawara
stands on the brown
lacquer and silver
table

Ballets-Russes' *Schéhérazade* (she had kept two little
reproductions of the Bakst designs), made the Pirogue sofa, a
kind of *lit-de-bateau* (boat bed) in lacquer and various
colors of tortoiseshell. The large cushions were in mat gold.
Eileen made three versions of this sofa. In 1982 one of the
Pirogue sofas sold for over six hundred sixty thousand francs
(one hundred thousand dollars) at an auction in Paris. The
other "unusual" piece was a low armchair in red lacquer
with rearing serpents in yellow dotted lacquer. It was
covered in pale salmon with thin stripes (not in black leather
as it was later, in Yves Saint Laurent's flat). There was also
a bookcase with three shelves which could be adjusted to the
height of the books—a sign of Eileen's practicality.

Another room, the bedroom-boudoir, had a sofa covered
in blue leather, a low table with three legs, and several
smaller screens. There was a mirror with drawers in

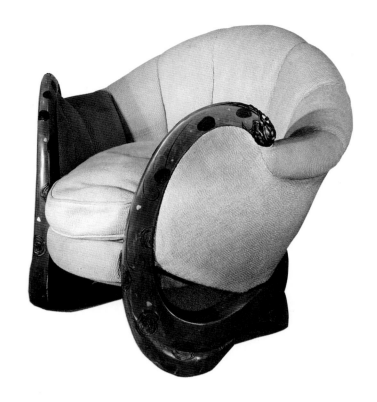

Serpent armchair
in red and yellow lac-
quer; it does not
appear in any early
photographs of the
rue de Lota apartment
but was probably
designed later

Sculptured wood bed
lacquered in orange
and chestnut brown
with silver, designed
for the rue de Lota
apartment

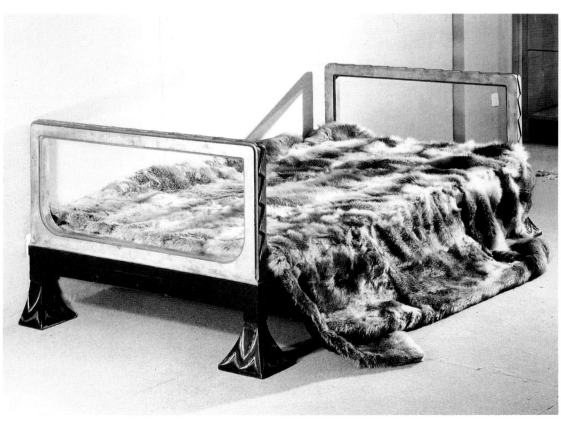

Ceiling light consisting of a cylinder pierced to emit light (and heat); one of a pair designed for the rue de Lota apartment

sycamore and ivory. Madame Mathieu-Lévy had asked for "discreet and relaxing lighting," so Eileen designed a number of ceiling lights and lanterns and one strange lamp of parchment.

Whatever she later thought about some of the pieces that she described as "unnecessarily theatrical," the luxury and the tonal refinement of the whole apartment was stunning. The bookshelves were in mat silver and so were the insides of the drawers of a black desk with ivory handles, echoing the silver of the walls. A black and white photograph can give only a hint of Eileen's subtle color scheme. In September 1920, *Harper's Bazaar* showed details of the apartment and wrote a long appraisal of the Lota flat:

> Paris and London are quite mad on the subject of lacquer rooms. The last word in interior decoration demands walls of lacquer with furnishings to match. Paris is still however ahead of the English capital for it possesses Miss Gray, admittedly the master of her difficult art. Her style is thoroughly modern although there is much feeling for the antique. There is also a reposeful dignity in her designs that is Egyptian in suggestion. While the designs are frequently startling and always mysterious such results are achieved by the simplest methods. Miss Gray's work stands out because of its beauty. . . . She was the first in the field to show an unusual perfection of workmanship. . . . Take the double doors of the room which she has just completed. The framework is of

black lacquer encrusted with gold while the long panels are of black. The walls might pose as studies from the latest Cubist exhibition. At least one panel might be "The Nude Descending the Staircase" [*sic*], but, in fact, the design is achieved by streaking the black lacquer with even tones of silver, slightly tarnished in places. Because of the softness of the silver tone, the effect is both interesting and peaceful. A great contrast here to the trays of our childhood. Of course one might imagine that the owner of a salon with a framework so apparently sombre, would choose brilliant colours for the furnishings. Not this owner nor this artist. The carpet is black and of a most luxurious depth and softness, the screen . . . is black touched with silver; incidentally the bold high points standing out on the screen are mountains, for this artist of the Occident finds mountains as responsive to her treatment as the Orientals found those faithful old dragons. The desk is a soft mellow black and so are most of the chairs.

In the same issue was a color reproduction of a "salle commune," which was in the Lota flat. It showed a large abstract screen, here wrongly reproduced in gold, which prompted Eileen to write furiously in the margin "Argent pas or, les couleurs sont fausses" ("Silver not gold, the colors are wrong").

Madame Mathieu-Lévy was very flattered by the public attention her new flat received. She had herself photographed sitting in an elegant pose on the Pirogue sofa. But her contentment did not prevent her, a couple of years later, asking the architect Paul Ruaud to redesign her place, using most of Eileen's furniture and settings. Ruaud was also responsible for the Doucet studio. Eileen too designed some new pieces for the Mathieu-Lévy flat: the Bibendum chair, some white brick screens, and a straightforward sofa flanked by two rectangular lacquer cubes. A second version of this sofa was made for her own apartment in the rue Bonaparte, but while Madame Mathieu-Lévy's sofa was tobacco color, she covered her own in red with a red lacquered cube on each side.

In 1933 the magazine *L'Illustration* reproduced the flat without even mentioning Eileen Gray's name; all the credit went to Ruaud. It was a repetition of the same magazine's treatment of her in connection with Doucet's studio. Eileen was not a fighter and certainly not for her own sake; she had a tendency to shrink away from painful confrontations. It was only one of many humiliations to come, so maybe it is not so astonishing that the relationship between the two women remained rather aloof and businesslike.

Madame Mathieu-Lévy was a famous society hostess, but

**Elegantly curved
bookcase in the rue
de Lota salon in buff
and chestnut-brown
lacquer with black,
gray, and silver. The
inlaid incisions
accentuate the long
line of the piece; the
shelves are adjustable**

Eileen never attended any of her dinner parties. The time
was long past when the *beau monde* would not invite dress
designers such as Jacques Doucet, or jewelers such as Cartier,
to their homes because they were *fournisseurs* (tradesmen).
On the contrary, dress designers and decorators were very
fashionable as guests, and Eileen with her budding fame,
elegant beauty, and aristocratic upbringing would have
graced any salon. But her usual shyness and a certain
arrogance and disdain for the world of fashionable people
made her keep herself to herself. She preferred to travel, and
in 1920 she visited Mexico for the first time. Eileen later
remembered little of this first visit, her memories being
tangled up with a second trip a few years later, but she
never missed a chance to ask anyone who had been there
about Mexico.

Around 1920, Eileen's fame began to spread beyond
France. In August 1921, *The London Times* reported that
"the love of lacquer, so dominant in the 17th century, is now
notable, and several remarkable artists have made lacquer
their own medium of expression. The best known are Miss
Gray and Mr Dunand." This was the first time that her
name was linked with France's leading lacquer artist. *The*

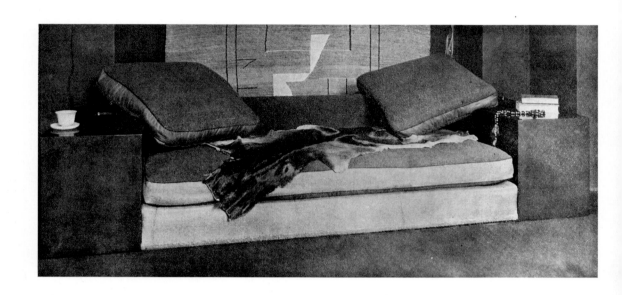

104 Rue de Lota

Opposite, top: A
daybed in tobacco
brown with arms of
deep-red lacquer
made a few years af-
ter the original de-
signed for Madame
Mathieu-Lévy in 1923

Above and opposite,
bottom: Photographs
from the magazine
L'Illustration, in
1933, showing
the rue de Lota
apartment after
redesigning by Paul
Ruaud. Eileen's
daybed-divan,
her white leather
Bibendum chairs, her
Serpent chair, brick
screen, and floor
lamp stand on a glass
floor lighted from
beneath

New York Herald, which was published in Paris but read all
over Europe, wrote June 20, 1922, about "Miss Gray, this
personal and original artist who does not hesitate in front of
modern forms and whose remarkable screens have
magnificent colours due to her studying the original lacquer
artists." More people became interested in her work.

The famous art critic Louis Vauxcelles wrote an article
about Eileen's lacquer work and sent it to her for review; it
gives a good insight into her working method: "In the field
of the applied arts talent is nothing without
professionalism. . . . Eileen Gray knows this. She works with
a wise and slow method for herself and for an elite. Frivolous
openings are not for her, in any case, they ignore who she is.
She aims higher and further. . . ." Vauxcelles describes in
minute detail Eileen's procedures: her choice of wood, "very
dry and very thin"; her way of gluing silk or gauze over it.
"The slightest error forces her to abandon the work and
start anew. An assiduous labor. What a paradox in our
frenetic times." He must have watched her work, or at least
talked to her at length about it:

She joins oil to the ordinary varnish, iron sulphate, rice vinegar,
then the colors, black, yellow, aventurine, red. She then measures
out carefully the gum, black animal dye, tea oil, pork bile,
cinnabar, cochineal, coromandel, orpiment. This is the reason for
her soft tones, like those of a night covered in stars, and the
lacquer work of our Irish woman is encrusted with mother-of-
pearl, corals, precious stones, lapis lazuli, all in harmony with the
material and the theme. Where does this admirable technique
come from? Not from Japan, vulgar race of virtuosi assimilators,
but from China, the true initiator.

Vauxcelles points out that Eileen frees herself from Oriental
influence in order to conquer new ground:

Does one dare to pronounce the word Cubism? Yes, one must.
Those combinations of lines, those geometrical syntheses, this
firm and singular precision is the equivalent of our logical
painters. We should not complain because the accents of human,
animal, or floral shapes have their place in the applied arts. . . .
The other merit of Miss Gray is that when she designs the
architecture of her furniture, she avoids extreme shapes; her
forms are simple, straightforward, and functional. Added to this

is the clarity of her precious woods. In this way the artist achieves
unity and richness, a hymn to geometry.

Eileen could not have asked for greater praise.

Unfortunately, the slow and painstaking process of
lacquer making was not to the liking of a rich and
demanding clientele, which was used to having their orders
executed as speedily as possible. Eileen worked day and
night. The endless visits from clients and workmen began to
exhaust her.

Luckily, she met someone who was able to entice her
away from her drawing board and show her once more a
Paris she seemed to have forgotten since the early years of
the century. Eileen had met Damia, the famous singer with
the raucous voice. Damia had been born, in 1892, Marie-
Louise Damien, one of eight children of a poor policeman.
After having "posed," scantily dressed, at the Bal Tabarin,
she worked as a walk-on at the Théâtre Châtelet. She was
discovered by an eccentric theater lover, Jacques Doherty,
who changed her name to Marisa Damia and transformed

her into a remarkable chanteuse. For a while she sang in small cafés garbed in mauve. The actor Sacha Guitry persuaded her to wear something somber, and she chose the black dress that became one of her hallmarks. By 1912 she was famous. Her records sold in the thousands, and her poster, by Paul Colin, displaying her with outstretched arms, her favorite pose, was all over the walls of Paris. After a concert at the Olympia, she was whisked off to America for a gigantic tour. Her reception was triumphant, but she was homesick and quickly returned to Paris, where she opened the Concert Damia. In an atmosphere of loucheness, she excited an audience consisting of "*drogués*," soldiers, and women without men with her "*chansons dramatiques et tristes*." She became the great *tragédienne de la chanson*, and her performance of the song "Le Fou"—in which she ran onto the stage, threw herself on the floor, and finished the song kneeling—reduced the audience to hysterical applause. She made several films, and Abel Gance asked her to sing the "Marseillaise" to accompany the film *Napoleon*.

Eileen had met Damia through Gaby Bloch and had, improbably, fallen in love with this green-eyed star of a world Eileen scarcely knew. When they met, Damia was in her thirties, Eileen in her forties. It was Eileen's last link with a more frivolous world. She bobbed her beautiful long auburn hair and had superbly tailored suits made at the *couturiers'*. She bought some stunning evening coats from Poiret and hats from Lanvin. She went with Damia to nightclubs and fashionable restaurants.

Damia often came to the rue Bonaparte, sometimes bringing her pet, a very handsome panther. Her laughter filled the house. She brought records, her own, and also "A Cottage for Sale," "Just a Little Drink," and "Foxtrot with Jack Hilton," the popular British band leader. She even prompted Eileen to try her hand at designing a ballet.

Under the influence of the Ballets-Russes, there was a great rush to design ballet sets and costumes. After Diaghilev's effort to employ the leading painters and sculptors, the Swedish industrialist Rolf de Maré, in 1920, created the Ballets Suédois and commissioned Théophile Steinlen, Fernand Léger, Pierre Bonnard, Foujita, and Francis Picabia to design for him. Even Gerald Murphy, a socialite and a client of Eileen's, designed a ballet, *Within the Quota*, danced to the music of Cole Porter. Another client, the Comte de Beaumont, rented the Théâtre de Pigalle in Montmartre for a series of ballets designed by Georges

Braque, André Derain, and Pablo Picasso. The lighting was entrusted to Loïe Fuller. Eileen of course saw quite a few of these performances, and they somehow must have prompted her to give in to Damia's suggestion. One page of her ballet scenario remains and a couple of drawings. She may never have got beyond that point. "Le chat s'ennuie. Je voudrais faire quelque chose pour le distraire . . ." ("The cat is bored. I would like to do something to amuse him. A ballet for animals, pardon, a ballet by animals [*bêtes*] for animals, or maybe a book").

During those years Eileen was sometimes persuaded to leave her work and to meet some of the literary ladies who formed the "charmed circle" of the American colony. Eileen met Natalie Clifford Barney and Gertrude Stein, the two American social and intellectual lionesses, after the war. Eileen did not care very much for these powerful lesbian ladies, whose salons were famous beyond the French border. Of course they all lived in the quarter and, "Sometimes," as Eileen put it, "we would have tea together."

The American writer Djuna Barnes created a monument to the many ladies of Paris in her *Lady's Almanach*, which she published anonymously and sold personally in the streets. The central character has often been identified as Natalie Barney. Eileen casually knew several of these—the journalist Janet Flanner and her friend Solita Solano, the writer Mina Loy, and Dolly Wilde, Oscar Wilde's niece—but their passion and domesticity were not for Eileen, who had not much time or liking for either. Seeing Janet Flanner, Solita Solano, and Djuna Barnes sitting at the Café Flore, wearing black tailored suits with white gloves and white silk scarves, and sipping martinis, always made her smile.

Among the Americans was the painter Romaine Brooks. She was an heiress from Pennsylvania born Beatrice Romaine Goddard, who had divorced John Ellingham Brooks, supposedly with the words, "One should be a slave to nothing but one's toothbrush." Romaine became a friend of Jean Cocteau and Gabriele D'Annunzio and most of all of Natalie Barney, who dreamed of founding a lesbian colony in Greece and ended up modestly with the famous Temple de l'Amitié in Paris. Her temple became the meeting place for artists and intellectuals. An Académie des Femmes, the female counterpart of the then all-male Académie Française, this closed circle included Djuna Barnes, and, of course, the Duchesse de Clermont-Tonnerre. André Gide was supposed to have said, "Natalie Barney is one of the

Eileen Gray 1916

> le chat s'ennuie. je voudrais faire quelque
> chose pour le distraire. Un Ballet. fait
> par les animaux pardon - par les Bêtes
> pour les bêtes.
> on fera un livre. des Images avec Inscription
> je commencerai par la Faufreluche.
>
> la Faufreluche
> Inscription.
> Réflexion faite et l'une dans l'autre
> je ne suis pas plus bête qu'une autre.
>
> la Paravesse
> Inscription
> Quand on me saisi je fiche le Camp
> car seul, je me nourris de l'air du temps.
>
> le Batiscope
> Inscription ça mangent des pierres
> les Batiscopes ça aiment la purée — d'Heliotrope.
>
> l'Inconnu
> Inscription
> ô femme regardez moi — me voyez vous
> 2 blanches 1 noir ça forme mon tout.
> on recherche l'auteur
>
> le Cerf vicieux.
> mes goûts sont un peu saugres
> j'adore semer la panique
> les Zopilotes les Axolotles les animaux étranges
> sans oublier le Mante Divine que personne ne dérange.
> Auteur Inconnu.
>
> le Mandibus.
> Inscription
> ô ménagères retenez bien ceci,
> on ne peut m'accomoder qu'avec du Riz.

people one ought to see if one has time." Natalie Barney's
Friday salon at 20 rue Jacob became famous; the hostess, in
a robe of white silk, presided over scores of illustrious guests.
Eileen saw her from time to time, but she always felt out of
place in the mirrored salon filled with furs and tapestries.
"She was the friend of man, and the lover of women, which
for people full of ardour and drive is better than the other
way round" was the epitaph Natalie Barney chose for herself.

Eileen much preferred Romaine Brooks, this withdrawn,
single-minded artist, who favored, for dresses as well as
canvases, the colors black and gray. Natalie Barney described
her as "un ange égaré, une étrangère partout." Romaine
Brooks had bought two Eileen Gray rugs for her apartment
on the rue Raynouard, where she regularly exhibited her
paintings to an invited group of celebrities from the worlds
of art and society. She had decorated her flat entirely in
shades of gray and black.

In 1929, Natalie Barney published *Aventures de l'Esprit*,
which included anecdotes about the writers and painters who
had come to her salon. She asked Romaine Brooks to
illustrate it. Romaine declined, so Natalie Barney did her

Ballot des Animaux
The Miscomforp
he walks backward

**Sketches for three of
the characters in the
ballet**

own childlike rendering of the Temple de l'Amitié. It shows a
table with cups, and around it some two hundred notable
names are inscribed: her "personal museum," her pantheon
of special admiration. It included not only Anatole France,
Guillaume Apollinaire, Rabindranath Tagore, James Joyce,
Rainer Maria Rilke, and André Gide, but also Eileen Grey
(*sic*), right next to the young poet René Crevel. Natalie
Barney greatly admired Eileen's work, although their contact
remained very formal. After Eileen spent an evening at 20
rue Jacob, December 20, 1919, Natalie Barney sent her a
book of her poems, with the inscription: "To Miss Gray—à
lire avec les trois cigarettes oubliés, her admirer always—and
perhaps at the same time her neighbour." The following year
Eileen was again sent a book, the famous *Pensées d'une
Amazone*, with the dedication "To Miss Gray, her voisine and
admiratrice, Natalie Barney." The poet Lucie Mardrus,
another friend and regular visitor to the Temple, also sent
Eileen her poetry, dedicated: "A Mademoiselle Grey [*sic*]

alchimiste du bois en admiration de son art impressionant."

Eileen did not remember precisely when she had met
Gertrude Stein—probably also right after the war, possibly
even earlier, since Kathleen Bruce sculptured a head of
Gertrude Stein. In *The Autobiography of Alice B. Toklas*,
Gertrude describes Kathleen Bruce as "a very beautiful, very
athletic English girl, a kind of sculptress," and remembers
visiting her in her studio. Eileen always liked the powerful
American lady with the impressive art collection. "She was
most determined, but I always thought her sympathetic."
Eileen kept seeing her sporadically on the rue de Fleurus,
where Miss Stein held court on Saturday, sitting
among the heavy Renaissance furniture so much at odds
with the walls covered with pictures by Picasso, Matisse,
Renoir, and Cézanne. The last time the two met, in 1938,
was after Gertrude Stein and Alice B. Toklas (whom Eileen
referred to as "the squaw") had moved to the rue Christine.
Eileen always mocked a little about these circles, but in later

life she was always eager to hear the gossip generated by these Amazons, whose biographies would flood the bookshops.

Eileen's relationship with most people was a distant acquaintance, not a kind of friendship. Her prejudices against anything Anglo-Saxon ran very deep. She had the habit of accusing the English of narrowness of culture and smugness. She would look into Sylvia Beach's famous bookshop, Shakespeare and Company, which published Joyce's *Ulysses*, and not speak to the owner. Daily, on the way to her own workshop, she would pass Nancy Cunard's gallery in the rue Guénégaud. She was naturally intrigued by the African masks in the window, the beautiful African clothes, and the Brazilian pieces Cunard exhibited, together with paintings by Yves Tanguy and Joan Miró. But she was too shy ever to speak to the elegant and extravagant-looking woman with the enormous ivory bracelets that covered both her arms.

Eileen's mind moved in a different world from that of any of the people who formed the international clique in the twenties. In fact one might suspect that it was precisely people of this sort who caused Eileen to keep more and more to herself. The American journalist and photographer Thérèse Bonney, who had come to Paris to write some articles on designers, summed her up as follows: "Eileen Gray was very quiet, unassuming, unexplosive, entirely consecrated. Of all the people I knew in that world, she gave the feeling of complete consecration."

During all this time Eileen kept her feelings for Damia very secret. Damia was quickly enthralled by people. One of her favorites was a designer called Rémy, who designed "chairs too high to sit on." He also had a car with "six places all one behind the other." On the other hand, Eileen and Damia and the panther driving around the streets of Paris also reduced Eileen to laughter. If Damia took Eileen out of her self-imposed solitude, Eileen gave the singer a kind of stability she lacked. Both of them spent their happiest hours in the countryside in the Forest of Fontainebleau, where they went for long walks together.

Shortly after the war, Eileen had bought a place there, in Samois-sur-Seine. Eileen had first acquired a little house on the corner of the rue du Bas and the quays. A little later, when the house next door became vacant, she bought that too in order to make a workroom for Sugawara. During the next few years Sugawara kept quite a few people employed there, many of them living in the house. People in the village referred to them as "the Chinese." Eventually, Eileen joined the two to make one large house. It stood right on the Seine, and with it came a little island that could be reached only by rowing across the river.

The house had a large living room and several bedrooms. She put in some Spanish furniture, and each of the guest rooms was decorated in a different color: one all yellow, the other all green. There was a big studio with a large refectory table that served as a worktable.

Eileen spent most weekends there. Sometimes there were a few guests: Damia, Jackie Raoul Duval, or Kate Weatherby. The women took baskets full of wine and food onto the island and picnicked there. Sometimes Eileen just put a large piece of lacquer on the garden table and served lunch under the magnificent wisteria that covered the house. But more often than not, while the guests enjoyed themselves, she sat in her studio drawing and designing.

Damia was fond of Eileen's lacquer work, and Eileen gave her a large mirror with a brown and silver frame. She taught her how to clean lacquer with a little bit of oil and absorbent cotton. Eileen also put some lacquer on Damia's furniture, lacquering the inside of a period dressing table and putting a pagoda design in black and red lacquer on a table. And Damia had a black armchair with gold figures designed by Eileen.

As always, Eileen soon got bored with the sort of life Damia led, and she stopped seeing her and her friends. In any case Damia had started to live with Gaby Bloch. Eileen was disappointed, hurt; she stopped going to Samois. Eileen loved the house and kept it for a few years, but after the war, she gave it up: "There were too many memories to cope with."

Friendship of any kind was difficult for her. Her character did not allow her to easily express feelings of confidence or love. Despite a great sensitivity and even passion, Eileen revealed little about her personality. She was incapable of breaking this barrier. In all her dealings with people, she preserved a vague and uncommitted tone that often gave the impression of distance and even coldness. Moreover, she would never do the expected if it did not accord with her own wishes. She had high standards, which often led her to harsh judgments, a certain censoriousness, and sometimes even bossiness.

Eileen could be quite querulous and rancorous. She

**Photograph of Damia
inscribed to Eileen**

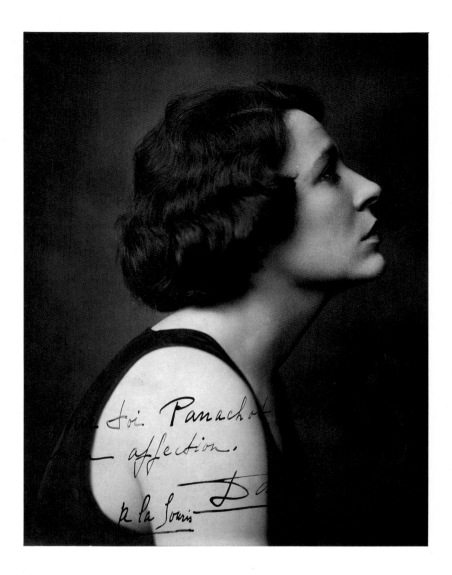

certainly never forgot when she had been wronged. Under
the polite exterior hid a much less pleasant personality. But
when it was pointed out to her that she was at fault, Eileen
would sulk a bit and then see reason. All her life she had
bouts of sudden rage which were as unnerving to others as
to herself. When she wanted, she could exude an
unforgettable charm, her eyes would twinkle and she would
break into girlish laughter. She was always able to cast a
certain spell over people who came into contact with her. It
was her extraordinary amiability, often expressed by the
interest she took in the circumstances and life of other
people, that touched those who met her.

On the other hand she was never at ease with other
people, always feeling slightly inadequate. "Plants and
animals," she once said, "appear to thrive and reach their
perfection naturally; the better the conditions, the better the

result. Man in too easy conditions degenerates, he has to go down into hell to progress, to deny himself, to struggle and lose his foothold, before he can be fulfilled." Eileen once more recognized what she knew all her life, that the freedom she longed for had to be paid for with an enduring isolation and that only by immersing herself in her work was she able to escape the perils of the pattern of life other people were drawing around her.

Eileen saw Damia once more, in 1950, when they ran into each other on the rue Bonaparte, a year after Damia had given her last recital, in the Salle Pleyel. She died in 1978 at the age of eighty-six. All her life Eileen kept the records, the dresses, the two evening coats by Poiret, and a couple of photographs of Damia inscribed "Pour toi Panachot avec toute mon affection," "A la souris," "Mon air aimable."

KEEPING A SHOP:
JEAN DÉSERT

In 1921, while still working on the rue de Lota flat, Eileen decided to enlarge her business. She wanted to get a proper outlet for her designs. She was tired of clients invading the privacy of her home. She also realized that producing custom-designed pieces was not economical.

For a while Sugawara and Eileen had been trying to sell from the rue Guénégaud. They had published a little leaflet offering "Sugawara lacquer maker, genuine Japanese lacquer, Screens, Modern Furniture," even "Repair of porcelain and objects of art. . . ." Sugawara obviously, not having enough work from Eileen, had begun to start his own independent business.

Gabrielle Bloch kept urging Eileen to open a shop. She started to search for a place. The fashionable area to have a gallery was around the Faubourg Saint-Honoré. Eileen was lucky; right opposite the Salle Pleyel was a place to rent. She took it immediately. The shop needed a name and Eileen had always been good at inventing names. Remembering her first trip to the desert and assuming that the name of a man would give a more serious tone, she called the gallery Jean Désert. (Eventually the frequency with which she received letters addressed to her as Monsieur Désert prompted her to print up some letter paper headed "Jean Désert et E. Gray.")

The classical facade, with its old-fashioned stucco lions would hardly have inspired anybody to look for a gallery of modern furniture, so she designed a new facade, entirely in black and white. The windows were enlarged and the black doors became three white lacquer panels. Above, in shiny lettering, she simply put the name of the gallery. She designed special slabs in blue glass to bring light into the basement, which allowed the passerby just a glimpse at what went on there. As usual, everything showed her tremendous refinement of taste combined with her practical sense. Inside, she ripped out the moldings and fittings and painted the walls all white. She put in a new modern staircase to the basement. At the back of the gallery was a little room large enough to serve as an office. She designed cards which read in bold letters: "Meubles, Laques, Paravents, Tapis d'Eileen

Gray" ("Furniture, Lacquer Work, Screens, Rugs by Eileen Gray"). Another card offered, in addition, "Décoration et Installation d'Appartements." With great enthusiasm, she filled the shop with her work.

Eileen used to take photographs of her own room settings. She had a great flair for display. Very rarely would she photograph a piece of furniture on its own; it was always part of a setting. In her new shop, too, Eileen put a large amber necklace on top of a table; other pieces of furniture displayed an open cigarette case or a small figure. In all her photographs one feels the presence of people. But her *mise en scène* was never elaborate, always just enough. Even a glass of water was always served on the right tray.

There was no question of Eileen herself selling in the gallery; she hated any contact with clients. An arrangement was made for Gaby Bloch to look after the business side, in return for 40 percent of the profits. Gaby had no intention of keeping shop either, so they took a saleswoman, Mademoiselle Larrousilh, the sister of a seamstress Eileen knew—not the very best choice for such sophisticated merchandise.

In the spring of 1922 there was an opening party; the invitations read: "Jean Désert opens May 17. You are invited to the opening, which will take place Tuesday, May 16, from 2:00 to 6:00, 217 rue du Faubourg Saint-Honoré."

Of course, other designers had opened small shops before her. Poiret had set up a shop he called Ateliers Martine as early as 1911; there he trained young women to become designers. He had visited the Wiener Werkstätte, and after his sales had reached a million francs (nearly two hundred thousand dollars) at his first couture collection, he decided to branch out into decorating. Francis Jourdain had opened the Ateliers Modernes in 1912. Louis Süe and André Mare had founded the Compagnie des Arts Français in 1919. In the same year Ruhlmann had opened a gallery where he sold his furniture. Maurice Dufrêne began a design studio, Maîtrise, in the Galeries Lafayette department store, and Paul Follot followed suit by opening one at the rival Bon Marché. In 1921, Jean Dunand also began exhibiting his first lacquer pieces and furniture at the Galerie Georges Petit.

It was certainly adventurous to start a decorating business in a world that had been hitherto exclusively filled by men. But Eileen Gray was not the only woman designer at that time. In the Anglo-Saxon world a number of other women had made names for themselves. There were Dolly

Rug design

Black lacquer desk
designed for the
Monte Carlo room,
1923. The drawers
had ivory handles
carved by Inagaki;
the bench in this
photograph was made
for Jean Désert, but
it resembles the one
originally shown with
the desk

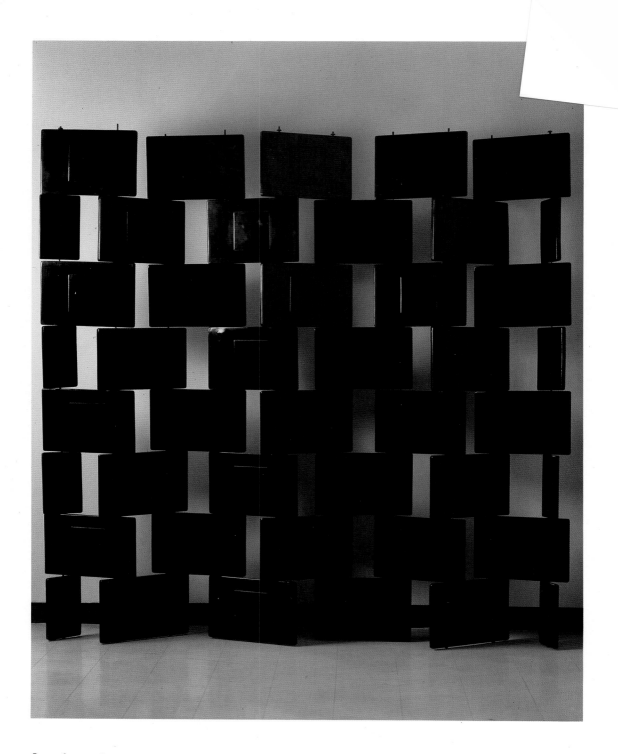

One of several ver-
sions of the brick
screen, here in black
lacquer; in the Monte
Carlo room it was
white

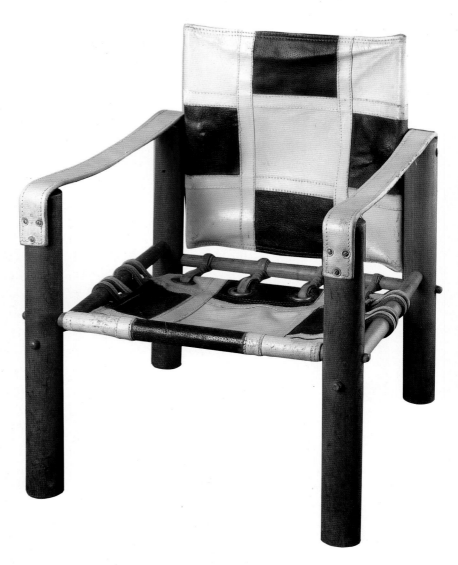

One of a pair of
armchairs with back
and seat of white and
black leather squares,
originally owned by
the car designer Jean-
Henri Labourdette

Pot rest or ashtray in
scorched wood,
probably
commissioned by
Labourdette

Mann, Sybil Colefax, and Betty Joel in London, and Dorothy Draper in America. Syrie Maugham, wife of Somerset, became all the rage, despite the fact that the formidable Elsie de Wolfe, America's number-one designer, had told her, "You are too late, dear, the decorating field is overcrowded."

In France, however, a woman decorator was the exception. In the first year business at Jean Désert was not brilliant. Eileen simply did not know how to deal with clients, nor did she know how to attract them. She had entered a field in which people had to act fast and be commercially skillful. She was incapable of throwing herself into the noisy and colorful happenings in the decorators' world. She was not clever, she lacked niceness and joviality, all talents necessary to assure herself a corner of the market. Eileen looked in amazement and with slight disdain at some other women decorators whose flamboyant lifestyles made them the center of attention among the rich and celebrated. Elsie de Wolfe, an actress, had turned to decoration when she was in her forties. Together with her friend Elisabeth Marbury, she had bought the Villa Trianon near Versailles. They moved in the right circles and entertained Sarah Bernhardt and Ellen Terry. They were friends of Edith Wharton, whose trend-setting book *The Decoration of Houses* had been published in 1897. In 1913, Elsie de Wolfe had written her own book, *The House in Good Taste*.

Eileen had no talent for self-promotion; the idea of gearing her social life to boost her sales would not have occurred to her, even if she had known how to do it. The people who bought her furniture almost totally ignored the person who designed it. So it is not surprising that in the first year she sold very little. The total sales, which were recorded in a large salesbook, amounted to nineteen thousand francs (less than four thousand dollars), hardly enough to pay the rent, the saleswoman, and Eileen's workers—not to mention materials. What sold best were the rugs, which were still woven in the rue Visconti by Evelyn Wyld and her people. The wool came from the Auvergne and was dyed in Paris. Each rug had a little label: "Designed by Eileen Gray at the workshop of Evelyn Wyld." The best-seller was a little rug called *Footit*, selling for one hundred fifty francs (about thirty dollars). It was named after a famous pair of clowns, Chocolat and Footit.

What was remarkable was the list of clients Eileen attracted during her first years. It included many famous names from French public life and the upper classes:

Premier Raymond Poincaré and the Communist politician Maurice Thorez, the writer Maurice Martin du Gard, Jenny Bradley, the translator and literary agent and a friend of Gertrude Stein, Gerald Murphy, Ezra Pound, James Joyce, and Sylvia Beach. There were the names from the French *beau monde*, and artists and architects like Henri Laurens, Henri Pacon, Charles Siclis, and Charles Moreux. The Vicomte Charles de Noailles purchased four large cushions and a dressing table, which was supposed to cost eighteen hundred francs (three hundred fifty dollars) but was reduced to sixteen hundred, which shows that wealth and breeding do not prevent people from bargaining. The most expensive item sold in the first year was a zebra skin purchased by the Comtesse de Behague. Pierre Meyer bought several rugs for his *hôtel particulier* on the avenue Montaigne, which was totally furnished by Legrain. Madame Tachard bought Eileen Gray's rugs for her villa at Saint-Cloud, also decorated by Legrain. Soon other designers and architects ordered from her shop: the jeweler André Leveillé, Jacques Rouché, who, in the years before the war, had staged shows at the Théâtre des Arts that linked the decorative arts with the theater, and Jean-Henri Labourdette, who built custom bodies for cars, and was thus the automotive equivalent of an *haut couturier*. In his shop, everything was custom made and fitted precisely to the client's taste: dashboard, upholstery, door knobs, every last detail. When he shopped for the modern furniture he collected, he wanted the same attention for himself. He taught Eileen about the use of aluminum and other metals. His flat contained important lacquer panels by Dunand, and he had bought a black lacquer desk from Eileen. He also owned armchairs, a lacquer table, a small stool, and an ostrich-egg lamp of hers. Eileen also sent some of her things abroad. There were some clients in England and Holland, even in Baltimore.

Now her work became the subject of articles in the popular press. In August 1921, the Paris correspondent of *The Times* reported to London on the lacquer work of Miss Eileen Gray and M. Jean Dunand. In June 1922, in *The Daily Mail* in London, Jean Désert shared the Paris news with the summer sales at the big French department stores:

> Lacquer is not a fashion but a passion in Paris. . . . Years of decorative art exhibitions have produced a cult for beauty and even when the home is restricted to the limits of a city flat, each object becomes the object of search and research. The influence of

**Interior of Jean
Désert, stairway to
basement**

JEAN DÉSERT
ouvre
le 17 mai.
MEUBLES
LAQUES
PARAVENTS
TAPIS
d'EILEEN GRAY

Vous êtes prié d'assister au Vernissage qui aura lieu le mardi
16 mai, de 2 heures 1/2 à 6 heures, 217, rue du faubourg Saint-Honoré.

JEAN DÉSERT
217, rue du Faubourg-St-Honoré

JEAN DÉSERT, 217, RUE DU FAUBOURG Sᵗ HONORÉ. TÉL.: ÉLYS. 26-88

MEUBLES
LAQUES
PARAVENTS
TAPIS

d'EILEEN GRAY

JEAN
DÉSERT

à
Paris

217,
rue du Faubourg-St-Honoré

JEAN DÉSERT
ET
E. GRAY

Laques
Meubles Modernes
Décoration.

217, FAUBOURG ST-HONORÉ.

Invitations and
announcements for
Jean Désert

Oriental art and artists is very apparent in modern Parisian products and finely lacquered work is used to make chairs and benches, while cabinets and screens show the rather heavy lines of Chinese furniture. An English artist working here turns out dark lacquered wood of great beauty, which she decorates with lightly engraved lines made luminous, in some cases, with a sparing use of mother-of-pearl. Her red lacquer is understated except by its own colour and flawless surface, but with deep brown she achieves furniture of great beauty that it would be extremely restful to live with. In one magnificent screen, this artist has produced a deep transparent blue lacquer like the atmosphere of a dark clear night. She has put specimens of her work displayed on a parquet floor with her hand-made rugs of undyed wools, into a depot built for them at 217 Faubourg St Honoré and the effect is as interesting as it is original.

In July 1922, the *Chicago Tribune* devoted an elated article to her work under the headline: "Furniture in Bizarre Forms and Styles." Praising Eileen's "unusual decorative perception and her rare grasp of detail and art," the reporter tells his readers that a visit to the shop of Jean Désert is "a sojourn into the never before seen, never before heard," and spends a whole paragraph praising the door handle Eileen put on the entrance door, "which performs its task of opening the door to abnormal perfection. . . . There are chairs oddly shaped for sitting, tables of fantastic attitudes, divans, lamps and screens in forms hitherto unguessed."

An equally flowery appraisal appeared in March 1922 in *Feuillets d'Art*. The writer was the Duchesse de Clermont-Tonnerre, who had closely followed Eileen's way of working. She tells us that the designer, "regardless of material costs and physical exhaustion rejects, begins again, not stopping until she has achieved the ideal line and the absolute ensemble. . . . This artist dreams up some totally harmonious settings . . . far removed from the bureaus of Louis XV. . . . She wants to create interiors suited to our existence, in proportion to our rooms and in accordance with our aspirations and feelings." "Les Laques d'Eileen Gray" was the first of several articles on Eileen to appear in France. Eileen had the habit of brushing aside any compliments, but the sudden public eulogy of her work pleased her enough to preserve the press clippings.

The publicity Jean Désert evoked was accompanied by invitations to exhibit—something her old friend Kate Weatherby had been prodding her to do for years: "Other people manage to get their work shown in the Salons," Kate kept repeating.

Rectangular wall
mirror in lacquer
with carved motifs,
about 1924

Finally, at the Salon d'Automne of 1922 Eileen showed a
screen in exotic wood and black lacquer, a chest of drawers
with a brown lacquer top, two carpets, and some wall
hangings. At the same Salon Le Corbusier showed his
Citrohan house. It was the first time that he exhibited a
design on *pilotis*, a system by which buildings were held up
by pillars, creating a space underneath. He also proposed a
standardized house to be mass-produced. Mallet-Stevens
exhibited his pavilion for the Aéro-Club. Eileen of course
saw both entries.

In the same year Eileen was also asked to participate in a group exhibition by French decorators in Amsterdam. She showed a black lacquer screen and a mirror. She later thought that her exhibit also included a deck-chair version of an armchair, the *fauteuil* Transatlantique, which became one of her most famous pieces of furniture. (Actually, her first sketches for the Transat chair date from 1924, although the design was not registered before 1930.) The one sent to Amsterdam could have been a first version. Eileen, as usual critical and fussy, disliked the way her furniture was displayed. She begged the Dutch architect Jan Wils to do something about it. On December 9, 1922, Wils reassured her in a letter that he had gone to the exhibition and done what she wanted. He sent her the catalogue and a drawing of her stand. In the same letter he told her that he found the whole exhibition of French furniture "sad" and that he was sorry to see her entry lost "in all those monstrosities. It is too fine and too restrained to be noticed." Eileen shared with Wils a distaste for much French furniture. Fifty years later, when shown a book featuring many of the interiors of the Art Deco period, she was prompted to write, "Lots of it makes me quite sick, as it made me feel then."

MONTE CARLO AND BEYOND

Eileen's Monte Carlo
room, the Bedroom-
boudoir exhibited in
the XIV Salon des
Artistes Décorateurs,
1923 (photograph
from *Wendingen*,
1924)

In 1923 Eileen was asked to exhibit an entire room in the
XIV Salon des Artistes Décorateurs. It opened in the spring,
and changed Eileen's life in more than one way.

She had never had a full-scale exhibition, so she was
naturally delighted. She had always liked the notion of a
bedroom-*cum*-living room: a room to sleep in but also a
place where one could write a letter or read a book. She had
made a bedroom-boudoir for Madame Mathieu-Lévy. Her
own bedroom on the rue Bonaparte contained library
shelves, a small writing desk, and two comfortable
armchairs. So for the exhibition she designed such a dual-
purpose room. Originally she called it simply Hall 1922, but
she changed the name to Bedroom-boudoir for Monte
Carlo—"to give it an exotic touch, 'Hall' being rather dull,
and Monte Carlo was all the rage." (When this room was
reproduced in *L'Architecture Vivante* in 1924 and in
Intérieurs Français in 1925, she reverted again to the
original name, Hall 1922.)

For the exhibition room Eileen took on a builder, and
together they constructed within the allotted space a whole
room, which measured 13 by 8¾ feet; they built steps and
walls, and Eileen helped with the painting. The room was
furnished much along the lines of her approved formula: a
fur-covered sofa that could be used as a bed in front of a
large screen; the bed was in black lacquer and stood on
white plaster legs. The structure of the divan-bed gave her
much trouble and she spent a lot of time making it. There
was a desk in black lacquer, a low table, some stools, a white
armchair, and some rugs, *Tarabos* and *Héliopolis*.

According to her own description, "The walls were white
and there were dark red and mat white lacquer panels
behind the bed. The door was very dull brown and dull gold
lacquer. There were two small white screens; the carpet was
dark blue and brown. The hanging lamp was made from
wood in dull gold lacquer and the ceiling lamp consisted of
circles shielding lights; the centre was illuminated." There
was also a lamp with blue and silver glass which she liked so
much that she hung one version in the rue Bonaparte flat.

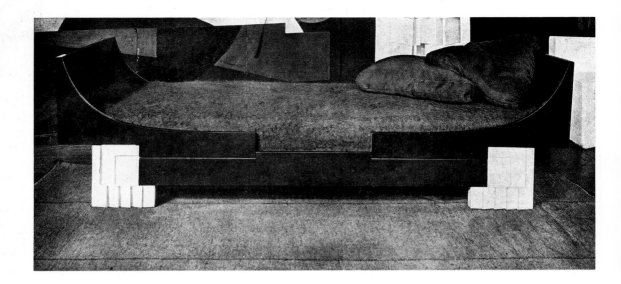

Daybed-divan in the Monte Carlo room; black lacquer with sculptured legs (all photographs on these two pages from *Wendingen*, 1924)

Conical ceiling lamp in parchment in "African" style

But it was the other lamps which aroused much controversy: "les appliqués aux aspects inquiétants" ("wall lights of unsettling appearance"), as one critic put it (*Art et Décoration*, 1923). The lamps which had so much unsettled the writer were made from parchment with different designs in red and white ivory. *Art et Décoration* also advised its readers to "take a look at the strange bedroom of Madame Eileen Gray. It is comical and it is abnormal. But it exudes an atmosphere, and one cannot deny its harmony and its extravagance; it reveals a talent and a sensitivity."

The whole room gave the feeling of austerity and rigor, despite the richness of the materials and colors used. This was a new language, much more formal than the one Eileen had used for the rue de Lota. Here was no client dictating a

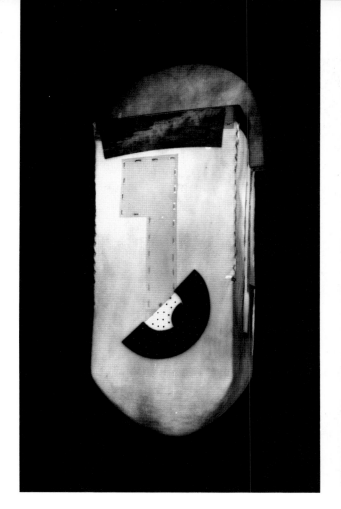
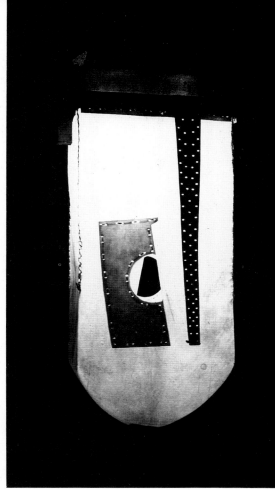

Parchment hanging
lights in red, white,
and ivory, with
appliquéd designs

certain style; Eileen did not have to make any concessions,
and she plunged headlong into a modern world, a world
which echoed Cubism. The art critic René Chavance, a man
not given to praising anything modern, wrote, "One can still
find some regrettable experiments with disquieting Cubism
in M. Pierre Legrain and Miss Eileen Gray, but nevertheless
the latter's room represents, in its eccentricity, a curious
harmony" (*Beaux Arts*, June 1, 1923).

The room with its daring furniture bore no resemblance
to the other room settings that surrounded it. And the
critical reaction that followed the exhibition was vehement.
Eileen had touched a nerve. One writer, comparing her room
to that of another designer, André Domin, which he called
"funereal, but of pleasing design," called "that of Madame
Grey [*sic*] for Monte Carlo maddening with its chrysalid
lamps in parchment and wrapping paper. It is the daughter
of Caligari in all its horror" (*L'Intransigeant*, May 5, 1923).

Eileen, as so often in her life, remembered the abuse she
received for this room and forgot that there was also quite a
lot of praise. An article on the Salon in the *Journal* (May 10,

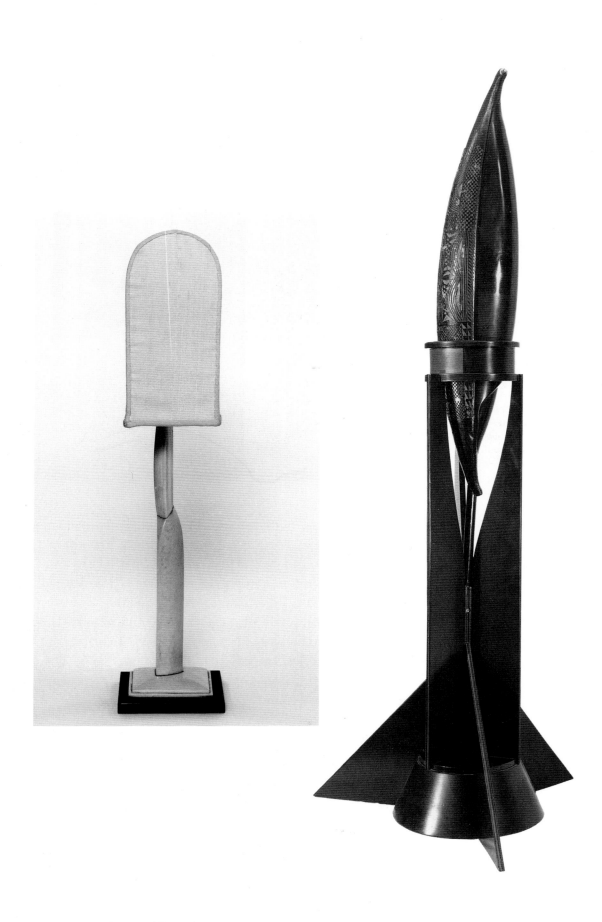

Right: Brown table lamp with ivory incrustations and Cubist motifs

Right: Table in oak described by Eileen as "painted black and white to imitate sycamore and ebony," 1922; it shows obvious similarities with De Stijl

Opposite, far left: Table lamp with an ivory base

Opposite, near left: Floor lamp with copper stem and black lacquered wood base; the shade is missing. Formerly owned by Damia

1923) singles out some of "the most outstanding exhibits": those of Edgar-William Brandt, René Lalique, Paul Follot, Bruno da Silva Bruhns, and Pierre Chareau. It also cites among them "a charming *coucher-boudoir* for the Côte d'Azur (and for fairy tales) by Mlle. Eileen Gray, who had the good sense not to show things which we have already seen." A writer in *Ere Nouvelle* (May 8, 1923) praises the "Monte Carlo room" for its "frank and energetic conception."

Another designer would have been quite happy with this public reception. Many papers linked Eileen's name with those of the top designers in France. But while the public praise gave her an official standing, the recognition from fellow designers was the greatest accolade. The architect Pierre Chareau spoke with admiration about her exhibit, an admiration which was mutual. Chareau was one of the first designers to aim at mass-produced pieces and rejected the idea of creating merely for the rich. The practical approach of a man who thought that a table is best designed by an architect was in accord with her budding ideas that each piece of furniture had to be worked out to its precise function. Another voice speaking for Eileen was Francis Jourdain, who said, "One can set up a room most luxuriously by emptying rather than furnishing it." Eileen did precisely this for the room in the 1923 exhibition. It was a room that, in its simplicity, pointed to her future development.

After the exhibition had opened, the architect Mallet-Stevens asked if she would like to work with him "because there is so little good modern stuff around." Eileen was very flattered, but she did not yet feel ready to work with anybody else. Her instinct told her that this was only the beginning of something she wanted to do and that she had to do it alone. Mallet-Stevens, who considered it an honor for anyone, however good, to work with him, felt rejected, and he would not likely forget this snub.

But the greatest praise, and the one that gave her the greatest pleasure, came from Holland. There were people who understood completely what she had tried to do. Ever since her exhibition in Amsterdam the previous year she had followed design in Holland with interest. In the *Bouwkundig Weekblad*, a Dutch magazine for architects, on July 14, 1923, appeared a reproduction of the Monte Carlo room with a review signed "V. R." The author was none other than the famous architect Sybold van Ravesteyn, a member of De Stijl movement, who wrote:

Originality is not one of the greatest aspects of French furniture designers: the three Louis and their descendants still hybridize architecture . . . however, coming as a surprise, there was also freshness. A room by Mlle. Eileen Gray touches us more and expresses balance between "searching" and "finding." The relationship with "De Stijl" is eye-catching, less orthodox, less pure: French virtues have not been disregarded and feminine frivolity makes itself felt. The work heralds the arrival of a Louis-free tendency even in France. . . .

Van Ravesteyn must have searched Eileen out, and she complained bitterly to him about the lack of understanding by the French. "En France, pour plaire, il faut le Hall luxe galerie [*sic*] Lafayette, le tout avec pieds Louis XVI" ("In France, in order to please, you need the luxurious hall of the Galeries Lafayette, and everything with Louis XVI feet")—a heartfelt cry she would repeat often. She added, "Your country is the only one to understand the art of our time." This was certainly exaggerated, but Eileen's enthusiasm for Holland and her disenchantment with France remained.

Her prejudices against French design and its practitioners strengthened the myth, which lingers on, that until the end of her life she was totally neglected. But in 1923 Eileen was also asked to exhibit some of her furniture in the Salon d'Automne. It was a very important Salon, featuring works by most leading designers of the period. Eileen had chosen very simple pieces, avoiding anything ornate. She showed a black lacquer version of her brick screen, a stool in the form of a cube with a hole created by a couple of small circles, a carpet in natural colors with a dark geometrical design, three lamps, plus a wealth of exotic cushions. Indeed, by 1924, Eileen had truly established herself as one of the leading designers in France. Henri Clouzot in *L'Amour de l'Art*, in 1924, points out that the Ballets-Russes and the avant-garde painters have renewed our vision and brought about a new taste in design. "The invention of cars has revealed a new sense of beauty . . . a pureness of line, a logicality of construction . . . decorators like Legrain, Poulet, Miss Gray, Francis Jourdain, Martine, to name only a few, are trying to give the furniture an expression which seems to be derived more from painting and sculpture and is not afraid of high-pitched notes or discordant elements. There are people of course who with the best intentions condemn them in the name of taste," and he adds a comment which must have pleased Eileen especially: "Let us not forget that good taste is a paralyzing element. One must dare and even dare to make mistakes." Eileen all her life was very aware of both.

In a substantial article in *Art et Décoration* in 1924, as an introduction to an exhibition of decorative arts, Guillaume Janneau, professor at the Ecole du Louvre and curator of the National Furniture Collection, tries to define the "modern spirit." Again Eileen's name figures among the leading designers: "What marks the decorative schemes of Pierre Chareau, Pierre Legrain, and Eileen Gray is that they are based not on taste, but on the permanence of their relationships to the environment. If Francis Jourdain, Pierre Chareau, Pierre Legrain, Eileen Gray, and René Herbst would publish manifestoes like the Futurists and Dadas, they would certainly choose for themselves the title 'Moderns.'" In 1925, in *Technique du Décor Intérieur Moderne*, published by Albert Morancé, Janneau linked her work with that of Jean Lurçat, who was also "producing large rugs of geometrical design." Janneau felt that both Lurçat and Gray were the first successful followers of Chareau, whose work he greatly admired. "Willingly or unwillingly," he wrote, "one is reminded of Baudelaire when one sees those tragic settings which Madame Eileen Grey [*sic*] creates with artistic refinement and taste, 'syncopated' black velvet wall hangings, low, wide beds, precious furs, unusual objects which are all wonderful." But Janneau has some criticism: "With these curious means some decorators distort Pierre Chareau's art. His followers are decorators, not architects; both Madame Eileen Grey and Pierre Legrain follow not his aesthetics, only his poetry." Soon Eileen would only too willingly admit that the room settings she created in the early part of her career did not take sufficient account of architectural aspects; only when she began studying architecture in earnest was she able to marry the decorator and the architect in herself to achieve room settings of great harmony. But if the outside world considered her part of the designers' world, there was something in Eileen which set her apart. She mistrusted many of her fellow designers. They were too much associated with a certain class and a certain way of life. She looked to Holland, hoping to find there, in the simpler handicraft tradition, a more congenial atmosphere.

De Stijl was founded in 1917, in the Dutch university city of Leiden, by Theo van Doesburg and Piet Mondrian, along with fellow painters Vilmos Huszár and Bart van der Leck. Van Doesburg's concern to improve society led him into architecture, and brought architects into De Stijl:

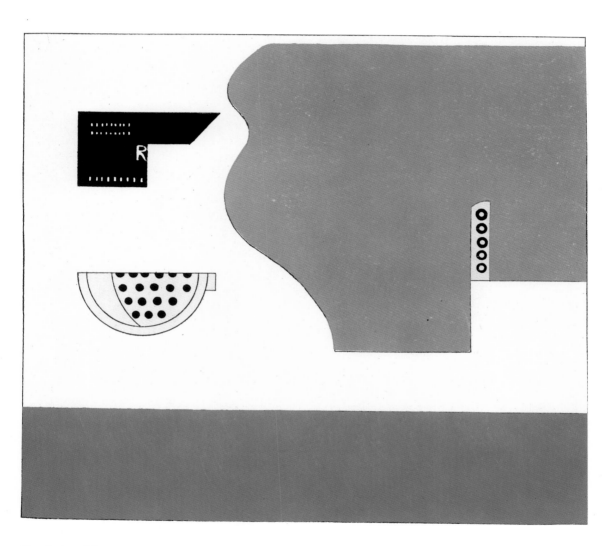

**Rug designed for
Eileen's first house,
E.1027**

...ered wood
...g lamp
...ed for the
... Carlo room;
the parchment shade
is modern

Satellite light,
made for the
Maharaja of Indore;
Eileen made another
version for herself
and hung it in her
workroom in the
apartment on the rue
Bonaparte

Ceiling light of white
lacquered wood with
an ostrich egg,
designed for the rue
de Lota apartment

Bernard Bijvoet, J. J. P. Oud and Jan Wils, and later Gerrit
Rietveld and Cornelis van Eesteren.

Their desire to free art and design from the constraint of
tradition and their constant search for truth struck a
familiar chord in Eileen. "All beautiful forms are mechanical
or functional, showing the thing without decor" was one of
their maxims. Until the end of her life Eileen spoke about
the liberating effect this movement had on her. Soon she met
some of the exponents of the movement. It has frequently
been stated that they became friends, which is not true.
They all knew Eileen's work and admired it. She personally
met Bijvoet, Van Ravesteyn, Oud, and Wils. She followed
Rietveld's work closely, but the two never met. Rietveld, who
started as a cabinetmaker, had designed his famous blue and
red chair in 1918. In 1924 he built the Schröder house in
Utrecht, aided by Madame Schröder herself. It influenced
Eileen's decision to become an architect. Eileen was not the
only designer attracted by the Dutch school, and the
attraction was mutual; the young Dutch architects looked
with enthusiasm at the budding work of Mallet-Stevens,
Pierre Chareau, and Eileen Gray.

In 1923, the same year Eileen exhibited her Monte Carlo
room, the Galerie de l'Effort Moderne, in Paris, owned by
Léonce Rosenberg, organized an exhibition entirely devoted
to Dutch architecture. Rosenberg had been negotiating for
several years with members of De Stijl, especially with Theo
van Doesburg, for the building of a house and gallery to be
designed jointly by all the Stijl artists. When this ambitious
project foundered, he decided to mount an exhibition in

order to introduce the movement to the French public. The exhibition, which lasted from October 15 to November 15, was an immense success. It summed up the architectural credo of the group. There were architectural drawings and models for houses by Van Eesteren and Van Doesburg, a model for a jeweler's shop by Rietveld, and designs by Huszár. Oud showed his drawings for the Purmerend Factory, and Wils his interiors of a women's residence in The Hague. There was also a model of a glass skyscraper by Mies van der Rohe.

Eileen was enthralled by what she saw. Van Doesburg and Van Eesteren took up residence in Paris, where Van Doesburg published his sixteen-point program "Toward a Plastic Architecture," which had a profound influence on Eileen's thinking about design. It asserted the primacy of architecture over painting and sculpture, because it is "the sum of all the arts, in their most elementary manifestation, as their essence."

The Dutch architect and writer A. Boeken had come to Paris to report about the Salon des Artistes Décorateurs. When he saw Eileen's exhibit, he was ecstatic: the abstract design of the furniture with its almost geometrical forms was something new. The lacquer surfaces, at times resembling a fantastic rich oxidized metal, were combined with beautifully grained wood; "without these indulgences, the nobility of her lacquer would be sterile," he wrote, in a glowing article in *Bouwkundig Weekblad*, in July. He also commented on a lamp in white parchment with black drawings, a lantern with blue and white glass, and a third lamp combining an ostrich eggshell with wrought iron and threaded ropes.

Boeken called on Eileen in her flat. She received him in her usual graceful manner. Their conversation was very lively. Eileen mentioned Ossip Zadkine to him and arranged for him to go and see the sculptor in his studio. They talked about architecture, and in his thank-you letter for the "delightful reception," Boeken mentioned a book published by the Bauhaus movement. "I am certain that you know all about it already." Eileen must have struck him as someone well informed in architectural matters. She was indeed gradually moving toward architecture. It was a logical step; her architectural forms were readily perceived in her furniture. It is not unusual for an architect to transform an object into architecture. Frank Lloyd Wright's point of departure for the Guggenheim Museum in New York was a coffee service designed in 1930 for the Netherlands Glass Company in London. Much of Eileen's earlier furniture contained strong architectural elements. The Monte Carlo daybed with its dark reclining elements sitting on a massive beige support suggests in its detailing some involvement with architecture. As one critic had acutely observed, in *Ere Nouvelle*, her furniture is treated "like simple complements to architectural structures." The evolution of Eileen's furniture toward more sculptural pieces showed clearly that she was ready for the next step of her career.

In *Bouwkundig Weekblad*, Boeken brushed aside the works by Francis Jourdain, Djo Bourgeois, Ruhlmann, Süe et Mare, and Martine, "who were doing very different works." Boeken simply stated "that the whole department of interior and furniture would be depressingly boring and would have no importance, were it not for three unpretentious entries, which attract one's attention. . . . Three interiors stood out for their depth of character as something new, strange, and so different from the rest of the atmosphere of the exhibition. The small contribution of Mlle. Eileen Gray, Pierre Chareau's small interior, and Robert Mallet-Stevens's bathroom." To be mentioned in the same sentence as these two architects was a great encouragement for Eileen. Boeken praised the lamps that had outraged the French critics: "Those wondrous lamps with their mysterious lighting; every analysis of the lamps comes to a halt. Are they modern works of art? Are they of this time? Her latest furniture in its geometrical abstraction, like her interiors, with their elementary contrasts, are certainly of this time. The lamps are much more than mere demonstrations of constructions and techniques of modern aesthetics. . . . Certain new things, a certain character, a purity, a strength bordering on perversity emerges which places the artist in a special category of her own." This was no longer the flowery praise of some magazine for fashionable amateurs, but the commendation of an architect in a professional publication.

But Boeken also criticized some of her furniture, especially the bookcase, which he felt was not driven by the same spirit of modernity. It had "the same weaknesses as much of the French design." Eileen did not need Boeken to tell her this, but she took his advice to heart. Most things she designed from then on had very little to do with the past. The period of the ornate lacquer pieces, the tassels, lay behind her. "I never felt really like doing these things. I did them because everybody wanted them. Already when I was in London [during the war], I looked back at most things I had done so far and I regretted many." Her heart lay in designs such as the one she did for the tea table, a kind of homage to the Stijl movement. It was one of her favorite pieces and stood in her own living room until her death.

It is not surprising that this small table caught the attention of the Stijl architects. The sculptural quality of this piece of furniture, its use of color, the logical construction were all elements that preoccupied De Stijl. It was the most remarkable piece among her exhibits. It was made of oak painted black and white "to imitate sycamore and ebony." Boeken was the first critic to point out the "abstract" qualities of her furniture, and nowhere was this more visible than in this table, which foreshadowed her architectural work to come. The search for a synthesis, the tendency to combine the most refined with the most clear and austere found its peak in this table. She often used two or more colors in the same piece of furniture to highlight the different use of material and to create a subtle balancing of different moods. This ambiguity gave almost all her furniture and later her architecture a particular dramatic tension and complexity. The step from this design for a table to pure architecture was now only a matter of time.

But the most important reason for the change to architecture was the encounter with a young architect, Jean Badovici, who had the most decisive influence on her entire career.

JEAN BADOVICI

Badovici was born Badoviso, in 1893, in Bucharest. His parents wanted him to study in Germany, but he insisted on going to Paris. When Eileen met Badovici, shortly after the First World War, he was a handsome young man in his twenties, almost penniless, working toward an architectural degree and "doing all sorts of evening jobs." Badovici studied first with Julien Guadet and Jean-Baptiste Paulin at the Ecole des Beaux-Arts, and then at the Ecole Supérieure d'Architecture from 1917 to 1919. He shared a garret with a friend, the Greek journalist Christian Zervos, at 48 avenue Denfert-Rochereau. They were not yet the successful critic and editor that they respectively would soon become. Both were passionately interested in modern architecture. They persuaded the publisher Albert Morancé to bring out a magazine on modern architecture. Called *L'Architecture Vivante*, it was published for the first time in 1923. In its ten years of existence it published twenty-one issues and in a short time became the most distinguished magazine of its kind.

Eileen was much taken by Badovici's enthusiastic manner, and Badovici, a man not without ambition, saw in her immediately a woman of great artistic talent and enough financial means to put his ideas into practice. Their relationship marked Eileen deeply, personally and professionally, and shifted her entire life into unforeseen directions. Through Badovici, Eileen came into contact with some of the most important architects of this century.

Paris was bursting with new ideas about architecture and design. Le Corbusier and Ozenfant had launched their review, *L'Esprit Nouveau*, in 1920. They also began working with Léger. Badovici soon became friendly with them, and through him Eileen met all three. Le Corbusier had not yet done much building, but with his cousin Pierre Jeanneret he had opened a studio at 35 rue de Sèvres, not far from where Eileen lived.

Besides editing *L'Architecture Vivante*, Badovici contributed articles to *Cahiers d'Art*, the magazine Zervos had begun to publish in 1926, and to the Dutch magazine *Wendingen*.

L'ARCHITECTURE VIVANTE

s'honore de la précieuse collaboration de :

A. BARTHOLOMÉ · L. BONNIER · E.-A. BOURDELLE · MAURICE DENIS
A. DERVAUX · JACQUES GRÉBER · LÉON JAUSSELY · FRANTZ JOURDAIN
A. et G. PERRET · CHARLES PLUMET · J.-E. RUHLMANN · H. SAUVAGE
LOUIS SOREL · SÜE et MARE · ANDRÉ VENTRE · ET DES MEMBRES DU
GROUPE DES ARCHITECTES MODERNES · H.-P. BERLAGE ET LES
ARCHITECTES DU GROUPE " DE STYL " (Hollande) · A. LOOS (Autriche)

SOMMAIRE DU FASCICULE D'HIVER 1923

Through Badovici and *L'Architecture Vivante*, which covered the whole spectrum of modern design and architecture, Eileen kept up with the major architectural trends in Holland, Germany, Russia, France, Belgium, and the United States. All the different movements—Constructivism, De Stijl, the Bauhaus, etc.—were widely discussed, and architects like Frank Lloyd Wright, Le Corbusier, Mies van der Rohe, Bruno Taut, Adolf Loos, and Gerrit Rietveld contributed to the magazine. It became Eileen's textbook. An example of how much Eileen learned from it is an architectural project which she did in 1923 for a small house. The same year *L'Architecture Vivante* had published a *petite maison* by Adolf Loos in which he tried to solve a problem that preoccupied him for years: how to achieve a pure space. Eileen experimented with this drawing and changed Loos's east facade completely. Realizing that this unsettled the whole plan, she redrew it completely, leaving only the terrace and the arrangement of the bedroom and bathroom from Loos's original idea. This can be considered a first attempt for a house, but it was more likely just an exercise in planning.

Eileen's drawing already shows some of her architectural preoccupations. There are built-in furniture and secondary entrances via staircase or terrace—both elements that would appear again and again later in her houses. This first surviving architectural sketch of hers shows remarkable

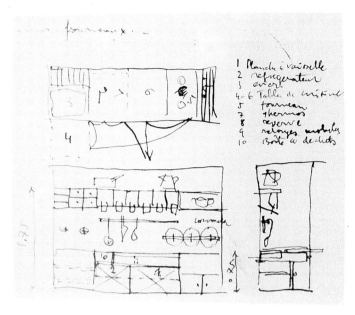

Three of Eileen's studies on the problem of architecture in a limited space. Above, left to right: her room at the Hotel Regis, Mexico City; small kitchen; right: her cabin on the boat she took to Mexico

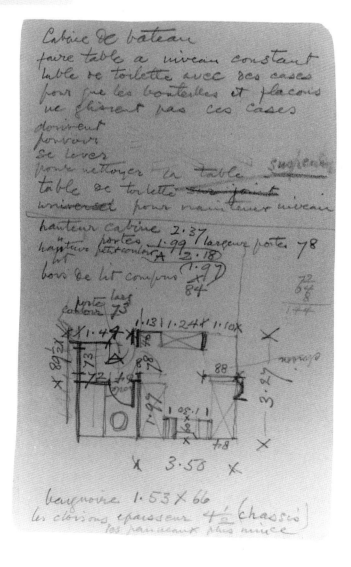

Dressing table
designed for Jean
Désert in oak and
sycamore stained
black, with two
pivoting side drawers
with ivory handles,
which were invisible
when closed; this was
the first time that
Eileen Gray used the
pivoting device, which
became one of her
hallmarks. The top
was glass, 1919–22

confidence in controlling space, but she still has trouble with the inner circulation of the house.

If architectural plans from fellow architects were one of Eileen's sources, she also learned from her immediate surroundings. Among her papers is a small sketch with her measurements of the cabin of the boat which took her to Mexico. In another she measured the dimensions of her hotel room. She was intrigued by the smallness of the two rooms, which seemed perfect subjects to study how to use limited spaces, a subject which in time she mastered superbly.

The preoccupation with architecture prompted her to look for new and more appropriate materials for her furniture. Everything in her told her she had to get away from the lacquer cult. From now on she increasingly used chrome and tubular steel. Exotic woods became also favorite materials. She used zebrawood and was always searching for unusual African woods. She would also try out new materials such as slate or the first synthetic resin, invented by Leo Hendrik Baekeland and known as Bakelite. She experimented furiously. She scorched wood with acid to achieve a rough texture. She made a sofa and a chest of drawers in "bois brûlé." She also designed a deceptively simple architect's cabinet in sycamore with chrome handles. It had an intricate system of different-sized drawers. She made one for the architect Henri Pacon and one for herself. It stood in her workroom until she died.

But the clients of Jean Désert did not let Eileen have her own way. A rich clientele was still looking for the old Eileen Gray, for the pieces they had seen in the smart salons of Paris, and Eileen had difficulty introducing new designs into her shop. Gradually taste changed in favor of simpler designs. The Duchesse de Clermont-Tonnerre gave up her big *hôtel particulier* in Passy and furnished a little villa, proclaiming: "All the things in my big apartment were made for a period which is crumbling, no more flowers, no more birds, the Chinese fish are dead. I have resolved not to hang onto the past and bravely to face the new epoch. Throwing overboard the decorated salons, I opt for the modern." The writer Maurice Sachs, a friend of Cocteau and Gide, decided "To make order in my room, and if the stock market continues to be good, I will redo it in modern; I have seen many good things with strict lines and one uses new woods—sycamore, citronwood, and elm."

Not everybody felt that the new "simplicity" was right. When he saw the austerity of Jean-Michel Frank's interiors,

Architect's cabinet in
sycamore with
chrome handles. The
drawers were
designed in varying
sizes to store files and
drawings; some
pivoted, others folded
out. Above the
cabinet a picture by
Eileen

Jean Cocteau remarked: "The young man is charming; pity he has been burgled." Eileen always liked Frank's interiors. Their restrained luxury appealed to her. When Elsa Schiaparelli became a *couturière*, he decorated her flat. Other designers Eileen liked were Djo Bourgeois and Edouard Benedictus, who, Eileen remembered, was "someone who was kind to her." As for the other fashionable designers, Eileen had few good things to say. Raymond Subes was "too commercial," Raymond Templier and Jean Puiforcat were "very conventional," and Maurice Dufrêne and Paul Follot "dreadful and ghastly." When Eileen made these rather harsh pronouncements, she was already in her nineties and she would not mince her words. Prejudices ran strongly in her and she would never forget an injury.

In the next few years Eileen's business improved slightly. Her list of clients included over forty people, many of them famous or rich, mostly both. Among them were the young Vicomte de Noailles and his new wife, Marie-Laure, daughter of the millionaire Maurice Bischoffsheim, a great patron of the arts and modern design. They had asked Mallet-Stevens to design them a small modernist house in Hyères. Mallet-Stevens began by building a modern house with five rooms. Eventually in the thirties, it was transformed into a castle, which would see as guests Alberto Giacometti, Man Ray, Cocteau, Buñuel, Gide, and many other famous people of literature and the arts. The interior was designed by Djo Bourgeois. It is supposed to have included some pieces by Eileen Gray which had been bought at Jean Désert.

In March 1923, *The Daily Mail* again praised the Jean Désert showroom and Miss Gray for her originality and the beauty of her lacquer. The increasing public awareness in France and abroad brought more clients. A designer from London named J. Duncan bought two white screens and put them in his showroom in Grosvenor Square. "You may trust us not to copy them," he wrote, and Eileen sent him some photographs of a black lacquer screen and some ideas for other screens.

In 1924, Eileen was invited by Pierre Chareau to show some of her work at his stand at the XV Salon des Artistes Décorateurs. Chareau had assembled an interior from various pieces by contemporary designers: a "Cubist" entrance hall by Mallet-Stevens, a heavily cushioned conservatory by Poiret. Other artists, according to a commentary by Gabriel Henriot in *Mobilier et Décoration d'Intérieur* for December 1924, "have enriched the apartment with wall hangings and carpets (that was the task of Madame Eileen Gray)."

But despite all this publicity Jean Désert did not do well. The only aspect of the gallery besides designing that gave her any pleasure was that she could give a few artists a chance to exhibit their work there. Her exhibitions started with her old friend Chana Orloff. Orloff had married the poet Ary Justman in 1916. Widowed two years later, she earned her living by making portraits of Parisian high society. She had exhibited at the Salon d'Automne in 1913 and at the Salon des Indépendants in 1918, but Eileen gave her her first one-man show, at Jean Désert. The invitation card read "Furniture by Eileen Gray and Woodcuts by Chana Orloff." Later Orloff became very famous, with shows in several galleries, and she became a *chevalier* of the Légion d'Honneur. She died in 1968, during a visit to Israel, where she had traveled for a retrospective of her work on her eightieth birthday.

Sugawara had also begun to make little wooden sculptures and Eileen exhibited them. But the most important artist Eileen showed at Jean Désert was Ossip Zadkine. Zadkine had come to Paris in 1909, and taken up lodgings in La Ruche. He had married Valentine Prax, an Algerian painter. In 1921, a small book by Maurice Raynal drew attention to his sculptures. Eileen had met Zadkine through Orloff and had immediately liked his solid stone figures. She invited him to show at Jean Désert.

Their relationship was distant, and sometimes strained. Eileen had bought one of his sculptures for herself, a beautiful stone head with painted lips, which she lent in 1926 to an exhibition in Brussels. Zadkine sent the catalogue with the following inscription, "To Miss Gray in remembrance," but he did not even sign it. Zadkine does not mention Eileen's name in his autobiography, or the fact that he exhibited in her gallery. Eileen was not used to much gratefulness or recognition in her life for personal favors. Surprisingly she still had no worldliness. There was something in her character that made people use and sometimes exploit her. In the end she became increasingly suspicious. But they stayed in contact, and later he visited her in her house in the south of France. During World War Two he taught in New York. In 1945 Zadkine returned to Paris, where he died in 1967.

There is a funny postscript. The Zadkine head always

stood on the mantelpiece in the rue Bonaparte. One day a zealous maid had decided to give it a good wash and to the horror of the culprit, and to the laughter of Eileen, the color of the painted lips disappeared. Zadkine cheerfully came around and restored the lips.

There was nothing unusual in shops displaying works of art. Paris in the twenties was full of little galleries and bookshops. Right around the corner from her flat was the Galerie Povolozky, where Chana Orloff had also exhibited and which also held a Picabia exhibition. Eileen was especially fond of Picabia and had bought a book of his work. The opening of the exhibition was attended by René Crevel, Erik Satie, and Picasso, with Tristan Tzara declaiming Dada songs and Cocteau and Auric playing music. Eileen's cook told her about the strange goings-on, but Eileen went the next day when the gay crowd had disappeared.

160   Jean Badovici

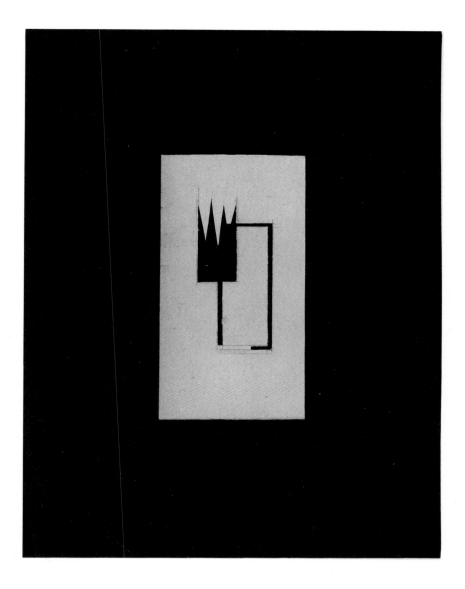

One side of the business that fared quite well was the
sale of Eileen's carpets. The success of her often stark,
abstract designs pleased her. It was at least some recognition
of the modernism of her art. Eileen made beautiful designs
on large sheets of paper, indicating exactly the color she
wanted to achieve. Those designs were then painstakingly
copied on the rue Visconti by Frenchwomen under the
supervision of Evelyn Wyld who "would weave away on their
looms." At one time business was so good that they had
eight women working there. Eileen, always fond of exotic
words, gave the rugs poetic names: *Héliogabale*, *Ulysse*,
Hannibal, *Macédoine*, *Pénélope*, *Fidèle*. There was one called
Tennis, another one *Casimir*, or *Biribi*. One was known by
the letter *E* and one by *D*, in homage to Damia and Eileen.
The cheapest cost one hundred fifty francs (under thirty

dollars); the most expensive, three thousand francs (about six hundred dollars).

But there was no one at the shop who knew how to run a business. Some clients did not pay, others exchanged the rugs several times because the "design did not go with their furniture." Decorators who had ordered designs for their clients complained that their merchandise was not delivered on the promised date. Eileen did not really care; her mind was on other things. She had begun to think of architecture.

TURNING POINT

In 1924 the Dutch magazine *Wendingen* (Turning Point) devoted a richly illustrated special issue to Eileen, with an introduction by Jan Wils and a long article by Jean Badovici. The texts of both architects give valuable insights into the way Eileen's mind worked. Jan Wils, recalling his visit to the Monte Carlo room, gave a lucid appreciation of Eileen's work:

EILEEN GRAY
Furniture and Interiors
Now that I have the pictures of Eileen Gray's work in front of me, my thoughts go back to the afternoon when, after experiencing the intoxicating charms of Paris for days on end, I came—by utter coincidence—across the place where this furniture was being exhibited. It was like stepping into another world; it was as if a fog had suddenly lifted, letting the sun shine down upon a landscape of unexpected beauty.

Here was peace: here one could breathe again, free of the passionate and artificial embrace of Paris. How clear the pretentiousness of narrow-minded Parisian life now appeared; how glaring the contrast with the natural simplicity and grace of furniture not designed to excite the senses.

I must admit that the change from the atmosphere of the boulevards to a place where each object had been so well placed was so great that the impression one got was undoubtedly more powerful than it would have been under other circumstances. That is why the difference between things seen elsewhere and so widely acclaimed was so strong, and there was no room for comparisons to be made by testing accepted formulas and merits.

It was a real joy to go from one piece of furniture to another, to observe it from all angles, and then to explore the luxuriousness of the material at close range. There was no question of logical reasoning or deep contemplation of the hows and whys; the armor of cool judgment and mathematical calculation of its future value did not pinch me for one moment. I know that later, when these tables, lamps, rugs, and screens are seen through the eyes of many friends, they will be seen in a different way from the way in which my eyes saw them. No doubt they will be thoroughly scrutinized: characteristics will be discovered which would suggest that the lifestyle of the observer is above suspicion. But I want nothing of them, for they would contaminate the pleasant memories I have of that afternoon. I also do not want anything to do with them because all those desperate, weighty arguments are neither here nor there. This furniture is the result of a dream; a dream which can only be experienced when one is in close contact with the furniture itself. Piece by piece, it has come into being, like full-blown flowers which have blossomed one after the other in all their splendor.

Sometimes it is like a soft, single chord, struck in a moment of oblivion; sometimes it can be compared to a strange, perfectly controlled movement, filled with vibration and deep emotion. It has not been created in the mind, but the hand has kneaded it as the soul directed at the moment of creation. This is why one piece is sober and streamlined while another, in sudden joy, became a complicated composition of line and form verging on exuberance.

Free of every tradition, taken from an inexhaustible storehouse of spiritual luxuries and desires, the treasures pile up, always different, just as the will of the creator brought them together in subtle distinction. Who inquires about the lifespan or the fulfillment of future longings? Is the enjoyment of a flower determined by the length of its life or by how many variations can be bred from it?

Eileen Gray is a very special, unique figure in the world of new form-finding. She is not one of those who, in an extreme of self-chastisement, is only in search of future happiness and prosperity. Neither is she one of those who aims to achieve a cheap success with the masses through pandering to them. Only the few who surround themselves with furniture of this kind will know the responsibilities involved.

Is it to be wondered at that there is no place for her in Paris? ". . . en France, pour plaire, il faut le Hall luxe galerie [*sic*] Lafayette, le tout avec pieds Louis XVI. . . ." But this furniture is noble. The pieces are as distinguished, refined, and gracious as a young queen whose posture and gestures are the result of a centuries-old culture, and on whom only the best characteristics of so many generations and races have descended. They are sometimes coquettish, their movement sometimes passionate and then softly gliding away. One feels a natural respect for them and one approaches them without exaggeration, lively gesture, or loud voice. They radiate a calm, dominating peace. Solitude they find preferable to the company of anything or anybody of inferior quality. The choice of the material and the way in which it is used do justice to these forms. They are like a well-used rug, its noble lines accentuated but its original value retained. In this way, spiritual content, form, and matter fuse together to form a unity of rare delight. They who know how to choose the material and decide how it is to be used should also be masters of their craft. She is the kind of artist of whom there are very few in existence today.

Badovici's article is the first comprehensive account of Eileen Gray as a designer:

THE ART OF EILEEN GRAY

Eileen Gray occupies the center of the modern movement. In all her tendencies, visions, and expressions she is modern; she rejects the feeling of the old aesthetics and mistrusts old forms.

She knows that our time, with its new possibilities of living, necessitates new ways of feeling. The formidable influence of technology has transformed our sensibilities. . . . All her work reflects a lyrical force, an enthusiasm, and the strength of feeling of this new civilization and spirit which are being forged little by little.

In yesterday's dead civilization, moral values and individual feelings dominated. In today's emerging civilization the individual is blotted out by geometry. This is not just the transformation of a detail or a partial change; it is a total change. . . .

The role of interior decoration is of no small importance in this general revision of values. It not only reflects man's way of living and his preoccupations, it also helps him to get a clearer picture of himself. Interior decoration helps him to strike the necessary balance between his most sacred and hidden desires and the outside world of his daily activities. He has to be in harmony with the new forms of architecture.

Eileen Gray has not retreated in the face of extreme difficulties; her creations testify to a rare audacity and reveal a singularly original vision. If she possessed a more sure and precise knowledge of architecture and relied a fraction less on her creative instinct, she might well be the most expressive artist of our time.

She wants the decorative arts to express the complexities of life, life tormented in its depths but with a quiet surface dominated by thought. Contemporary man's life mixes dream and reality, fuses them in the rhythm of a dance of lines. Violent vibrations and peaceful chants join in a dance of ideal arabesques. In our age of the machine Eileen Gray has remained thoroughly romantic . . . but she refuses to let herself glide into a state of impressionableness without control. She dominates and she dominates herself. She is fond of an architecture which reflects the precise laws and the new necessities, an architecture which expresses the strong will of modern man.

Eileen Gray confirms in her designs the conflict between ideas and material form. She is not interested in presenting mere natural form, she wants to find the geometric equivalent. The beauty of her work does not stem from scientific laws, it is derived from an original and lyrical *élan* which gives her objects their profound unity. Her designs may have a dry, geometric appearance, but their harmony is evident. Sometimes it can be charged that they lack depth and that lyrical intensity dominates the scientific element too much. . . . But a systematic unity gives all her designs a unique, architectonic significance. Furniture, wall hangings, the general mood seem to be like the components of a soul, the soul of its inhabitant, whose outside form corresponds to its inner rhythm.

We find in her compositions those marvelous abstract geometric elements which are the charm of modern furniture. Instead of presenting each piece separately, she makes them complement each other. Lines of individual pieces are no longer frontiers; they extend into the lines of a wall. It is a richly realized totality of space. . . . This is a decoration of ambience, the space is organized through masses and zones in accordance with a purely intellectual order. Form and color have a totally new role, dictated by a visionary understanding of modern ideas and the need of the modern soul for truth.

This is the reason that Eileen Gray denies a tradition which used only one kind of material. She uses all materials which have the capacity to add to the richness and harmony of her design schemes. This is the result of a total conception: glass, cardboard, wood, cement, concrete, leather, fabric, horsehair, mirror glass, etc. . . . Sometimes her materials are precious and handled with great care, the result of painstaking work and knowledge, in which one recognizes the hand of the creator of the beautiful lacquer work—Eileen Gray. Sometimes, on the contrary, this artist uses natural wool for her rugs, simple untreated wood for her furniture. She varies the details in accordance with the character of the whole design scheme. She always exhausts all possibilities. . . . The colors white, gray, black underline a mass, suggesting strength. Other colors, chosen for their contrast or

Chest of drawers in zebra wood scorched in the Japanese manner, with ivory or bone handles; on the black lacquer top, a "fictitious" architectural model, 1919–22

their similarities, add profundity and mystery to the total composition. Subtle emotive nuances complete the harmony of line and lend it strength. Eileen Gray loves smooth materials, . . . silks that shine in the light.

. . . She is often criticized because her art is not cerebral. It is, on the contrary, the expression of a sensibility which vibrates with new and rich forms reflecting the new way of life. It is born of a strong and powerful élan. It shows a will to build purely ideal spaces. . . .

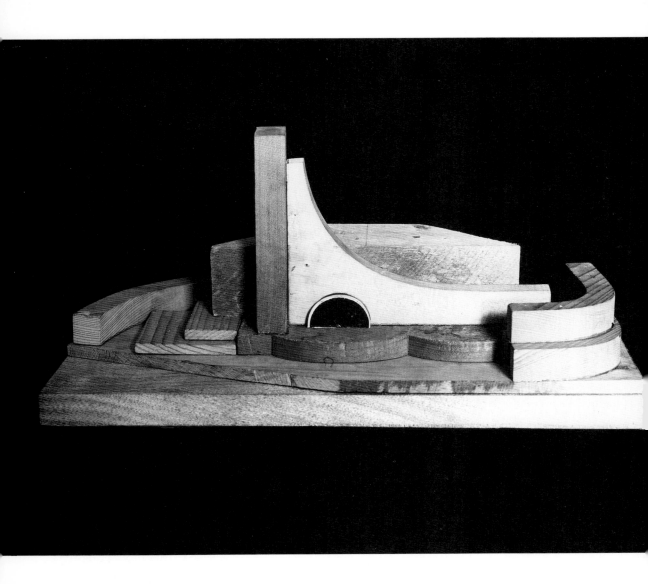

Model of the House with a Small Factory

This article, despite Badovici's characteristic excursions into philosophical fields, shows a clear understanding of Eileen's mind and the nature of her work. Both he and Wils stressed the fact that Eileen created for the "modern man." The modern man for Eileen was the one who combined the highest degree of sensibility with reason, a combination she herself possessed to the highest degree. Both articles, and Badovici's in particular, stressed what Boeken had only hinted at in *Bouwkundig Weekblad*: the fact that her work was closely linked with architecture, that it was conceived in terms of constructive elements. This was the aspect of her work Eileen would henceforth concentrate on. It is in this sense that one has to understand Wils's remark that "Eileen Gray is a very special, unique figure in the world of new form-finding." Here were two architects who publicly and clearly pronounced her modern. It was this which pleased her most and compensated for the many humiliations and disappointments of her past professional life.

This edition of *Wendingen* created quite a sensation when it appeared in Holland. The press attacked the magazine, as usual. The *Handelsblad* called Eileen Gray "an Irish woman working in Paris, more bizarre than beautiful," and the *Telegraaf* accused *Wendingen* of once again showing "bizarreries." Badovici's article took the full brunt: "calling the designs abstract, metaphysical, was like Plato expressing himself in a dinner tray." But the architectural world looked up to her. J. J. P. Oud, after seeing *Wendingen*, wrote her a postcard (in English) sending it to Ireland. "I am highly interested in it and should like to see any more of your works. Could you perhaps send me a number of a revue [*sic*] containing your works. I would be highly obliged by it as I saw until now, very few good modern interiors," and he added a P.S. (referring to Ireland): "Do you have any modern 'movement' in your country?" Eileen's reply is unfortunately lost, but she kept Oud's postcard.

Wendingen also included a model of a House with a Small Factory, which must count among Eileen's first architectural designs. The model was of solid wood, with a large chimney and one entrance. This small object is a curious mix of architecture and sculpture. It is a study in architectural form, not yet a real building. As such it is not unlike the Russian Constructivist "Architectons" of Kasimir Malevich, who also made architectural fictions of this kind as form studies. It was probably done on advice from Badovici, who, having recognized Eileen's talent for building, had suggested that she do something more lasting than decorations and become an architect. "Why don't you build?" he said. When she protested that she had no training, he brushed her scruples aside. It was Badovici who insisted that she learn the basic facts of architecture. Like Kate Weatherby, who had pushed her into making furniture, Eileen had again found somebody with confidence in her who forced her into a new direction. "Vous friez" ("You are frittering away your time"), he said. "Make a door that will last." When this happened, Eileen was forty-six years old.

TOWARD AN ARCHITECTURE

Much of Eileen's previous work—screens, furniture, the apartment for Madame Mathieu-Lévy, her carpets, the Monte Carlo boudoir—had in their concept, attitude, and realization pointed toward architecture. All were marked by clear structural conception and daring innovation. Eileen had very carefully prepared herself for the next endeavor. There was something within her that told her that this was the most important step of her life. She was determined but did not dare to expect too much. *L'Architecture Vivante* was now in its second year and counted among its collaborators Fernand Léger, Piet Mondrian, Amédée Ozenfant, and the architects of De Stijl. Badovici had also become very friendly with Le Corbusier, and kept meeting many more modern architects, and Eileen did so also. She was able to witness or read about most of the leading architectural activities in France, Holland, and America. For this, *L'Architecture Vivante* was still her foremost textbook. Eileen worked closely with Badovici on it and sometimes helped him with the choice of illustrations and with the writing of articles, and so was very familiar with all the material he published. Among her papers are a couple of layout pages for *L'Architecture Vivante*, which suggests that she was sometimes actively involved with that aspect of the magazine.

During the next years, Eileen and Jean traveled together to Holland and Germany, looking at buildings by Gerrit Rietveld, Bruno Taut, Ludwig Mies van der Rohe, Walter Gropius, and many others. In 1924 *L'Architecture Vivante* reproduced three rooms by Vilmos Huszár and Rietveld for the Greater Berlin Exhibition. It was there that Rietveld exhibited his Berlin chair. But there were other sources of information. Le Corbusier and Ozenfant began in 1920 to publish the magazine *L'Esprit Nouveau*. Eileen was one of the early subscribers. It started with a series of articles on architecture, which, when later published in book form, became one of the most influential architectural books of the twentieth century: Le Corbusier's *Vers une Architecture*.

Eileen was building a library containing also specific

works on architectural problems such as Planat's *Manuel de Perspective et Tracé des Ombres à l'Usage des Architectes et Ingénieurs et des Elèves des Ecoles Spéciales* and Fredrik Macody Lund's *Ad Quadratum, Etude des Bases Géométriques de l'Architecture Religieuse dans l'Antiquité et au Moyen Age Découvertes dans la Cathédrale de Nidaros.* The subjects of these books showed with what tenacity she pursued her studies.

Eileen also began some practical studies. Badovici introduced her to a young architect, Adrienne Gorska, who had been born in Russia in 1898 of a Polish family. Adrienne had met Badovici at the Ecole Supérieure d'Architecture, where they were both students. Now Adrienne had just obtained her degree and was working on a building site. She took Eileen along and taught her the first steps in architectural drawing. Feeling very much like an amateur, Eileen kept her studies quite secret. She realized that she needed some practice, but she "would rather have died" than ask any of the architects she knew for help. She could have talked to Mallet-Stevens or Pierre Legrain, who had both asked her to work with them, but she—probably rightly—knew that as a woman and an amateur she would have found little professional understanding. She could have turned to her friends from De Stijl, but she did not dare. So she felt she had no one really she could turn to.

As in her adaptation of the Adolf Loos house, she continued to practice by making plans for imaginary houses. She later mentioned that she "regretted not having learned more about facades, but there were not many people from whom I could learn." Eileen had been, from her early student years, interested in architecture, but she was entirely self-taught; she never had any formal architectural training.

Badovici had a very good theoretical knowledge of architecture, but his coaching was not entirely altruistic. In 1924, Eileen had furnished a house for him, which he had purchased and modernized in the little town of Vézelay, about two hundred miles from Paris. He now wanted Eileen to build him a "little refuge" in the south of France. Eileen realized that the best way of learning her new trade was by practicing. She also was infatuated with the very persuasive, good-looking Jean. So early in 1925 they drove in her little car down to the south to look for a plot. They took a room in Saint-Raphaël. Badovici left her there and Eileen began to explore the area. She first opted for the peninsula of Saint-Tropez. It was there, many years earlier, before the Great

La Bastide Blanche, Eileen's favorite place, near Saint-Tropez; she took this photograph in the early twenties

War, that she had fallen in love with a most enchanting place, only a couple of miles from the sleepy little town.

Saint-Tropez had always been a favorite of artists. Liszt had stayed there and Cosima Wagner. Maupassant had written a eulogy about the little fishing port. In 1902 it had only two hotels, and the artists met at the old Café Frédéric at the port. When Eileen had arrived around 1910—with Kate Weatherby and Evelyn Wyld—Pierre Bonnard, Paul Signac, Henri Manguin, and Henri Matisse lived in the area. There was still an old railway linking Toulon and Saint-Raphaël with Saint-Tropez. There were few tourists.

Eileen and her friends had decided to explore the coast around Saint-Tropez on foot. They hired a donkey to carry their bags in Croix-Valmer. Crossing the mountains, they had come across a beautiful beach, stretching out along green vineyards. It was getting dark and thunder threatened. They were looking for shelter, but there was only one farmhouse and an old customs outpost by the name of La Bastide Blanche. The officer in charge did not consider the customs house a suitable place for three women. But the farmer, Monsieur Lebrun, put the extraordinary English women, with their donkey, up for the night. He could not anticipate that he would see them for the next fifty years. La Bastide Blanche became for Eileen a paradisical spot to which she would always return. The last time, when she was ninety-seven years old, she climbed happily the fences of the villas which had now been built there, still considering it "her place." After the Great War, Kate and Evelyn had bought a house there, and the three friends spent many summers in this blissful place.

Eileen saw all the changes of Saint-Tropez, right up to the ones Brigitte Bardot and Françoise Sagan brought. But she stuck it out, loving it despite all the terrible transformations, still finding corners which were those Colette described: "I knew another Saint-Tropez . . . the old harbor, soberly tricolored blue sea. Facades a faded pink, sky milky as the edge of the desert. Five o'clock by the church bell. . . ."

In the twenties Saint-Tropez began to become popular. Cars brought the first summer tourists. Boutiques opened. Soon a Parisian, Jeanne Duc, transformed a cellar into the first nightclub—Escale. Colette, who continued to live on her lovely property, La Treille Muscate, among the vines, would write: "Pajama, bare backs, nightclubs for rich tourists, cocktails, champagne on the yachts on the quays."

Eileen loved Saint-Tropez at all times, so it was not surprising that she wanted to build her first house there. Searching for a suitable plot, she must have strayed far away from La Bastide Blanche—maybe on purpose. Her relationship with Evelyn Wyld had become rather strained, and she thought it better to be a little farther away from a certain part of her life. One day she drove as far as a little place called Roquebrune, on the coast between Menton and Nice. She had heard of land which was cut off so that one could not drive to it.

She walked along the railway track from the small station at Roquebrune and came to a rocky terrain a hundred feet above the Mediterranean Sea, inaccessible and not overlooked from anywhere. Of course this part of the coast was not very much built up yet, but even then a plot like this was a rarity. It had the kind of savage atmosphere that Eileen always preferred to the lush, gentler landscape. If she had any doubts earlier, she suddenly "knew that I was going to build and I was going to build here."

She called Badovici, and he and Zervos came down.

Badovici loved the place and Eileen bought it in his name.
The three of them returned to Paris, and Eileen started to
make architectural plans. She realized that if she was ever
going to succeed, she had to go about it in her own way.
However much she valued Badovici's expertise, she knew her
own temperament very well. She was unable to do anything
with somebody hovering over her, especially someone like
Badovici. As usual she resented the slightest restraint. She
returned to Saint-Raphaël, driving often to the plot of land.
Not knowing how to draw an architectural plan properly, she
did what she would always do: she made a model.

After two months, she returned to Paris and showed
Badovici the model for the little refuge he had asked for.
Badovici liked what she had done, but urged her to make it
larger, so that they "would have a house they could show to
future clients and maybe use it for a place to work in."
Together they decided that it should have at least two
bedrooms. Eileen went back to the south and altered and
enlarged the model. When she finally showed it to Badovici,
he accepted it as it was, but he suggested the bedrooms
should be underneath and that the house should be put on
pilotis.

From time to time she had to go to Paris; things at Jean
Désert were not going well, despite continuing publicity. In
1924, *Les Arts de la Maison* had reproduced three of her
most recent pieces (a bookcase in lacquer and silver, a
writing table, and a brown lacquer table with a screen), and
Badovici had brought out three publications on French
interiors: *Intérieurs de Süe et Mare*; *Harmonies: Intérieurs
de Ruhlmann*; and finally *Intérieurs Français*, which
included interiors by Chareau, Groult, Jourdain, Martine,
Mallet-Stevens, Ruhlmann, Süe et Mare, and Eileen Gray.
Under the heading "Our Decorators," the preface states that
"we have tried to study as impartially and completely as
possible, the decorative art of our time. We have limited our
choice to those we consider the pioneers." A short piece
introduced each of the eight designers. Eileen's own copy of
this edition of *Intérieurs Français* has a personal dedication
by Morancé, thanking her especially "for her valuable
collaboration on this publication."

Nineteen twenty-five was the year of the big exhibition of
Arts Décoratifs, with its enormous pavilions displaying
several thousand modern works by designers and architects
from all over the world. The show covered several parts of
Paris, with barges in the River Seine, decorated by Poiret,

mooring between the Pont Alexandre III and the Pont des Invalides, where the majority of events took place. The whole show was described by one critic as "orgies of lacquer furniture in rare woods and sometimes covered in shagreen. Textiles and wallpapers, either blinding like the decor of one of the early Russian ballets, or as chaste as a drawing-board diagram, panels with dryly geometric outlines."

Strangely enough, nobody invited Eileen Gray to participate in this vast show. To ignore her work seems today an almost unbelievable omission. The only explanation one can offer is that this exhibition was set up by countries, and Eileen, as an English designer living in France, had no sponsor. She might have taken some consolation, if she needed any, in the sad fact that Le Corbusier was given a section safely tucked away from the rest so as not to offend by the austerity of his work. The exhibition commission was so worried by his building that they erected a fence almost twenty feet high around it; the fence was removed only once, for the day of the official opening by the minister of Fine Arts. Le Corbusier's Pavillon de *L'Esprit Nouveau*, with murals by Léger, earned mostly abuse and had no end of difficulties from the authorities. People were hardly ready for the wares exposed in the main exhibition halls; how could his gesture of faith in a machine age hope to find a public?

But there were a few voices who found the display of decorative luxury immoral and asocial. "The Société des Artistes Décorateurs has given the measure of the spirit in which our architects and designers work," wrote Waldemar George in *L'Art Vivant* (1925). "They are reactionaries not only because of their devotion to money but also because of their lack of understanding of the needs imposed by modern life. . . . Architects and furniture designers ignore the triple principle of economy: economy of space, economy of material, and economy of money."

Most architects, even the best ones, had failed to respond to modern times. There were of course the exceptions, and those were the ones Eileen learned from: "The theater of Perret, the two pavilions of Mallet-Stevens, the pavilion of the U.S.S.R. [by Konstantin Melnikov], and the villa of L'Esprit Nouveau [by Le Corbusier, Ozenfant, and Jeanneret] were the only buildings which could be considered modern" was the final and not totally unjust verdict of Waldemar George.

This great exhibition was the watershed of two worlds, one still clinging to the old values of bourgeois taste, with its

Right: Lamp with
chromed metal base,
designed in the
thirties

Below: Floor lamp
with a "Cubist" foot
designed for the
Monte Carlo room

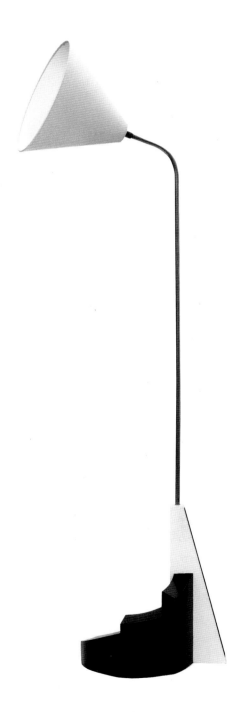

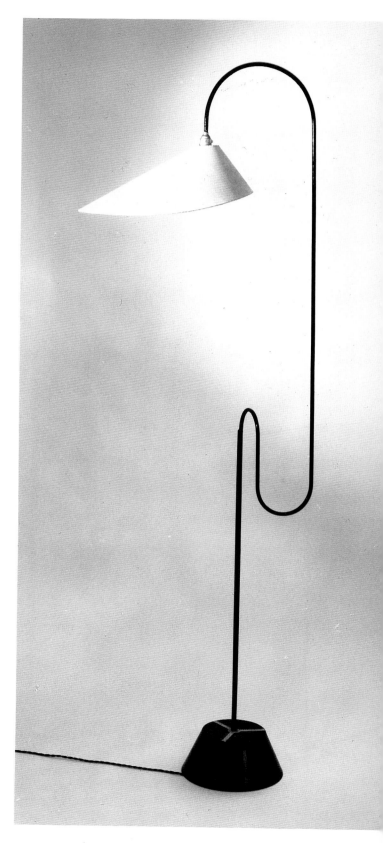

Model of the House for an Engineer. The project uses the whole vocabulary of modern architecture: roofed-over terrace, *pilotis*, long windows, white walls. One enters via the terrace, which is protected by a low wall from outside viewing

delight in luxury, and the other already pointing at the future and a new way of living. There was no doubt in Eileen's mind which way she had to look: "The future projects light, the past only shadows" was her own dictum.

While drafting Roquebrune, Eileen had made another project, a small house for an engineer, situated on the Mediterranean. Two floor plans, three elevations, and some photographs of the model survive. It certainly uses the first draft for the house for Badovici, with which it shares some startling similarities. The series of linked terraces, the entrance, and an indoor and outdoor kitchen are all ideas which recur in the final house. It had two living rooms and a kitchen on the ground floor, and two bedrooms, one with an office, on the next floor. There was a central staircase; it stood on *pilotis*. Although it was also not as complex and refined as the house she would eventually build—facades and ground plan are not totally in harmony—it had her stamp, which contradicts the general belief that Eileen created more on the building site itself than on the drawing board. There was the same open feeling which would characterize her next

houses. It is evident that Eileen worked on the engineer's
house before she found the land for Badovici's house, because
it was conceived for a flat site.

The project shows some influence of other architects,
notably Van Doesburg, Van Eesteren, Le Corbusier, and even
Mies van der Rohe, but it also already displayed a high
degree of conceptual independence, which is remarkable for a
beginner and autodidact. Its design is contemporaneous with
those of Le Corbusier's Maison Cook and Maison Guiette. It
precedes Mies van der Rohe's Barcelona Pavilion (1929) and
the Tugendhat House (1930), which are both astonishingly
similar to the ground plan of the engineer's house. The study
of the plan reveals that right from the start Eileen was
willing to face quite complex and new problems such as the
right balance between outer and inner space, the relationship
between architecture and furniture, and the control of light
and heating.

Eileen began building the house at Roquebrune in 1926.
It was constructed exactly as she had designed it. Most
houses on the Côte d'Azur were either copies of Provençal

**House for an
Engineer, elevation
and ground plans
First floor: a. Entrance,
b. Kitchen, c. Dining
area, d. Living
room, e. Terrace;
second floor (linked
by a central staircase):
f. Study/Office,
g. Bedroom,
h. Bathroom,
i. Bedroom,
j. Terrace**

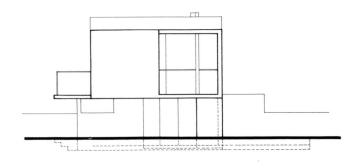

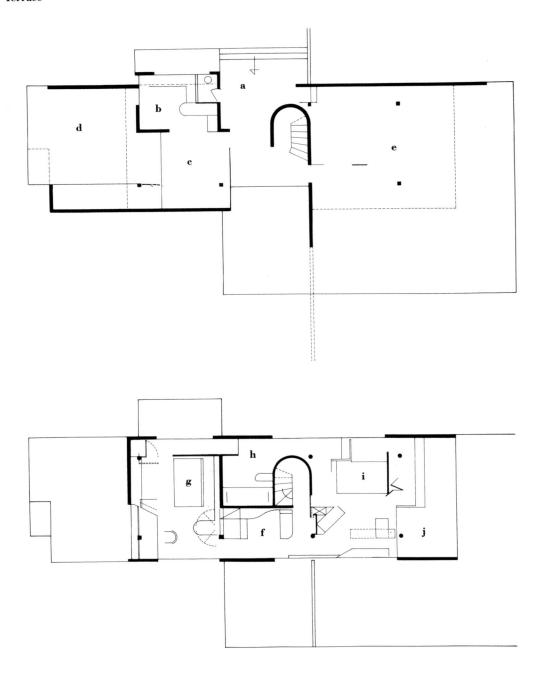

farmhouses, or villas copying the styles of previous centuries. Eileen remembered that it came as quite a shock to the local people who saw it grow, "but I was determined not to make any compromise."

Badovici did not have much time to keep an eye on Roquebrune. He was very busy with his magazine, endlessly traveling to Germany and Holland for his articles, but he continued to bring back new and interesting architectural ideas which stimulated the budding architect.

For the building Eileen had hired a mason who was an expert in reinforced concrete; with the help of two assistants he built the entire house. The relationship between architect and builders was excellent; between Badovici and the builders it was less so, and Eileen "was glad that Jean kept away." Eileen had found a little flat in Roquebrune and remained in the south for most of the next three years.

During the summer months Jean Désert closed. Eileen was in Roquebrune working on her new project, which took all her energy and enthusiasm. Very little else mattered to her now. There were other changes in her life. Evelyn Wyld had started to design her own carpets. While supervising the making of Eileen's designs, she had begun to "explore her own pattern and design." She was no longer content just to make Eileen's.

Evelyn had met a stunning-looking twenty-seven-year-old American painter and designer, Elizabeth de Lanux, who was writing a monthly column for an American magazine: "Letters of Elizabeth." She was the wife of the writer Pierre de Lanux, a friend of Jean Cocteau, who, as a young man, had been private secretary to André Gide. The Lanuxes moved in the right circles. They were friends of Man Ray, Eluard, Aragon, and Breton. They were also friends of the Duchesse de Clermont-Tonnerre and frequent visitors to Natalie Barney's salon. Elizabeth ("Lise," as she was known to her friends) was doing some research into new Paris designers and had naturally come across Jean Désert. She was introduced to Evelyn Wyld. Shortly afterward the two women decided to set up a shop together. Elizabeth took the name of her grandfather William Eyre as her professional name, and made a career as Eyre de Lanux. Eyre de Lanux began as a painter and later changed to furniture design. She exhibited her drawings together with Chana Orloff's woodcuts at Natalie Barney's house. Natalie Barney had commissioned Eyre to do a portrait of her friend the famous courtesan Liane de Pugy.

Around 1924 Eyre decided to turn her back on the smart world, which included her husband, and she moved in with Evelyn Wyld.

Eileen and Evelyn parted, not on the best of terms. They had been friends since childhood and partners for seventeen years. Evelyn kept half the looms and remained on the rue Visconti. Eileen moved the other half into the basement of the rue du Faubourg Saint-Honoré. Eileen always claimed that Evelyn did not design any carpets. This is not exactly true. What is certain is that some of the carpets sold under Evelyn Wyld's name are in fact from Eileen Gray's designs. Evelyn, not wanting to have the original drawings in the studio, had carefully copied the original Eileen Gray designs for the women to make the carpets. It is these copies—which are among Evelyn Wyld's scrapbooks, left to the Royal Institute of British Architects—that led to this confusion. Evelyn Wyld's own carpet designs are easily recognizable and very different from Eileen Gray's. They are far more flowery and are very remote from Eileen's stark abstract style.

Eyre and Evelyn first worked on the rue Visconti. Eyre's many contacts in French society gave them their first clients. A wealthy American engaged them to decorate her flat. The result was written up in *Town and Country*. Eileen watched all these activities with personal and professional jealousy, which prevented her all her life from acknowledging Evelyn Wyld's activities once they had separated.

In 1929 Evelyn and Eyre moved down to La Bastide Blanche. Soon afterward they settled in a house Evelyn had bought in the hills behind Cannes—La Bastide Caillenco—and opened a decorator's shop in Cannes, called Décor, at 2 quai Saint-Pierre. They collaborated on various interiors, Eyre doing lacquer furniture, some of it with the help of Sugawara. But the shop soon closed. The next year they showed another room setting at the Salon des Artistes Décorateurs (their first had been in 1928) and some of Evelyn's rugs were exhibited in 1931 at the Curtis Moffat Gallery in London, in a show organized by Madge Garland (the *Vogue* editor who had promoted Eileen's work back in 1917) that also included carpets by Da Silva Bruhns and Marian Dorn.

Eyre left Evelyn eventually and moved to Rome. Evelyn, having lost both her creative mentors, gave up designing altogether and became a market gardener in the south of France. The rift between Eileen and Evelyn began slowly to heal but was never completely repaired.

Rugs designed
probably in the
twenties. Top: *Tour de
Nesle*; bottom:
Centimètre

Eileen photographed by Berenice Abbott in Paris in 1926

Eileen had had no real reason for any professional jealousy of Evelyn. Despite the commercial disaster of Jean Désert, Eileen was well established. In 1926 she was photographed by Berenice Abbott, whom Sylvia Beach, in her book *Shakespeare and Company*, described with Man Ray, as "the official portraitists of 'the Crowd.' To be 'done' by Man Ray or Berenice Abbott meant you were rated as somebody." Abbott, then a young photographer, had studied with Man Ray. By the time she took Eileen's photograph Abbott had moved out of Man Ray's studio and had opened her own place on the rue Dauphine. In June 1926 Eileen had seen the exhibition of Abbott's photographs in the Galerie du Sacre du Printemps, which included some of her famous early portraits, among them James Joyce, André Gide, Jean Cocteau, Sylvia Beach, and Marie Laurencin. Soon after Abbott took the first photographs of Eileen. In the following

year, she was again photographed by Abbott, who by then
had achieved fame on her own.

The other important change happened in Eileen's home
life. In 1927, Eileen engaged a maid who remained with her
for the rest of her life, Louise Dany. Céleste for Proust,
Pauline for Colette, Berthe for Natalie Barney: one day
someone will have to write a book about these faithful
creatures who devoted a lifetime to their employers, more
loving, more committed than most husbands and wives.
Their faithfulness has survived the lives of those they served,
prisoners of a strange social situation, much needed, much
cared for, and yet often abused. "J'ai mangé du pain blanc,
mais aussi du pain noir" ("I've eaten white bread, but also
black") was one of Louise's favorite sayings.

Louise Dany had come to Paris to visit an aunt and to
scout out work possibilities. She was eighteen and had not

Louise Dany in a
photograph made
during the Second
World War

seen much of the world. When she spotted a little note in a
shop window offering a job as a maid, she presented herself
at the first floor of the rue Bonaparte, carrying a little
basket which held most of her belongings. Eileen's old cook,
Madame Berger, let her into the elegant salon and asked her
to wait. Louise waited for what seemed to her an eternity
and was just going to run from this strange environment
when a lady in a trouser suit with a silk blouse and short
auburn hair entered, followed by what seemed to Louise to be
a gentleman: it was Gaby Bloch. Louise politely said,
"Bonjour, madame. Bonjour, monsieur." Eileen asked her,
"Can you cook?" "No." "Can you iron?" Louise shook her
head. "Have you ever cleaned flats?" Louise shrugged her
shoulders. Then something must have pleased Eileen. She
gave a friendly tap to Louise's shoulder. "How about
trying?" Louise was engaged. The first night she slept on
the sofa in the big salon. To describe her as "La Bonne,"
which is what she became known as, is an injustice to this
great lady, who shared more of Eileen's often cumbersome
life than anybody else. It was a turbulent relationship,
spurred on by mutual obstinacy, but Louise survived all
Eileen's other maids, some with such marvelous names as
Modeste and Tranquille.

Louise helped in the Jean Désert shop and handled all
the dealings with suppliers and workmen. She looked after
Eileen when she was interned as a resident alien during the

Second World War. It was Louise who slept in the armchair in the small hospital room when Eileen had a major operation in 1968. And it was Louise who finally set the little plaque at Père Lachaise, a simple black marble slab with the name Eileen Gray on it and the date of her death. It left out her date of birth, "because Mademoiselle did not like to speak of her age." The love and loyalty to Mademoiselle survived all fights and changes.

Eileen's carpets were now woven in the basement of Jean Désert, and Louise soon was in charge of delivering them to the clients. It was exciting for her to meet people whose names she had read in the papers: the ex-premier Poincaré and the famous singer Damia, to whom she had to deliver a lacquer tea table. She kept busy; at Madame Regnier's sixty-seven hundred francs (thirteen hundred dollars) had to be collected. The writer Maurice Martin du Gard bought an oak desk, and the jewelry designer André Leveillé bought a bench in red lacquer. Often people did not pay. One day money was running so short that they did not know how to pay the workers. Louise was sent to the house of Madame Thorez, wife of the Communist leader, where a large debt was outstanding. Louise could be very insistent and finally managed to get a check. Madame Thorez sent a letter of complaint about the impertinent behavior of Jean Désert's employees. Eileen, who could be quite stern, always insisting on good behavior, had a strong inbuilt sense of justice and backed Louise up totally. A good way to keep peace in the house, but not a way to keep difficult clients.

The most extraordinary client came from India. Louise thought she had entered *The Thousand and One Nights*. In 1925 the twenty-five-year-old Prince Yeshwant Rao Holkar Bahadur was invested as the new Maharaja of Indore, an ancient kingdom that belongs now to the vast state of Madhya Pradesh and is situated about three hundred fifty miles northeast of Bombay. As was customary, the young monarch studied at Oxford, where his tutor introduced him to European art. Also up at Oxford was the son of the German architect Hermann Muthesius, the founder of the Deutsche Werkbund. The godfather of Eckhart Muthesius was none other than Charles Rennie Mackintosh. So it was not surprising that the twenty-four-year-old Eckhart had only one desire: to build and to design furniture. The young Indian and the budding German architect became friends and soon plotted the building of a modern palace in India. Muthesius, together with his collaborator, Klemens Weigel,

Bedroom in the palace of the Maharaja of Indore; Eileen's Transat chair is at right

was invited to go there and the plans for the palace advanced further.

Manik Bagh—Garden of Rubies—took four years to build; it was a jewel of Art Deco. Besides the private apartment of the Maharaja, there was a banquet hall, a ballroom, numerous guest suites, and a music room. The majority of the furniture was designed by Eckhart Muthesius. Muthesius traveled with the Maharaja to Paris to find other designers. The writer Henri-Pierre Roché was asked to help to put together a collection of the best of French design. Roché, who knew Eileen from Doucet's time, was a great friend of Gertrude Stein. It was he who introduced Picasso to her. And so she described him: "this very noble, very enthusiastic man was a kind of introducer, he knew everybody."

The Maharaja ordered carpets from Da Silva Bruhns, crystal chandeliers from Lalique, silver from Puiforcat, and furniture from Ruhlmann, Le Corbusier, Charlotte Perriand, and Eileen Gray. Eileen provided two of her Transat chairs, which she had designed for her house at Roquebrune, and a lamp described in her franglais in an invoice as "lustre rondelles et cones, métals chromés et lacqués plus two light-bulbs." Three entire shiploads of furniture, steel doors, and marble left Hamburg for Indore. A special glue had to be applied to all the wooden pieces to enable them to withstand the heat. The Maharaja's palace was one of the most amazing monuments to the modern style. Eileen had always hoped that she would be able to go there one day, and see the place where her Transat stood in the Maharaja's bedroom, next to the bed by Ruhlmann. In 1970, the Maharaja's heirs asked Eileen to design some more furniture for the pools. She was then in her nineties and still willing to design, but she was too weak to travel all that way, and "it was impossible to invent furniture for a place she had not seen." She gave permission for the old Transat to be reproduced in a summer version. On May 25, 1980, the contents of the palace were sold at auction at Monte Carlo. At the same sale, most of the furniture from Eileen's own flat fell under the hammer.

E.1027*

During all those years Eileen was building her first house. While Jean Désert fought for survival, Eileen, for almost three years, led a very solitary existence, living in the south of France, on site or in a little hotel room. She saw hardly anyone for months on end. The work was terribly hard. As there was no road, all the material had to be brought on wheelbarrows to the site. Eileen remembered how lonely and tired she was at the end of each day. The only diversion was the daily swim in the crystal-clear water right underneath the house. There was no one to talk to, and she took most of her meals alone, sometimes sharing a sandwich with the workers who lived on the site. "I had very little encouragement. I was strong and keen but often it was difficult and very hard to get one's enthusiasm going."

Badovici, in the meantime, moved about. He spent part of the summer with Le Corbusier in Arcachon. Sometimes he came down to look at the progress, to give her some advice (it was Badovici who suggested the spiral staircase, wanting it to lead up to the roof), and to make sure that there were no structural mistakes. Asked later about the authorship, she simply said, "We were associated. It is no use differentiating now. He had ideas for the roof and the staircase." Because of her generous nature she always gave him some credit for the building. Without his initial encouragement, she would never have undertaken the task at all, and she never forgot that. She shared the authorship of the house and called it E.1027, not with a "wink at machinism," as has been suggested, but simply after Badovici and herself: *E* for "Eileen," *10* for "J" (the tenth letter of the alphabet), *2* for "B," and *7* for "G." It was finished in 1929. It was her first house; she was fifty-one years old.

During the months of preparation, she had studied the terrain with its different levels and decided not to alter the topography, but to let the house embrace the natural

*The quoted passages in the captions in this chapter come from a special issue of *L'Architecture Vivante* entitled *E.1027: Maison en Bord de Mer*, which was published in 1929.

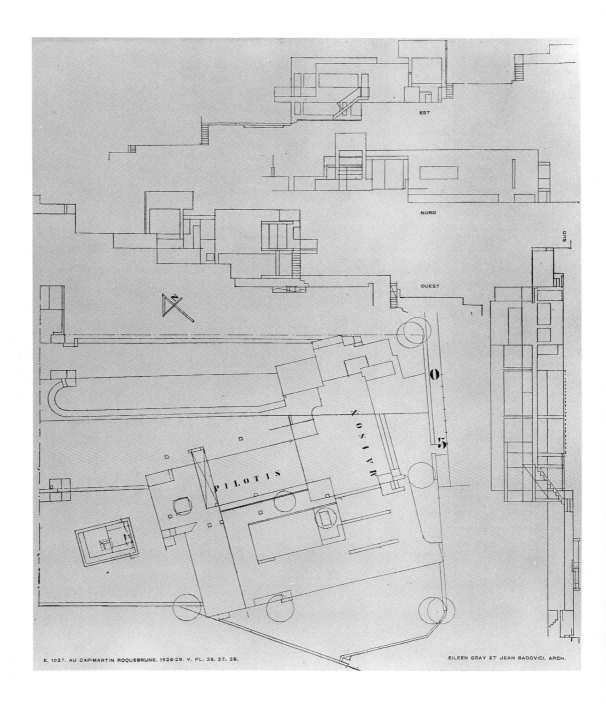

E. 1027. AU CAP-MARTIN ROQUEBRUNE. 1926-29. V. PL. 26, 27, 28.

EILEEN GRAY ET JEAN BADOVICI, ARCH.

Facades from the four sides

contours. She looked at the light and studied the wind to make use of all elements.

The house consisted basically of a large living room, extended by a terrace, and two small bedrooms—one conceived as a study/bedroom with its own small terrace with an outdoor daybed, the other with a staircase giving direct access to the garden. The whole was on two floors linked by a central staircase. It was a small house—sixteen hundred square feet on the ground level, twelve hundred on the first. But nowhere did one get the feeling of smallness.

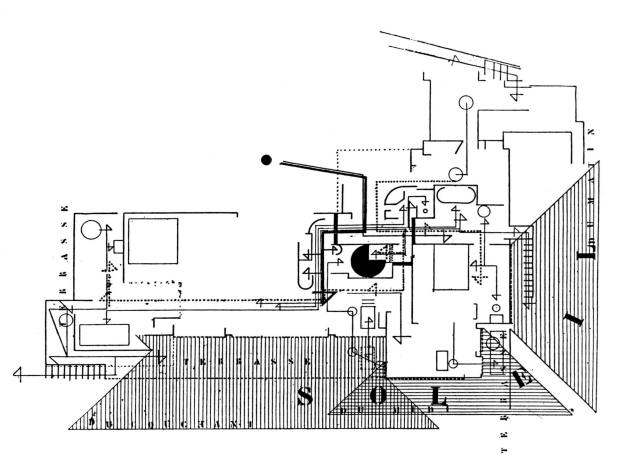

Eileen worked out the
precise passage of the
sun before she settled
on the orientation of
the house

Inside and outside are one whole, and give the feeling of spaciousness. Around a central core formed by the large living room are situated terraces, loggias, kitchen, and bathrooms.

It was in every sense a truly modern house in line with those built by Mallet-Stevens and Le Corbusier. It can almost be seen as a manifesto house formulated on the basis of Le Corbusier's "5 Points of the New Architecture" from 1926:

1. It stands on *pilotis*.
2. The roof is reached via a staircase.
3. Open-plan living is achieved by the mixture of free-standing and fixed walls.
4. The windows are oriented horizontally.
5. The south window creates an open facade.

There is no doubt that Eileen owes much to Le Corbusier's teaching.

E.1027 has almost no wasted space. The areas are simply divided by movable or light partition walls. The use

Above: On the west side, steps lead directly from the garden to the living room. A gate—echoing a Constructivist painting—"keeps dogs out." A small terrace allows total privacy for sunning or reading

Opposite: Views of the sea
Top: Over the rooftop
Bottom: From the upper terrace

of built-in furniture and the small scale of the house reflect the social ideas of housing of the time. E.1027 has been described as a "maison minimum." Many people were trying to solve the housing shortage resulting from the wartime destruction by creating smaller houses which could be used as prototypes. The Bauhaus architects in Germany, the Constructivists in Russia, and especially Le Corbusier all worked on "maisons minimums" or on "machines à habiter." Le Corbusier's Maison Dom-Ino (1914–15), Troyes (1919), Monot (1920), and Citrohan (1922) are all studies in small and concentrated scales.

Standardization of housing became the great battle cry from Gropius to Le Corbusier. However individual, Eileen's small residences could easily be adapted and multiplied on a much larger scale. Just as her furniture was all prototypes for later production, so were her houses. The use of prefabricated elements in wall panels, windows, even doors underlines this point and shows how much she moved toward industrialization. While still building E.1027, Eileen began to experiment with metal houses, an idea which she would later realize.

Eileen regarded the "dwelling as a living organism" in

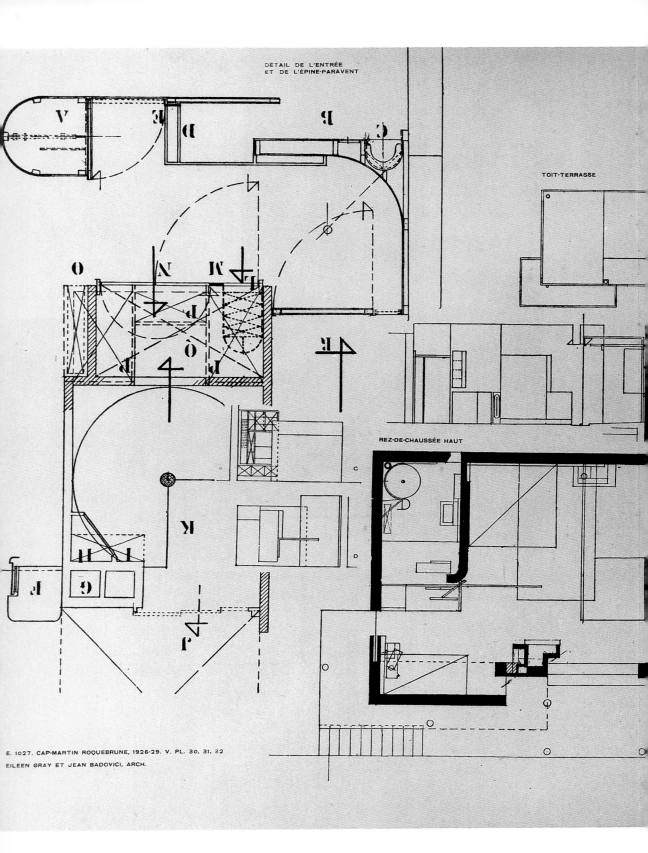

TOIT-TERRASSE

REZ-DE-CHAUSSÉE HAUT

E. 1027. CAP-MARTIN ROQUEBRUNE, 1926-29. V. PL. 30, 31, 32
EILEEN GRAY ET JEAN BADOVICI, ARCH.

**Plans of the upper
ground floor,
entrance, and roof
terrace**

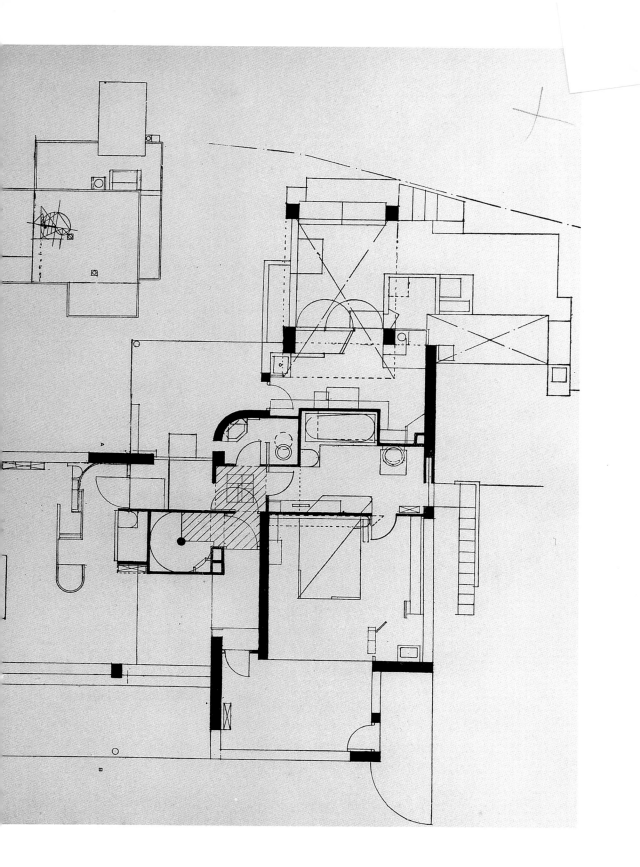

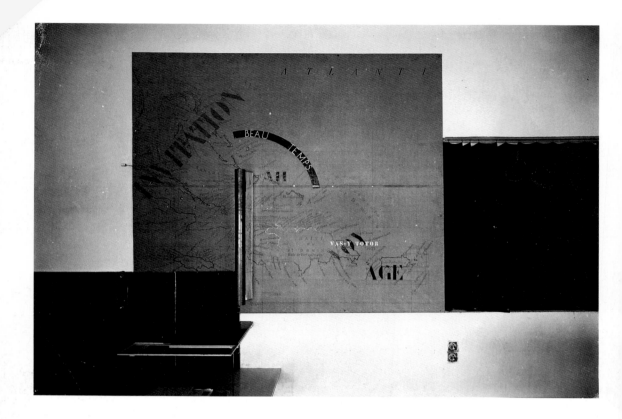

"INVITATION AU
VOYAGE" reads a
marine chart on the
north wall of the living
room. The inscription
"VAS-Y TOTOR" refers
to Eileen's car

which "each of the inhabitants could, if need be, find total independence and an atmosphere of solitude and concentration." "The interior plan should not be the incidental result of the facade; it should live a complete, harmonious, and logical life," she had written. Eileen demanded that the inside control the outside and not the other way around. She wanted to create an interior space which "as in Gothic times [was] a homogeneous whole built for man, to the human scale, and balanced in all its parts."

Eileen's garden and the arrangement of terraces make them an extension of the building. They are often organized like the inside of a house. The structure flows into the garden, and outside and inside become one. There is a footpath on the terrace, and deck chairs are used indoors and outdoors, creating a unity between both worlds. There is a kitchen for outdoor cooking. All this reflects, of course, the southern lifestyle.

Everything is logically organized. The entrance is marked by use of a distinguishing color: red. The curved wall leads one into the house. Here again the transition between outside and inside is effortless. Black square tiles provide a pause; then the house takes one over. In the entrance hall the inscription on the wall, "ENTREZ

The spacious living room, 21 by 46 feet, is conceived for maximum flexibility. A partition at one end "conceals a complete dressing room with shower, linen cabinets, a cupboard, etc. Against the full wall a large divan . . . can be converted into a bed. The cushion supports can be placed [on . . . the floor] to extend the divan" to a total of 13 feet

LENTEMENT," is more than just a witty pun, it is also part of the logical organization of the house. It warns the visitor that there is more than one choice between two doors, one that leads into the service area, one that leads into the living room.

The living room is screened off from the entrance hall by a cupboard in transparent celluloid, a device she had already envisaged in her adaptation of the Loos drawing. The movement in space was important to her. She made a little sketch showing all possible movements of the act of entering by little arrows. In chronological order she traced the entrance from putting down the umbrella in a specially designed umbrella stand to hanging up overcoats and hats.

The living room fulfills multiple purposes: eating, resting, reading, relaxing. Screens and built-in furniture mark the various areas. Architecture and furniture

Entrance leads into a hall. There, "set into the wall of the staircase . . . [is] the hat niche, a half-cylinder in transparent celluloid [with] shelves made of string nets with broad meshes on which the dust cannot settle. A rod running the length of the spine holds overcoats." The hangers are stored in a drum. A sliding system allows one to pick them up easily upon arrival. Underneath the niche is storage space for spare chairs

complement each other perfectly, interacting and enhancing each other.

As is appropriate for the Mediterranean setting, Eileen makes much use of the maritime style. Railings, the use of sailcloth in awnings and deck chairs, the extensive use of white, the built-in headboards for the beds, even the flagpole on the roof, everything recalls the architecture of boats and their cabins. Even the color of the rugs suggests the color of the sea; their shape, the sea's horizon.

An intricate system of shutters regulated ventilation and natural light. No less care was taken with artificial light. Concealed ceiling lights illuminated the bottles in the bar. Other lights were fixed behind mirrors or diffused behind frosted glass.

There were special mirrors which enlarged the face for shaving. Others were to serve "Madame petite et coquette," and "Monsieur qui aime se regarder la nuque." This was Eileen: practical and witty. It was this mocking spirit which prompted her to call the fat chair Bibendum and the chair with one armrest Nonconformist. These little touches were more important to her than a signature on the back. At a

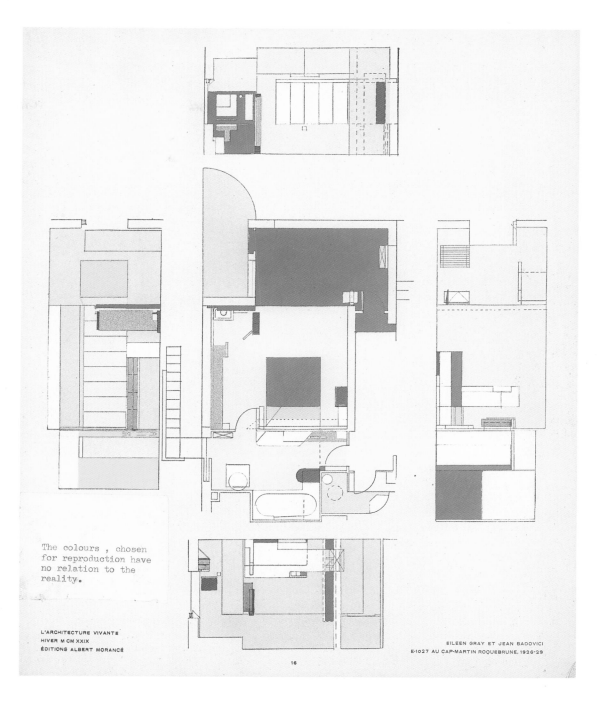

The colours , chosen
for reproduction have
no relation to the
reality.

L'ARCHITECTURE VIVANTE
HIVER M CM XXIX
ÉDITIONS ALBERT MORANCÉ

EILEEN GRAY ET JEAN BADOVICI
E-1027 AU CAP-MARTIN ROQUEBRUNE, 1926-29

16

**Plan of the main
bedroom and studio
with Eileen's type-
written comments, in
one of her copies of
E.1027: Maison en
Bord de Mer: "The
colours, chosen for
reproduction have no
relation to the
reality"**

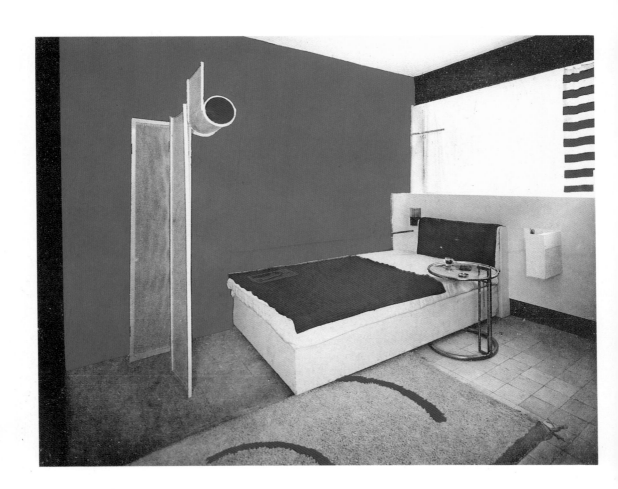

The guest room

Opposite, top: It "is independent and has its own direct exit to the garden and terrace. . . . The bed is a stock divan. . . . A movable partition [at the foot of the bed] eliminates drafts" from the mistral wind. Eileen noted on a copy of *E.1027: Maison en Bord de Mer:* "The colours are not exact. The green should be a bright but pale 'Nile' green, the blue very dark & the brown more subdued"

Opposite, bottom: A writing desk is concealed in a cabinet which contains multiple drawers and bookshelves and built-in lighting

Right: The E.1027 table—one of Eileen's most famous creations—is a bedside table in steel tubing that can be lowered and raised to bring the tray to the desired height

Below: The writing desk open

glance, from the bed one could see if the mail had arrived in the letterbox. The tea trolley was cork-covered, so that no noise would wake the sleeper. There were special places around the bed for books and even a hot-water bottle. Mosquito nets protected one from insects, and a little sand-filled pool on the terrace allowed one to cool or warm one's feet, without, as water would, attracting mosquitoes. There was wit and nostalgia; in the headboard of the bed the blue night lights reminded one of a night in a sleeping car on a train transporting one to faraway places. The decoration on the wall in the living room, a marine chart, read: "INVITATION AU VOYAGE." Another inscription, in the entrance, warned: "DÉFENSE DE RIRE" ("No laughing").

E.1027 was beautiful but also full of tenderness and attentiveness, a formidable present to her mentor. "Comme une musique, une oeuvre ne vaut que par l'amour dont elle témoigne" ("Like music, a work acquires its value only through the love it manifests"), she had written in one of her notebooks. The house she built for the man she esteemed, and maybe even loved, was "submitted to the feeling of well-being down to the smallest detail." "L'oeuvre belle est plus vraie que l'artiste" ("A beautiful work speaks more truth than the artist"). What she could not, would not, say in words she expressed in the house. Everything in it added to the *joie de vivre*. There are few modern houses which are so humane and so cheerful as E.1027.

Eileen had thought of everything: The balustrade on the terrace was made of removable canvas so "that in the winter one could warm one's legs in the heat of the sun." Eileen's slightly prim sense of order can be seen in the directive for the bed: "It has colored sheets, so that the disorder will not be noticed when the bed has not been made."

She had a scenario for dealing with the weather as well: "When the sea is rough and the horizon gloomy, one has only to close the large bay window to the south, draw the curtain, and then open the small bay window to the north, which gives on to a garden of lemon trees and the old village, to find a new horizon where masses of greenery replace the broad expanses of blue and gray."

All the furniture in the house was especially designed by Eileen. In her designs she explored all the possible uses a piece of furniture could have: Tables and chairs, cupboards and mirrors, everything was highly flexible; a simple gesture could rotate a cake tray. Bending and folding of elements created a mechanical ballet that became a hallmark of her

design. Her practical sense found extraordinary aesthetic solutions: cupboards were hung at eye level and had translucent fronts. Her knowledge of the craft of making things coupled with an intellectual gamesmanship made her explore until she found the right material, the right shape, which led the design to its logical conclusion. She often borrowed from the most unlikely sources—she even used metal screens made from the sheets used in flour mills to sift the flour.

The moment Eileen began working on architecture she began also to modify her designs for furniture. She was no longer interested in creating beautifully executed one-of-a-kind pieces. From now on her furniture is all prototypes, easily adaptable, easily reproduced for sale at Jean Désert. It

Right: A large glass wall separates the living room from the terrace. "The fireplace [in the foreground] set against the light, allows one to enjoy both firelight and natural light simultaneously." In the background at left is an elliptical closet (shown close up opposite)

is inexpensive or allows for an inexpensive version to be made. Eileen designed many pieces of furniture for E.1027 in the so-called camping style. "The house built for a man who loves his work, sports, and entertaining friends" had to be completely flexible. "Only the camping style made it possible to resolve this." Her research into the problems of architecture went hand in hand with that into the problems of furniture. Metal with its flexibility and pliability takes increasingly the place of wood, which is more rigid. During the years 1926 to 1929, Eileen designed a number of important pieces of furniture using metal tubing. Many of her chrome designs preceded those of Le Corbusier (who showed his first chrome furniture in 1928), Mies van der Rohe, Marcel Breuer, and Charlotte Perriand.

Cantilevered bedside
table with pivoting
arms and adjustable
reading stand. The
word stenciled on the
cupboard means
"CUSHIONS"

Right and below:
Cupboard with
pivoting drawers which
stands against the
living room windows
alongside the fireplace
(also visible on page
207)

Right: Dining room with its built-in bar in fluted aluminum. During meals it is a serving table, but it can be folded down out of the way. The sideboard has hinged drawers. "The ceiling of the bar slants in two sections . . . creating the effect of light on the bottles"

Below: "The gateleg tea table is made of tubing that can be folded and is covered with a sheet of cork designed to avoid noise and shocks to fragile cups." Disklike trays in aluminum for fruit and cakes can be rotated to put the plates in easy reach. The cups can be placed on the narrower end of the table, which extends its length

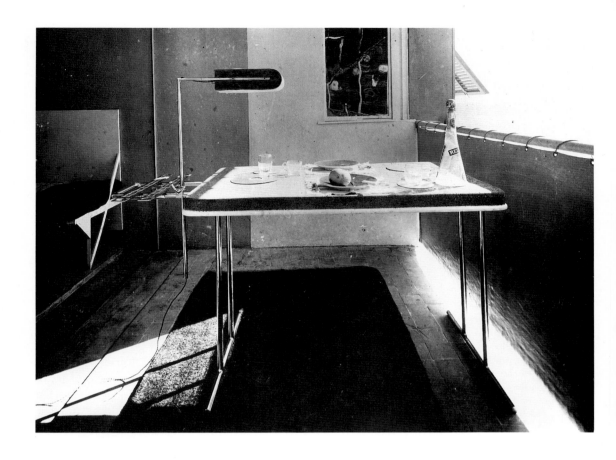

But while Eileen's furniture was becoming simpler and "purer," it was very distinct from that of her contemporaries. She accepted the basic ideas of the modern movement with its belief in hygiene, purity, and machine thinking, but she implanted her own thought as well. For Eileen a piece of furniture had to be practical and comfortable; it was never the mere carrier of an idea or an aesthetic. At the same time her furniture was never purely functional. She always added a touch of humor or irony to her design. The Nonconformist chair or the Bibendum was comfortable but it was also witty. It is this quality which distinguishes Eileen from her more earnest male colleagues. There is a playfulness, sometimes even a bit of mania in all those elements which bend, rotate, or tilt. Some of Eileen's furniture was totally integrated into the architecture. Other pieces were precisely the opposite; they were without a fixed position within a room or even in the house. They were light enough to be transported from one place to another. Some had a neutrality which made them at home in any room; others had a kind of sculptural quality which created an interesting accent in a fairly neutral space. But in both cases Eileen found the right

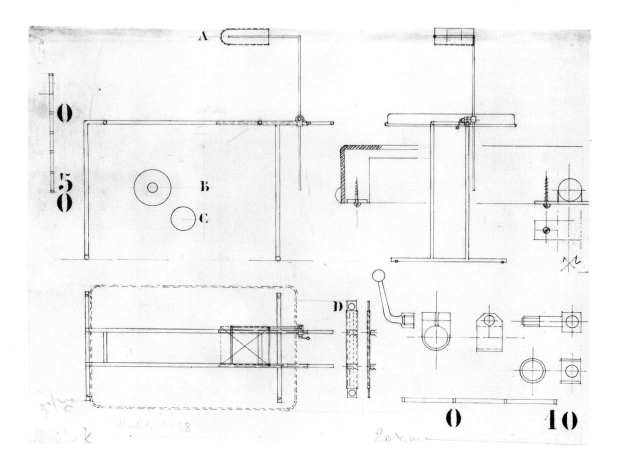

Technical drawing for the dining table

balance between the aesthetic and the practical. They make living easy. There is an amazing honesty about her designs; they are instantly readable.

The same kind of honesty is also applied in the treatment of wash basins, even electrical wiring. Eileen saw no need to disguise them. The use of industrial pieces for door handles or shutter railings or for screens or filing shelves is openly admitted. She did not believe that these designs were a solution for every interior, "simply . . . a convenient method for an exceptional circumstance," "or that this [was] the style for tomorrow." She considered "Steel tubing, as conceived and used by avant-garde architects . . . expensive, fragile, and cold." She consciously set herself apart from her contemporaries, firmly believing that each circumstance demanded its own design. "The practice of employing uniform and standardized models is . . . contrary to good taste, even to good sense."

In 1925 Le Corbusier had called for "built-in storage spaces which are at hand at the precise place where they have to be felt." Eileen had taken up his dictum that furniture is not added to architecture but that it is

Nonconformist chair, made from a continuous steel tube, is covered in beige stitched canvas. "We have eliminated one of the elbow rests to allow more freedom to the body, which can lean to one side, bend, or turn the other way without any difficulty"

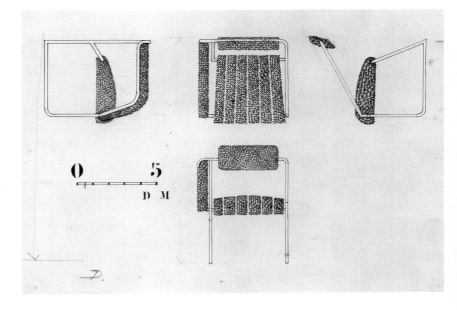

Technical drawing for the Nonconformist chair

architecture. But all her pieces, however simple, had a distinct individuality. Her feminine imagination prevented her from following slavishly Le Corbusier's demand for "standard furniture, fabricated by industry without any characteristics of art or decoration charged with meaning" (*L'Esprit Nouveau*). From the richness of her lacquer pieces she had come to metal, glass, and plain wood without falling into the trap of mere functionalism.

Trolley with several
functions: it can be
used in serving or
take the gramophone
out onto the terrace

"The kitchen . . . should be of easy access and yet isolated enough so that no odors can penetrate the living spaces." "The arrangement of the kitchen has been dictated by the habit of peasant women who prepare their meals outside in the summer, inside in the winter. . . . [It] can be transformed into an open-air kitchen by a partition made of glass panels that fold flat. When . . . opened, the kitchen is nothing more than an alcove in the courtyard"

Again and again one is struck by the architectural quality of her furniture, beginning with her screens, the most architectural of objects: part wall, part furniture; separating and yet communicating between two spaces. The architectural quality of her screens is heightened by the use of squares and linear designs.

If comfort was one feeling she sought, freedom was the other. Tables could be pushed together to form a large dining surface, their legs lengthened or shortened according to the height of the sitters. With one movement, a writing desk could be changed into a low coffee table. There were large spaces and small ones, giving its inhabitants oases of independence and intimacy so important to Eileen. "Even in the smallest house each person must feel alone, completely alone."

There was one room that seems sadly neglected: the kitchen. Roquebrune had, like many southern houses, a lovely place for outdoor cooking. But the kitchen was really only a galley, with things stored so high that one could not reach them. Many jokes passed between Eileen and Louise, who all her life had to suffer the inadequacies of Eileen's kitchens. Eileen simply had no idea how to run a household. "Oh, how I abominate housework." She was almost incapable of boiling herself an egg, or rather she chose to be incapable. But she did design for Louise the most wonderful-looking toaster. Alas, it kept going wrong, blowing fuses in the entire house and always having to be repaired.

Food was just not one of Eileen's priorities; her preferences in that regard were simple. She had a great liking for wine. She avoided strong alcohol and rather stuck to apéritifs, which she always referred to as "cocktails," serving them in pretty glasses designed by Poiret. She was a heavy smoker, sometimes smoking up to three packs a day. In later years, when she was supposed to give up smoking, much time was spent opening the windows in an attempt to fan out the smoke before Louise entered with the usual cold remark: "Mademoiselle has sinned again," to which Eileen, pretending to find her impertinent, just said, "Eh, bien."

If Eileen's neglect of any domesticity is seen in her design for the kitchen, her design for the maid's room reveals how much she was still—despite her inbuilt sense of social justice—part of an older era. For the maid she devised what she called the perfect "*smallest living cell*, [which] despite its very reduced dimensions, achieves quite sufficient comfort." This room might serve as a model for all servants' and

**Plans of the servant's
room and lower
ground floor**

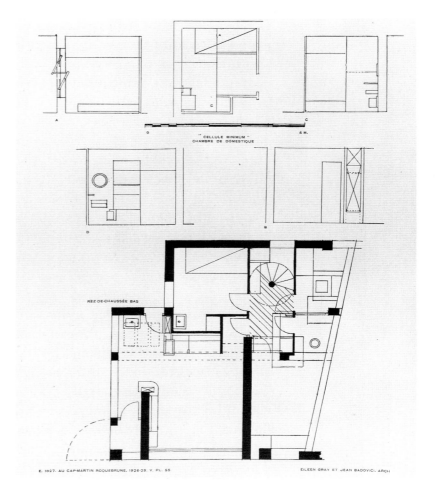

"CELLULE MINIMUM"
CHAMBRE DE DOMESTIQUE

REZ-DE-CHAUSSÉE BAS

E. 1027. AU CAP-MARTIN ROQUEBRUNE, 1926-29. V. PL. 55

EILEEN GRAY ET JEAN BADOVICI. ARCH

children's rooms, where only basic comfort is sought. Both
species in Eileen's mind could obviously exist in "reduced"
circumstances.

The house was permeated in every aspect, inside and out,
by an intense desire to reconcile the aesthetic principle with
human needs. Walking through the rooms, looking at the
many personal touches of comfort, wit, and romanticism
(and some of its minor shortcomings) is like looking into the
mind of the person who conceived it. This house on Cap
Martin reveals more of Eileen Gray than any object, piece of
furniture, or anecdote. "The poverty of modern
architecture," she wrote in the forties, "stems from the
atrophy of sensuality. Everything is dominated by reason in
order to create amazement without proper research. The art
of the engineer is not enough if it is not guided by the
primitive needs of men. Reason without instinct. We must
mistrust merely pictorial elements if they are not assimilated
by instinct."

The double desire to make things not only look right, but
also feel right never left her. It was part of her nature. With

an obstinacy which was both exasperating and admirable, she would not rest until she got it right. No two designs of hers ever look alike. She always kept changing, rejecting, altering, improving, sometimes wavering, making it more comfortable. When in 1970 she reupholstered the dining chairs she had designed in the twenties, she insisted on changing the little crossbar at the back, because "it didn't feel right."

Eileen's superior intelligence was always warmed by a deep romanticism. Whenever one visited a new building with her, one was made aware that for her a building was an emanation of some continuous life force, a romantic idea in which nature seems to manifest itself in art through form and structure.

Eileen was always concerned about the impression a house should give to the one who arrives. At E.1027 the entrance was "a large, covered space, a sort of atrium . . . welcoming, not like those small narrow doors that one only wants to open reluctantly." But a swinging screen prevented the visitor from looking into the living room once the front door was open. For Eileen a door is an opening to a surprise. Le Corbusier saw in a door "merely a space through which a man could enter" (Introduction to the catalogue for the Pavillon de *L'Esprit Nouveau*). He had said about his Roche house (1923), "This house will be like an architectural promenade, one enters and the architectural vista presents itself immediately to view; one follows a set route and a great variety of perspectives present themselves." Eileen expected her architectural route to be more mysterious. In some notes she made in later years, she describes how one should enter a house. "Le désir de pénétrer . . . une transition qui garde le mystère de l'objet à voir, qui tient en haleine le plaisir" ("The desire to penetrate . . . a transition which still keeps the mystery of the object one is going to see, which keeps the pleasure in suspense"). "The movement in building should follow the walls in such a natural way that the pictorial objects inside reveal themselves gradually to the spectator." "Entering a house is like the sensation of entering a mouth which will close behind you . . . or like the sensation of pleasure when one arrives with a boat in a harbour, the feeling of being enclosed but free to circulate." "The individual should have the feeling of penetrating without effort a place where he feels protected," and she cited the example of the sadness of two travelers who enter the restaurant of a hotel with "200 places eternally set."

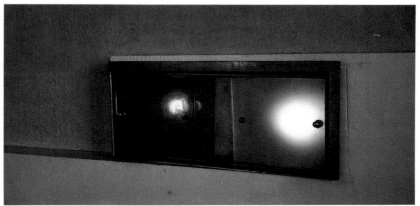

The principal bedroom

Opposite, top: It "consists of a studio and sitting room." The two parts are clearly marked by different treatments of the floor: "black sandstone for the studio, white sandstone for the bedroom"—an elegant solution which gives a dramatic touch to this small room, where the colors are kept to the minimum. Since it gets sunshine from morning to night, windows are designed so that "the influx of light and air can be regulated . . . like the shutters of a camera. . . ."

Opposite, bottom: Plywood headboard, which is fastened to the wall, contains "a white light [for reading] and a blue night light . . . [an alarm] clock with a luminous dial, and outlets for an electric kettle and a foot warmer"

Right: Studio area contains a writing table with a central part which can be lifted to form a lectern. There is "a very low source of diffused light behind frosted glass." The door on the left leads to a "small private terrace with an outdoor daybed. . . . An aluminum and cork dressing cupboard conceals the washstand and extends to form a screen"

Le Corbusier admired the Eileen Gray house. When in 1938 the South African architect Rex Martienssen visited him, the two went to Roquebrune to see E.1027. Martienssen in an article in the South African journal *SA Architectural Record*, October 1941, described Eileen's house as follows:

> let us consider a solution which employs a technique that is a product of the general movement fostered by Le Corbusier. This is the house at Cap Martin Roquebrune, by Eileen Gray and Jean Badovici. This house displays a conceptual origin and a high degree of abstract arrangement which are the antithesis of an approach through the vernacular, yet attempts to go beyond the apparent frigidity of a purely intellectual solution to the instinctively emotional demand which the passions and desires of the individual and the romantically evocative site demand.

Martienssen rightly recognized that E.1027 was neither simply an example of vernacular Mediterranean architecture nor the result of the modern movement. It was a congenial and individual house which did not grow out of any idea other than that of living. Le Corbusier probably recognized that with this house Eileen had set herself apart from the world of her contemporaries. E.1027 was free of any overintellectualizing approach. This was one of its main attractions to him. As Eileen said in *L'Architecture Vivante* in 1929, "It is not a matter of simply constructing beautiful ensembles of lines, but above all *dwellings for people.*"

Her own personal need for isolation, for protection, and also her strong desire for freedom found here, in E.1027, their most telling expression. "L'homme civilisé a besoin d'une certaine rélevance formée; il connait la pudeur de certains gestes; il a besoin de s'isoler" ("The civilized man needs coherent form; he knows the modesty of certain acts, he needs to isolate himself").

During her lifetime E.1027 received little official praise. For her it was always simply a house she had built that, in a very deep sense, corresponded to her character. Today it seems still unbelievable that an untrained person could almost singlehandedly build a house which has become a classic of modern architecture, anticipating many tendencies adopted by later generations. Despite Le Corbusier's early admiration, E.1027 is only now receiving more and more studies assessing its originality. It is often cited as an example of modern architecture, but Eileen Gray's practical sense prevented it from becoming simply the manifestation of some architectural ideas. Eileen did not consider E.1027 "a perfect house," able to solve all the problems which preoccupied her. With her usual modesty she stated: "It is only an attempt. . . . If some of the innovations . . . can be regarded as definitive and ought to be adopted everywhere, others still need to be improved, and some can probably be discarded." E.1027 was for her a prototype, a research project for modern living.

> For me, a model house is merely a house whose construction has been carried out in accordance with the best and least costly technical procedures, and whose architecture attains the maximum of perfection for a given situation; that is to say, it is like a model that is not to be infinitely reproduced, but which will inspire the construction of other houses in the same spirit.

In 1929 Badovici published a special issue of his architectural review devoted to E.1027. It was called *E.1027: Maison en Bord de Mer,* a title Eileen had suggested which presented simply how she felt about the house at the

The cover of *E.1027:
Maison en Bord de
Mer,* the issue of
L'Architecture Vivante
devoted to E.1027,
winter 1929

Aluminum and cork
dressing cupboard.
The drawers pivot or
fold down for easy
access. The back of
the cupboard serves
as a screen. The
doors are mirrored
inside. There is also
concealed lighting.
Eileen considered
"aluminum an
excellent material
whose coolness is
agreeable in warm
countries"

Wash corner in the
principal bedroom
has a wire basket for
tissues, a barstool,
and a perforated felt
rug on the floor. The
windows are on tracks
and fold to one side
(Jean Badovici
patented this design
in 1929). The hinged
mirror allows one to
see oneself from the
sides. It is held in the
wall by screws fitted
to little hinges

"The bathroom [in the principal bedroom] is very small but provided with all the necessary accessories. Ventilation is assured by the door with slats . . . and by a large sash window that opens above the tub. . . . On the wall . . . a cupboard contains a shelf for shoes, and bath towels (with a special system for drying), and a large cupboard . . . serves for underwear and pajamas." Cupboards over the doors hold suitcases. On the floor are perforated white felt mats. The bidet cover forms a seat. The tub "has been covered with a coat of aluminum, which gives . . . an agreeable . . . bright touch"

Left: Kitchen cabinet
of wood painted gray
with ribbed aluminum
pivoting drawers

Right: This
deceptively simple
wooden cupboard of
painted black and
white is influenced by
De Stijl. An intricate
system of doors and
drawers forms a
decorative pattern

edge of the sea. Eileen has written very little about her own work. We are fortunate to have here Eileen's own thoughts and plans concerning the house. The preface of *E.1027: Maison en Bord de Mer*, signed by Eileen Gray and Jean Badovici, is a discourse between two people: Badovici and Eileen Gray. While the interviewer takes the role of the rationalist, the other voice, Eileen's, pleads for the return of feeling: "Formulas are nothing, life is everything." In other words, "Nowhere did we search for a line or a formula, for its own sake, everywhere we thought of the human being, his sensitivity and his need."

The first time Badovici had used the dialogue form was in *Intérieurs Français* (May 1925), which was also published by Albert Morancé, the publisher of *L'Architecture Vivante*. Eileen was involved also in this earlier issue. In the introductory dialogue the interviewer talks to someone who pleads for the presence of human nature in all ideas, even in the most contradictory passions. One can probably detect Eileen's voice in the partner who sees the proper balance and the domination of oneself as the source of beauty and the sign of a superior intelligence: "Man has not only a soul and a will, he has also a body." The interviewer replies, "Yes, the task of Art is to show man in his totality." This is also

The guest room

Opposite, top: The wardrobe is made of wood painted with Ripolin. The interior is covered with coated celluloid and the shelves are glass. Glass panels in the ceiling give shadow-less illumination to the wardrobe as well as the wash corner. The Satellite mirror (close up at right), another version of the hinged mirror, is above the sink. Its small mirror "makes it possible to shave the back of one's neck: a lamp is set in the center of [this] illuminating mirror so that everything is lighted equally, without shadows"

Opposite, bottom: Corner of the wardrobe—here closed—contains a group of pivoting drawers

Right: A small movable dressing table is made of steel tubing. The first version had two pivoting drawers and a small cupboard. The top was made of leather; in this second version, the top is of rosewood veneer

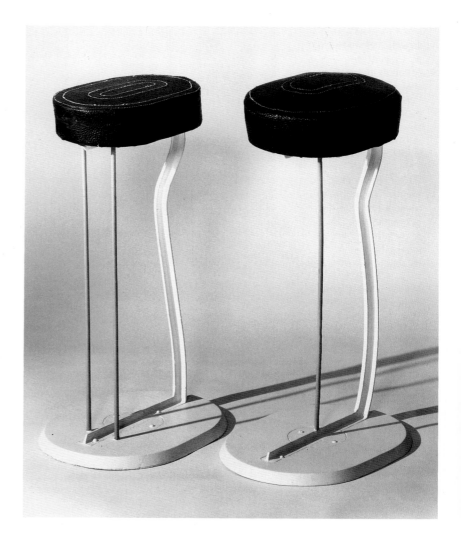

clearly a conversation between Jean Badovici and Eileen Gray. We find in it many passages reminiscent of what Badovici wrote about Eileen in *Wendingen* and some of the observations Eileen made in her notebooks.

Badovici wrote: "You often told me not to look backward. Greek art . . ."

The Eileen-like character rejoins: "I don't want to bring back Greek art, but the balance of the Greek spirit . . . with its sense of measure and its profound sense of order. . . . Beauty is lasting and can be understood only bit by bit. I am sure that our future will preserve the flower of our civilization and art will manifest it."

Both speakers continue trying to define genius: those among the creators who "translate the most unconscious

Eileen made several of these chrome dining chairs. She was very fond of them and used them in all her apartments. Some were covered in green plastic; this one is done in brown suede. The crossbars on the back are slightly more curved than in the first series, for greater comfort. Rosewood tips were also added to the legs

aspirations which correspond fully to the real nature of things and the human spirit." While the dialogue continues, the interviewer is gradually won over. He sees that modern design must find its own expression, not that of a previous period, and ends up elatedly praising concrete and iron as materials: "Yes, they alone have the necessary facility to find the proper balance, they offer infinite possibilities. Industry can now put material at the disposal of the artist, which allows him to create homogeneous and harmonious works that reflect the soul of our time."

In 1926, Badovici again used dialogue in an article in *L'Architecture Vivante* entitled "Utilitarian Architecture." A conversation between the rational and sensitive artist was only beginning. With the third discourse, "From Eclecticism

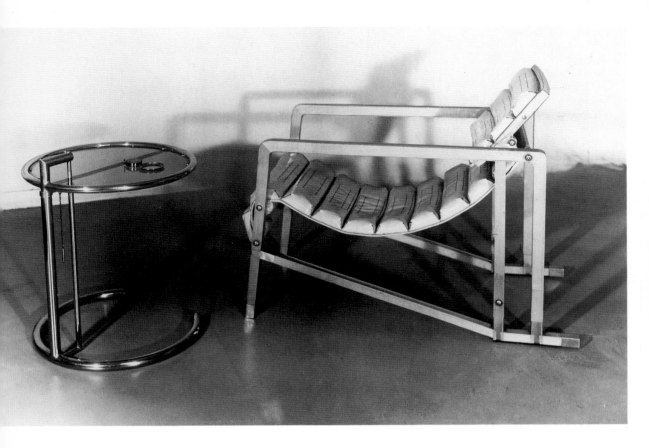

The Transat
(= Transatlantique)
armchair exists in
several versions. It
was designed for
E.1027 and sold
through Jean Désert.
The first one was
designed around
1924, but it was not
patented until 1930.
The frame was made
of lacquered wood
and had chromed
connectors. The seat
was slung into the
frame like a
hammock, and the
headrest tilted.
Although the Transat
was constructed with
rigorous geometry, it
was very flexible

Above: The E.1027
table with the Transat
chair in white

Right: The Transat in
ponyskin

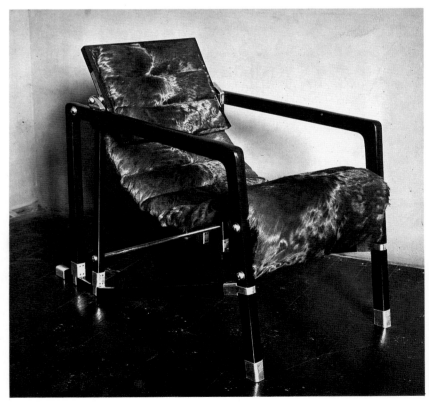

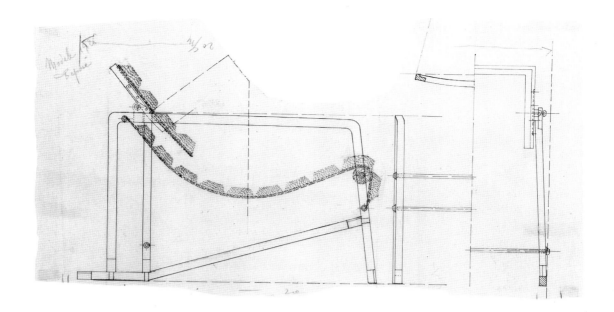

Above: Technical drawing for the Transat chair

Right: The Transat chair in patent leather

**Filing and tool
cabinet made from
perforated industrial
metal**

to Doubt," in 1929, the argument had taken on a further
dimension, attacking the cold calculation of the false
intellectualism of the avant-garde. It was Eileen's creed, her
belief in the supremacy of instinct and emotion over mere
intellectual speculation, the supremacy of the artist over the
technician. This last dialogue finally carried both signatures.

FROM ECLECTICISM TO DOUBT*

[Eileen Gray]: . . . We had to get rid of the old oppression in
order to be conscious again of freedom. But the intellectual
coldness that ensued, and which corresponds all too well to the
harsh laws of modern machinery, can be only a transition. It is
necessary to rediscover once more the human being in the plastic

*Extract from the preface to *E.1027: Maison en Bord de Mer*. The
identifications "G" and "B" have been added. — P. A.

form, the human will under the material appearance, and the pathos of modern life. . . . The pathos that is inseparable from all real life.

[JEAN BADOVICI]: You intend to rediscover emotion.

G: Yes, a purified emotion and one that can be expressed in countless ways . . . an emotion purified by knowledge, enriched by ideas. This does not exclude the knowledge and appreciation of scientific achievements. All one has to ask of artists is to be of their time. . . . All it takes sometimes is to choose a material beautiful in itself and worked with sincere simplicity. . . . A beautiful work speaks more truth than the artist.

B: But how does one express a period, and especially a period like ours, so full of contradictions? . . .

G: Every work of art is symbolic. It conveys, it suggests the essential rather than representing it. It is up to artists to find, in this multitude of contradictory elements, the one that gives intellectual and emotional support to both the individual and the social man.

B: Do you think that inspiration will ever be up to such a task?

G: It is life itself, the meaning of life, that is the inspiration. . . .

B: You demand of the architect a universal mind?

G: Almost! What is essential is that he understands the meaning of each thing, and that he knows how to be simple and sound. By not neglecting any means of expression, he will be able in turn to make use of the most diverse material. By the judicious use of materials and architectural structure he will be able to express what he wishes of the life surrounding him.

B: There's a word you haven't spoken but that all your statements lead me to expect: it is unity. For it is quite obvious that this diversity of the sources of inspiration and the diversity of the elements of execution would lead only to chaotic disorder if the architect did not coordinate them all and direct them toward a common goal.

G: Actually there is no architectural creation in the true sense of the word that is not an organic unity. But while formerly the unity was completely exterior, it is now necessary to make it interior also, right down to the slightest details.

Exterior architecture seems to have interested avant-garde architects at the expense of the interior. As though a house ought to be conceived more for the pleasure of the eyes than for the comfort of its inhabitants. . . . The thing constructed has more importance than the way it is constructed, and the process is subordinate to the plan, *not the plan to the process.* It is not a matter of simply constructing beautiful ensembles of lines, but above all *dwellings for people.* [The preceding paragraph is from the "Description" of the house, in the same issue.]

The spiral staircase in E.1027 is a piece of architectural bravura. It is "as small . . . as possible, but with wide, hollowed-out steps. The stairwell is much larger than the spiral staircase itself [allowing for a series of cupboards, reached by the staircase itself, which thus] . . . serves as a ladder." Through the skylight one gains access to the roof. The staircase ends in a sculptural metal and glass elevation on the roof. It also anchors the house in the ground, a piece of naked rock visible inside the house

Opposite, top: "A window without shutters is like an eye without eyelids." Having discovered that "all existing combinations [of shutters] give . . . insufficient ventilation when . . . closed," Eileen decided to create a variety of shutters which allowed "free and ample intake of outside air while keeping out excess light." The number of different solutions in this single house is amazing. Extremely sophisticated, each opening has found its own autonomous solution, according to its need and position

Opposite, bottom: Side view (east facade): on the roof the top of the staircase sits like a piece of sculpture in glass

[In this dialogue Eileen also turns against the overintellectualizing of modern architecture, which simply followed fashion and reduced everything to a mathematical formula.]

G: . . . art is founded on habit, but not on the fleeting or rather artificial habit that creates fashion. What is necessary is to give the object the form best suited to the spontaneous gesture or instinctive reflex which corresponds to its use. . . .

Think of those exaggerations such as introducing camping furniture, deck chairs, and folding chairs into a room meant for rest or working at home. No more intimacy, no more atmosphere! They simplified everything to death. Simplicity does not always mean simplification, and especially not such crude simplification. Formulas are nothing, life is everything. And life is simultaneously mind and heart.

B: In short, you want to react against the fashionable formulas and turn back.

G: No, on the contrary, I want to develop those formulas and push them to the point where they reestablish contact with life; I

want to enrich them, make some reality penetrate their abstraction. . . .

B: You want architecture to be a symphony in which all forms of the inner life find themselves expressed.

G: Exactly. Dream and action find equal support in it.

B: The decoration could be a powerful help.

G: It is architecture that must be its own decoration. The play of lines and colors should be such, it should correspond so exactly to the needs of the interior atmosphere, that any detached painting, any picture, will seem not only useless but detrimental to the overall harmony.

B: Isn't that what so-called avant-garde architecture has tried to do?

G: In a sense, yes, but only in a sense. Because for them architectural creation is supposed to be self-sufficient without regard for the atmosphere required by the inner life. It is a creation of proportions that are sometimes knowledgeable, but detached from its main object, which is the living human being.

It utilizes the occasional, the accidental, while it is universal feelings alone that should be conveyed and fulfilled. . . . It is too intellectualistic: an art of thought and calculation in which the heart is lacking.

B: It's true that many works are a little cold, but isn't that because we are still under the influence of the recent past? And aren't the principles of hygiene in themselves somewhat responsible for that coldness that offends us?

G: Yes! Hygiene to bore you to death! Hygiene poorly understood. Because hygiene doesn't exclude either comfort or activity. No, they are intoxicated by the machine. But the machine isn't everything. The world is full of living allusions, living symmetries, hard to find, but real. Their excessive intellectuality would like to suppress whatever is marvelous in life, just as their poorly understood concern for hygiene makes hygiene unbearable. Their wish for rigid precision has made them neglect the beauty of all these forms: disks, cylinders, wavy and zigzag lines, ellipsoidal lines, which are like straight lines in motion. Avant-garde architecture has no soul. . . .

Technique isn't everything. It is only the means. One must build for man, so that he may rediscover in the architectural construction the joy of feeling himself, as in a whole that extends him and completes him. So that the very furniture, losing its individuality, merges with the architectural ensemble. . . .

Normalization and rationalization, excellent means of reducing cost prices, will only, if we are not careful, give us constructions still more destitute of soul and individuality than what we have seen so far. It is much more a type of architecture that is being sought than a true style. . . .

EILEEN GRAY and JEAN BADOVICI

"We have avoided a pond, which would have attracted mosquitoes, but have provided a sort of divan in sloping slabs for sunbathing, a trough for sandbathing, a glass-topped table for cocktails, and benches on each side for conversation"

The publication of a special edition of *L'Architecture Vivante* pleased Eileen. This kind of accolade so far had been given only to Le Corbusier and Jeanneret by this most distinguished magazine. Outside of some reproductions of houses by Gropius and Taut and a cinema by Poelzig, the issue was almost exclusively devoted to her house. It included thirty-four photographs of E.1027, a detailed description, and some plans. Most of the photographs were Eileen's own. Again one is struck by the care she took. These photographs are not just to show off a piece of furniture, cold and clinical, as is so often the case nowadays in magazines. Eileen was not interested in merely displaying the design; her photographs of furniture always included the presence of a person. An open book, two cups of tea, a plate with an apple, a cigarette case, a hairbrush and combs—items she considered contributing to a feeling of well-being; small but significant gestures, staged by her to say, "All this is made for the art of living."

As usual Eileen's joy over the special edition was mixed with her own censoriousness. "A technical difficulty made it impossible to reproduce the colors used in the house. Those shown in the book are inaccurate and have little connection with the reality," she wrote in her own scrapbook twenty years later. And her disappointment was also voiced in comments she pasted directly on the pictures. One could still sense the anger she had felt when the issue was published. It was not easy to please her.

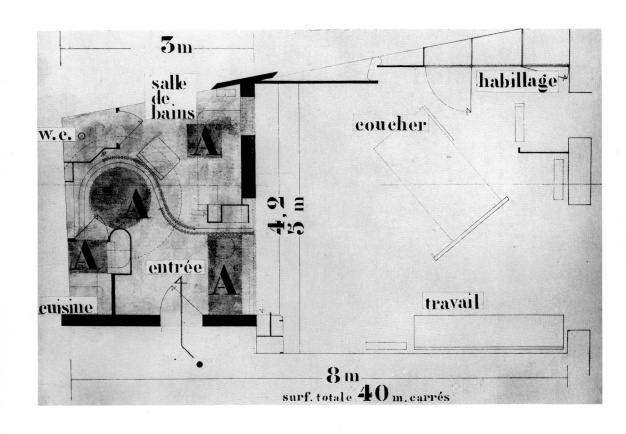

3 m

salle
de
bains

w.c.

coucher

habillage

A

A

entrée

cuisine

A

A°

4,2
5 m

travail

8 m

surf. totale 40 m. carrés

LIFE AS AN ARCHITECT

When Eileen returned to Paris, she was determined to give up Jean Désert. The shop seemed to her part of a life she was no longer interested in. She considered herself, quite rightly now, an architect. The year 1929, with the crash on Wall Street, was not a good year to sell expensive furniture, and Eileen's was not the only decorator's shop to close its doors. She had been keeping on Sugawara, who by now had five or six people working for him, among them a Japanese, Ouzada. Louise used to cook lunch for them, but sometimes she had too much work. Then she fetched some readymade dishes from a little restaurant around the corner. From time to time Eileen asked Sugawara to join her for lunch in the rue Bonaparte, where, over their food, they would discuss new designs.

Since the beginning of E.1027, when Eileen had started to experiment with tubular furniture, she showed some of the pieces at Jean Désert, such as the Bibendum chair made from chrome and rolls of white leather, which was bought by Madame Mathieu-Lévy for her refurnished salon, or a blue leather sofa in chrome, very similar to the one she had designed for E.1027.

But on the whole Eileen was tired of designing for the clients of Jean Désert. She wanted to get away from the shop, which contained remnants of a part of her life that was finished, and she could not get away fast enough. She still had ten lacquer screens left, ranging in price from a little black screen for twenty-five hundred francs (five hundred dollars) to a large one costing forty-nine thousand francs (nearly ten thousand dollars). It was more than nine feet high and consisted of ten panels, the largest she had ever attempted. She decided to split it and sell it off as two screens with five panels each. There was also a silver screen for which she was asking thirty-nine thousand francs (seventy-five hundred dollars), a couple of smaller tables, a big lacquer table, a bookcase, and a tea table.

In order to get rid of the stock she drafted a letter to her best clients inviting them to come and buy the furniture "at the old prices." She managed to sell seventeen items.

Armchair in steel tubing, covered in beige stitched canvas, with a tilting back-rest. This was created for E.1027; another stood in Eileen's Paris apartment

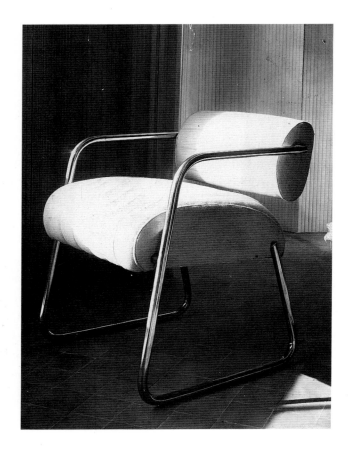

Bibendum chair in white leather and chrome was designed for E.1027 and sold at Jean Désert

Three pieces of chrome furniture Eileen first showed at Jean Désert. The divan at center had a built-in table which could slide along the curve of the frame. Since she could not sell the divans or the freestanding aluminum table, she used them in her own homes

Unfortunately, many of these pieces are lost or cannot be traced. (The salesbook with the names of clients became more and more unreliable during the last years.) After the sale she still had many pieces left—fifty-nine to be precise—so she reduced prices further.

She sold four more Bibendum chairs at twenty-two hundred francs (four hundred twenty-five dollars) each. Two went to Pierre Meyer, and two to the designer Labourdette, who probably bought them on behalf of Madame Tachard. The architect Henri Pacon bought a large black lacquer screen for fifty-five hundred francs (a thousand dollars). The *couturière* Madame Schiaparelli bought an armchair painted white, a smart-looking mattress in black shiny cotton, and a mirror with a metal frame. Madame Mathieu-Lévy bought a black painted armchair, a table, and hesitated between a black or a white cotton-covered mattress. It was almost the last time that Eileen would have to go through the "torture" of dealing with difficult clients. From now on, she would work and design for herself. February 3, 1930, she closed the books. She broke off with Gaby Bloch and sold the shop to Madame Cécile Maifflard *dite* Sartoris, according to the official sales papers. The remaining items were stored in her own flat on the rue Bonaparte.

As a personal souvenir she took a little piece of metal, with the initials J. D. (Jean Désert), from which she made the legs for a little table in burnt pine, a material she had grown to like, and placed it in her own house. She gave up the second-floor flat in the rue Guénégaud which she had used as a workshop since 1919. The tiny flat on the top floor was kept for Louise to live in after Eileen's death.

Jean Désert had lasted almost ten years. It had brought her some fame and many headaches. It made and lost her a few friends and cost her a great deal of money. But Eileen had few regrets. The ironical ending of this episode was that the rue Bonaparte was now totally cluttered with screens, pieces of furniture, table legs, and various other carcasses. Eileen and Louise kept falling over them, cursing each other, until Eileen decided to give all the "stuff nobody wants any more" to an orphanage in Auteuil. If Eileen was very stubborn by nature, Louise, always a hoarder, could be more so, and threw a fit. Louise managed to sell some of the tables at the beginning of World War Two for as little as five hundred francs (eleven dollars), and a shoe designer who had just opened a new shop on the rue Pasquier took the rest to display her shoes on.

The years that followed the building of E.1027 and the closing of Jean Désert were good years. Eileen was as happy as she could ever be. Maybe it was of those years she was thinking when, almost at the end of her life, she said, "One must never look for happiness. It passes you on your way, but always in the opposite direction. Sometimes I recognized it."

She had built her first house, an achievement that satisfied even her critical mind, and for the first time she had designed some furniture that corresponded completely to her own ideas and not to those of some clients or a certain fashion. The Bibendum, the Transat chair, the table later called (after the house) E.1027, the dining chairs, the dressing tables, some mirrors (the one with the corner and the Satellite), and the amusing version of the armchair of continuous metal tubing later known as the Nonconformist chair were prototypes that she hoped would be reproduced in large quantities. Unfortunately, Eileen Gray did not live to see this happen, although a modest beginning was made with three pieces during the last few years of her life when Zeff Aram in London began to reproduce her furniture. She never lived to see the French designer Andrée Putman's formidable effort to make her name internationally known, although the two had missed each other by a second when Eileen went to take a look at a new shop Putman had opened in Paris. Only after her death did production of her pieces begin in earnest. In the nineteen eighties they proved to be as timeless as they had been when they were conceived.

Eileen had also begun to make a name for herself in architectural circles. Not that architectural papers or the profession took any great notice. There were some reports and photographs in the German magazine *Der Baumeister* in October 1930, which, under the title "New Interiors," featured two houses: the Villa Savoye by Le Corbusier and the house on Cap Martin by Gray and Badovici. With so much going on in modern architecture, the building of one house was not really an earthshaking event. In 1928 the Congrès Internationaux d'Architecture Moderne (CIAM) was founded in Switzerland, and there were so many exciting new buildings in the next few years to talk about or review that it is only too easy to understand how Eileen's got lost. Hans Poelzig built his I. G. Farben building in Frankfurt (1928–31), Le Corbusier the Villa Savoye in Poissy (1929); people talked about Richard Neutra's Lovell House in Los Angeles (1927–29) and the Barcelona Pavilion of Mies van der Rohe (1929); and from 1928 to 1932, Pierre Chareau was building his Maison de Verre for Dr. Jean Dalsace in collaboration with Bernard Bijvoet.

In 1929, Eileen had become a founding member of the Union des Artistes Modernes. UAM's other founding members were Sonia Delaunay, Pierre Chareau, the sculptors Jean and Joël Martel, Le Corbusier, René Herbst, Gustav Miklós, and Jean Prouvé; the first president was Robert Mallet-Stevens. However different the style of their work, they had one thing in common: the determination to free design from its past ornaments in order to create something beautiful and useful. No longer was furniture thought of as separate from architecture. Eileen's E.1027 fitted well into the program of UAM. It offered Eileen a chance to renew contacts with architects she had met before, many of whom admired her work. The first exhibition of UAM, held in the Pavillon Marsan in 1930, showed photographs of the plans for the E.1027 house. Among the sponsors of this exhibition were three old clients: Jacques Rouché, the Vicomte de Noailles, and André Leveillé. In the catalogue Eileen was listed as an "active member," not just a "guest." A new chapter in her life had begun, or so it seemed.

Rug design with "UAM 100" woven into the background

Two rug designs by
Eileen, the one at
bottom called
Castellar

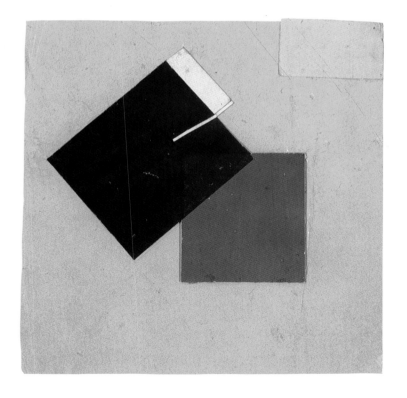

**The Transat chair in
light blue**

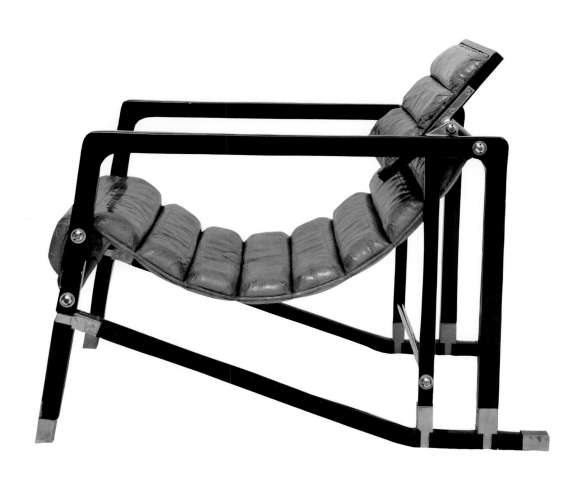

The Transat chair
with a black lacquer
frame and brass
fittings, upholstered
in brown leather

**Gouaches painted by
Eileen during the
Second World War**

la Maison hantée

Robert Mallet-Stevens began to launch work groups which united such designers as Charlotte Perriand, Chareau, and Herbst. Despite this formidable chance for her to work with other architects and designers, Eileen seems to have kept apart, preferring for the most part to work alone. In 1931, together with Badovici, she presented a study for a tent consisting of a metal structure in the form of an umbrella which could be folded, and "rational systems for storage in modern houses" at the first general assembly of UAM, but her relationship with UAM was not a happy one. She even stopped paying her membership fees. By 1934 her name was no longer on its list, and it did not appear again until 1952. One does not know why. Eileen could never be persuaded to talk about it. The architect René Herbst, a president of UAM, speculated later that one could not ask Eileen Gray to participate in anything based on group work. "She was far too individualistic. I never asked her, she needed nobody, she was the most gifted of our generation." This belated accolade, however generous, does not at all reflect the realities. Eileen needed help, if only her shy and modest nature had not prevented her from taking the first step. It is true that in earlier years Mallet-Stevens had asked her to work with him, but that was at a time when she was not ready. Her association with Badovici gave her a certain standing since few architects could afford not to be on good terms with the editor of such an influential magazine as *L'Architecture Vivante*, but otherwise she had no help.

In fact at the first UAM exhibition, at the Pavillon Marsan, she was given a "terrible place," and when she complained to Herbst, an even worse one. She suddenly discovered that her exhibits had been replaced by the jewelry of Jean Fouquet. At the second exhibition, which took place in 1931 at the Gallery Georges Petit, she exhibited only some photographs of the flat in the rue Chateaubriand which she designed for Badovici. She finally gave up exhibiting with UAM. In 1933 she showed furniture in the XXIV Salon des Artistes Décorateurs, which also included a model and photos of E.1027. She also showed at the Salon d'Automne that year.

Again and again Eileen was made to feel that for a woman, a mere amateur, there was little room among the elitist male-oriented group of architects. There was much in-talk and Eileen, because of temperament and also lack of professional training, would not participate. So again, she was marginal. "I was not a pusher and maybe that's the reason I did not get the place I should have had," she said, "but then everybody was so busy promoting their own work." Maybe this explanation does not give a true picture, but when questioned later about her stand, she had been eaten away by injuries and preferred to forget about it.

But there were many happy occasions, most of them linked with travel. Whenever she could, she accompanied Badovici to the numerous architectural exhibitions in Europe. They traveled to Stuttgart in 1927 to see the exhibition of the Werkbund, where they visited the famous Weissenhof Siedlung. There, under the auspices of Mies van der Rohe, the international elite of architects were assembled to present their ideas about habitat and housing prototypes. Two houses were constructed by Le Corbusier, others by Walter Gropius and Bruno Taut. The next year Jean and Eileen were in Frankfurt to see an exhibition dealing with cheap living accommodations in new towns. In 1930 the Deutsche Werkbund came to Paris, invited by the XX Salon des Artistes Décorateurs. Its exhibition, which was presented by Gropius, caused quite a sensation. Many people saw for the first time steel furniture by Marcel Breuer, Gropius, and Herbert Bayer. For Eileen it was a chance to renew acquaintances from her travels. In 1931, Eileen and Jean went to Berlin, and the following year he wrote a study of Erich Mendelsohn. At the Building Exhibition in Berlin, Eileen met many of the leading architects and saw the buildings of Gropius, Lilly Reich, Mies van der Rohe, Breuer, and many others. She took a special liking to Gropius, and they lunched together.

The Berlin exhibition was formidable and made a lasting impression on Eileen. There were seventeen large rooms dealing with modern architecture outside Germany, thirteen rooms dealing with the problems of urbanism in Germany, and twelve more devoted to interior design. Eileen and Jean were especially fascinated by the glass and steel furniture— the work of Marcel Breuer and Lilly Reich.

Much of the exhibition was devoted to small spaces. Eileen saw the solution Mies van der Rohe had found to use each volume to its maximum of possibilities by multiple usage of every corner. She and Jean liked the low house by the brothers Hans and Wassily Luckhardt and Alfons Anker. Eileen also brought home a number of suggestions that she would later apply when she designed her vacation and cultural centers. A considerable part of the exhibition was devoted to collective living. There were vast auditoriums for multiple use and vacation and recreation facilities.

Eileen, like most architects, borrowed freely from all available sources without literally copying—especially when she admired the work of an architect. She always spoke highly of Neutra, of Lilly Reich, of Mart Stam, Oud, Wils, and Bijvoet. She was also fascinated by the great Russian architects of the first years of the Revolution: Melnikov and the Vesnin brothers.

Not many of the people she met were aware of her talents or her achievements. Badovici was a great talker and preoccupied with getting articles for his magazine. It was hardly in his interest to make too much of Eileen as an architect or to let all the world know that they had built the house together. He could hardly admit to the people he considered his colleagues his true role in E.1027. Eileen never complained about it later; she merely said, "He was the big man and he did all the talking." Anyway, she was glad to be there, to see and to learn.

Of course there was much bitter rivalry among architects, as among all professional groups. At one time Eileen had become quite friendly with the Spanish architect Josep Lluis Sert. She used to go to see him in his studio and look at his models. It was through Badovici that Eileen had met Sert, who worked as a collaborator with Le Corbusier and Jeanneret. Badovici did not care very much for Eileen's visits to Sert's studio; a mixture of personal and professional jealousy made him resent his pupil's becoming independent. When Badovici, Zervos, Léger, Le Corbusier, Charlotte Perriand, Chareau, and others went in 1933 on the famous boat trip from Marseilles to Athens for CIAM, when the Athens Charter was drafted, Eileen remained behind. She was not invited.

In 1929 Eileen and Jean went to Peru. It was an exciting trip, from which Eileen brought back beautiful pots and memories that remained with her for the rest of her life. She not only called her last house Lou Pérou, but she also pinned an old map of Peru on the wall.

But there was also work. In 1929, Jean Badovici took a place in Paris on the rue Chateaubriand. It was a small irregularly shaped room of only four hundred thirty square feet. He asked Eileen to transform this rather conventional flat into a modern studio. Eileen set to work with great gusto. She realized at once that in this confined space she was able to apply her many principles of storage and ingenious planning. As soon as E.1027 was finished, she

Rue Chateaubriand apartment

Right: The working corner with a built-in desk. An adjustable tube light was set on corkboard. The Transat chair is in black leather

Below: A large divan-bed was placed diagonally through the room, linking working and living space. It had Eileen's usual pivoting table attached to the headboard, an E.1027 table, and built-in lighting. On one side of the bed was a mirrored wall which gave the illusion of spaciousness

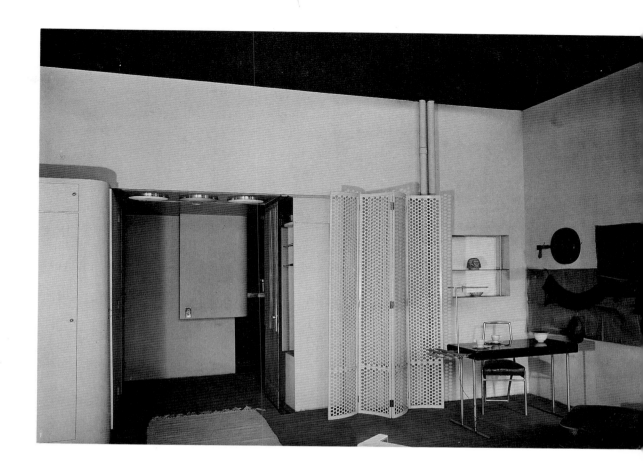

The entrance was
concealed behind a
perforated white
metal screen on the
left side and a large
wardrobe screen in
aluminum and cork,
which provided a
strong visual accent.
For the dining corner
Eileen had designed a
table with an
adjustable lamp
similar to the one for
E.1027. The
entrance was marked
by a pool of light
from three spotlights
fixed in the ceiling

began to draw up the plans for the studio, and the work began in 1930. Eileen furnished it "to the last tooth mug." There was a sofa that could easily be transformed into a bed. Many of the favorite pieces of furniture she had designed for E.1027 were reproduced for Badovici's studio. The firm of Aixia in Paris made most of the metal pieces for tables, *poufs*, chairs. The charge was twenty-five hundred francs (one hundred dollars), a considerable sum at this time—another formidable present from the generous Eileen. She called it "a single room, organized as a habitat of only 40 sq. m. [430 square feet]." It contained an entrance, a kitchenette, a bar, and a bathroom—all hidden behind curved walls. Mirrors gave the illusion of space. The most ingenious invention was a false ceiling, which hid some storage space. "In small rooms it is important not to encumber the available space. This can sometimes be realised by mechanical means, obtaining several uses for the same object," she wrote in her scrapbook.

Badovici moved in in March 1931. He was very happy with the result. He now had an exciting studio in Paris and a large place in the south of France. He was thirty-seven years old, and his magazine was a success. Sometimes he tried to sell some of Eileen's furniture from his studio; "For some reason he refused to bring potential clients to the rue Bonaparte." So Eileen sent some pieces to the rue Chateaubriand. Nothing was ever sold, but neither did Eileen get anything back again. Badovici once wanted her to design furniture for a hotel. Eileen did not like to do contract furniture, so she refused.

He gave up the studio after the war. It is now an office. When it was last seen, a number of years ago, it still had Eileen's swiveling mirror and some of her light fixtures in the bathroom. There was also one of Eileen's lacquer-brick screens, which someone had covered with color reproductions and postcards. When Eileen was told this, she burst into laughter.

Badovici spent much time now in Vézelay, where as early as 1923 he had begun to buy up some old derelict houses. Eileen helped him to finance his purchases (and had furnished one house for him), and over the next few years he acquired five houses, restoring them and giving them some Corbusian features. He was dreaming of forming an artists' colony there. Zervos had also bought a house there, and Le Corbusier often came to stay with Badovici. There were theater evenings, and quite a lot of heavy drinking. Eileen was only part of this venture. Some of her weavers for the carpets lived in one of the houses. But on the whole, the usual jollity and free living of the whole group, and Badovici's constant affairs with local women, made her uncomfortable.

In 1938 Badovici bought another house in Vézelay just to receive friends. Fernand Léger was a frequent guest in this house. Jean Follain, in *Cahiers d'Art*, in 1940, remembered that he had met Léger "in Vézelay in the house of the architect Badovici," who asked Léger to paint a wall—a wall without life, which blocked a whole vista and closed off a small courtyard. Léger had consented. "He pulverized the wall under a burst of red color, and in the playfulness of the tonal values, there were some simple and graceful objects which expressed all the power of their magic volume. They belonged to the Universe and at the same time kept a magnificent isolation."

Eileen and Jean lived most of the summer months together in Roquebrune. Louise looked after the household. There were quite a few visitors. Zervos, Le Corbusier, and his wife came for tea. Fernand Léger came from Antibes,

Above: Metallic
curtain which
separated the shower
room from the rest of
the apartment

Below: Circular
storage space in the
ceiling (visible to left
of the metallic screen
above) was furnished
with glass shelves and
sliding screens. It was
reached by a retract-
able ladder (see page
273)

House in Vézelay modernized by Jean Badovici. He renovated five houses in the old pilgrimage town

the writer Claude Roger-Marx, who now worked for Badovici's publisher, Morancé, was also a frequent guest. Eileen, with her impeccable sense of style, saw to it that the table was always beautifully set with dishes of transparent glass. In a large blue bowl she put white yucca flowers. The guests all used to go down to the sea to swim. There was much laughter and a lot of animated conversation, mostly about architecture. Zervos would bring the latest news from the world of painting and sculpture, and others arriving from Paris reported on the latest films: Buñuel's *Un Chien Andalou*, *Le Million* by Réné Clair, Pabst's *Threepenny Opera*, Cocteau's *Sang d'un Poète*, Eisenstein's *Potemkin*, or the first sound movie from America, *The Jazz Singer*. Eileen was fascinated by films and whenever she was in Paris went to see them.

But somehow Eileen's relationship with Badovici was not happy. Eileen was in her fifties. He was fourteen years younger, drank heavily, and was a great womanizer. However fond Eileen might have been of him, she certainly was not jealous in the conventional way, but her sense of dignity and discretion could not tolerate a situation penetrated by "lies and silliness," the silliness probably weighing heavier than the lies. Also, she got bored with leading a life which was not hers, seeing people who were not her friends, "the endless exercise in futility." She had spent almost forty years of her life living alone and was not cut out for any kind of communal life. Of course she suffered; once more she had invested much time, energy, and money in a relationship, and she felt her friendship betrayed. She knew that for someone of her temperament, permanent content could only come from work. Also she wanted to build again. She decided to go.

It was a difficult decision nevertheless. "Inside oneself, if one cuts away all sensitivity, one cuts away a large bit of human being." So, as in so many situations before, she packed up. Or to be precise she left, since Eileen never seemed to pack up at all, always leaving most of her belongings behind. As she once said, "Memories do cling to things, so it is better to start anew."

But it was not only for sentimental reasons that she always moved on. She was always thinking of selling her houses the minute she finished them: "I like doing the things, but I hate possessions."

A HOUSE FOR HERSELF: TEMPE À PAILLA

The idea of building a house all for herself must have occurred to Eileen quite early. While still building E.1027, she had bought some land in Castellar. It was a very small plot on the chemin de Belvessasa, the steep and winding road from Menton up the mountain. It had a superb view right down the valley: on one side the Alps, on the other the sea. The highway that now spoils the marvelous panorama did not exist. Eileen always liked long wide vistas and this land gave her precisely that. She purchased two other plots right next to hers. On April 24, 1926, a sales contract was signed between "Jean Baptiste J. Viale, farmer, and Mademoiselle Eileen Moray Gray, without profession." Eileen paid sixty-eight thousand francs (about thirteen thousand dollars) for the three parcels. The main one was occupied by a so-called *maison rurale*, a small single-story farm building, mostly used for tools or shelter. This building—known in the south as a *cabanon*, really a place for shepherds to keep their sheep in, or for farmers to house their tools—stood above a cellar. There were also three water tanks. The *cabanon* stood right on the edge of the road. In order to prevent people from building and spoiling her view, Eileen also bought the small piece of land right on the other side of the road with seventy-three lemon trees on it. All together Eileen had one and a half acres of land. In 1932 she bought another little plot of vines.

The first thing Eileen did was to paint the little house, which was called Le Bateau, all white. She did not undertake any alterations. In 1932 she asked for official permission to build a house there. She had spent the previous year planning and designing. Permission was granted four months later. The *cabanon* was pulled down. Le Bateau Blanc or, as it came to be known, Castellar was Eileen's work alone. "The only suggestion from Badovici was to make the 'passerelle' [bridge] fairly large, which I did."

The house had to be built right on the road. It therefore could not take advantage of the same free-standing position as E.1027. But Eileen made good use of the awkward terrain. She built on the existing water tanks, which gave the

house a dominating position. The first tank became a
garage, the second a cellar, accessible from the dining room,
and the last one kept its original function as a reservoir for
rainwater. Eileen did not need to build this house on *pilotis*.
She could construct here on the natural element of stone.

People have always asked why she chose such a difficult
site to build on. There was no shortage of affordable plots
around. It is true that Eileen adored the view. It is also true
that she desperately wanted to have her own place, and the
faster the better, but most of all the building of Castellar
presented a challenge. That was something she could never
resist. On the contrary she wanted to explore the duality and
the contradiction fully. She wanted to create a dramatic
dialogue between the house and its site. She was never
seduced by the merely picturesque.

At first glance Castellar does not appear as harmonious
as E.1027. It seems to be more fragmented. This has
certainly something to do with the fact that Eileen built here
on an existing structure. But the transition between the old
and new is flawless. The new building almost floats on the
old foundations, both embracing the curve of the road. The
way she integrated terrain, water tanks, and new building is
masterly. She created a house which stands in complete
contrast to its surroundings and thus achieves a unique
strength. Again it was a small house. Everything in her told

Street facade with the
entrance next to the
garage. Behind the
gate is an outside
staircase which leads
to a bridge—a
practical and exciting
solution for a difficult
terrain which
heightens the feeling
of arrival. Above the
garage, the terrace

her to reduce rather than to enlarge her environment. For
herself she was content with a living-working cell, a *machine
à habiter*. It was much smaller than E.1027, only a little
more than a thousand square feet of habitable surface. It
had a large living room of two hundred thirty-five square
feet extended by a terrace of three hundred fifty square feet.
There were two small bedrooms of only sixty-five and
seventy-five square feet respectively, and a dining room on
the first floor, and a third bedroom on the lower level.

The first floor was reached by an outside concrete
staircase and a bridge, again built in concrete. Both features
dominated the architecture and allowed access to the
garden. Eileen, as in E.1027, took her cues from ship
architecture. On the bridge was a wooden flag mast reaching
sixteen and a half feet above the roof. It was a true house of
the south: outside and inside were treated in almost the
same manner and formed one unit. The same shutters, the

**Above: Entrance via
the terrace, which is
treated like a second
living room and
roofed over with a
concrete awning. The
outer wall, giving on
to the road, has
sliding shutters which
shield the terrace
from the outside.
There is also a
sunbed in black tiles.
At the far end, the
windows to the living
room**

**Right: Terrace seen
from the garden**

Above: Terrace seen from the bridge

Right: Entrance to the kitchen

Top: Floor plan. One reaches the terrace (H) via the bridge (I) that leads from the garden (J). A large window gives access to the living room (A). Off the living room are the dining room (B), service area (C), and the bedroom (E). A second bedroom (G) is hidden behind a small hall. Both bedrooms have access to the small bathroom (F). The kitchen (D) has two entrances: one from the public path and another from a small courtyard (K)

Center: Elevation

Bottom: South facade. Underneath the terrace is a third little bedroom, which is also lighted through an opening in the ceiling that is concealed in the tiled sunbed above

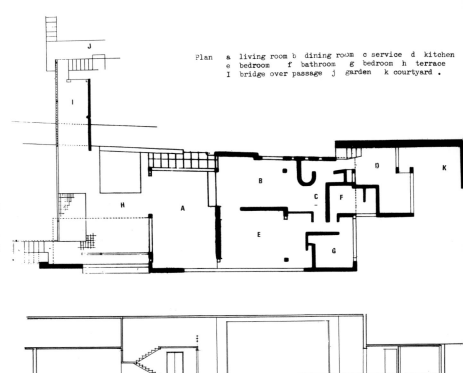

Plan a living room b dining room c service d kitchen
e bedroom f bathroom g bedroom h terrace
I bridge over passage j garden k courtyard .

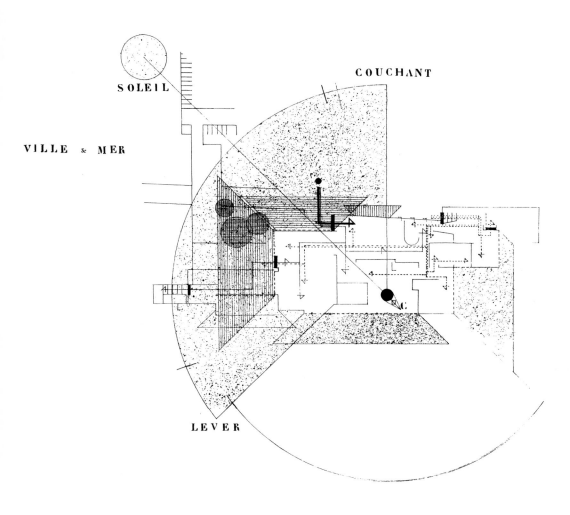

SOLEIL

COUCHANT

VILLE & MER

LEVER

MONTAGNE

**Orientation of the
house showing town,
sea, mountain, and
passage of the sun**

Study side of the living room. Movable metal shutters at ceiling height and a large window (see photo above) give light. The floor is of white tiles, which continue under the built-in desk. The writing table can be folded against the wall, hiding the bulletin board. A commercial gooseneck lamp is mounted on a piece of scorched wood and fixed on the wall, next to a reproduction of an ancient Mexican head

same light fixtures, the same treatment of the floor and walls for the rooms and the terrace, which thus became a second living room.

The inside of the house was simple, almost spartan. Next to the large living room was the dining room and, behind, a hall, a bedroom, a bathroom, and the kitchen. The kitchen had direct access to the outside. The orientation of the rooms is similar to that of E.1027. The living room faced south, the bedroom windows east.

Of course, building a second house was much easier than building the first one. Having lived on the site in daily contact with the builder, she had gained a tremendous amount of practical experience about building. She engaged once more her old mason, and André-Joseph Roattino, the carpenter, who lived in Castellar and executed most of the furniture.

Roattino remembers Eileen driving around in a little MG, wearing a trouser suit with a neat bow tie, fussing over

Entertaining side of
the living room. A
spare sofa bed is
placed on a raised
platform. The dark
panel behind the
radiator can slide to
the side to reveal a
window giving on to
the street

everything and never stopping until she had precisely what
she wanted. Eileen hated being contradicted and could be
quite firm and demanding. But the workmen liked her very
much, although they resented Badovici, who sometimes came
along and usually pushed people around. But Eileen was
grateful for Badovici's help when dealing with suppliers—or
occasionally the workmen—became increasingly difficult.
Letters and telegrams went back and forth between Paris
and the south.

Again, Eileen was not only building a house but
designing the entire interior. She collected ideas, borrowing
freely. She had seen a garage door which tilted, made by a
firm called Eclair. This was a fairly new idea. The doors,
when finally installed, created quite a stir, and Roattino
remembers people driving up the small road "to see the
funny doors on the funny house." In 1933 she had also
ordered some sliding windows from a firm called Wanner,
which Le Corbusier had recommended to her after he had
used them in Switzerland for his Clarté apartment building

Terrace seen from the
living room. The tiled
sunbed is visible just
beyond the sliding
doors

in Geneva, which he built in 1928. Wanner made shutters, lamps, airplane doors, etc. She had seen a door of a telephone booth in New York and adopted it also.

Castellar revealed again Eileen Gray's extraordinary architectural conception, her refinement and mastership, rare in an autodidact. She solved effortlessly very complex problems such as achieving balance between inside and outside, or the perfect interaction between the different functions of the rooms. It is as if her lack of academic training had led to a much freer and more imaginative execution of her task. Eileen's conception grew on the object itself, on the drawings, and on the models. Since her mind was uncluttered by too much knowledge and preconceived ideas, the line between the idea and the execution was fine, while her critical capacities were sharpened by the immediacy of the task. Also here was an architect building for herself. Her house was not obliged to enter any polemic,

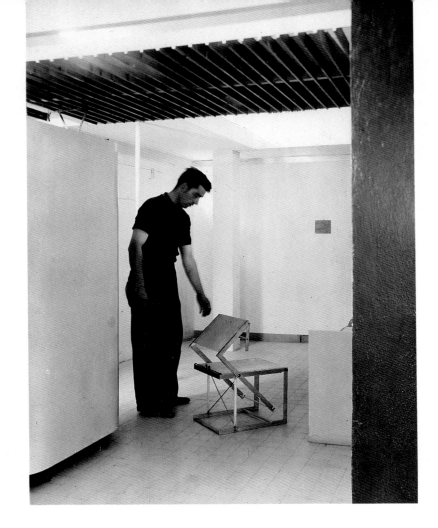

André-Joseph Roattino, the carpenter, demonstrating a metal seat which could be made into a stepladder

did not have to manifest any style or tendency. It was the purest and most self-centered task. This gave the house its homogeneity.

As in E.1027, Eileen designed every piece of furniture herself, but here it is even more integrated with the architecture. A multitude of folding and sliding systems create ingenious storage spaces. Metal cupboards serve also as architectural screens. As in the rue Chateaubriand flat, space was used to its maximum. A false ceiling in the dining area hid some storage space above wooden slats. A bench folded back to reveal steps leading into the cellar. In the hall another storage space could be reached by a stepladder that folded back into the wall. Every corner was used in the most imaginative way. Metal screens hid objects; a central niche concealed the bottles for the much-liked apéritif. But the most inventive object was a huge cupboard whose size could be reduced or enlarged with a simple gesture according to need. Again her furniture served many functions; it could be expanded or shrunk, heightened or lowered.

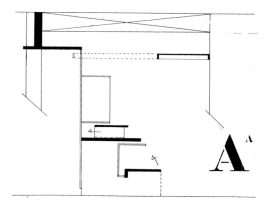

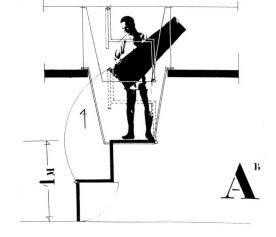

**Top: Opening in the
ceiling for storage:
the metal grid simply
folds back to give
access**

**Above and right:
Three diagrams
showing methods of
access to concealed
storage**

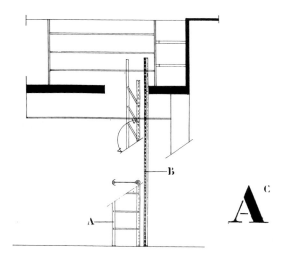

Large extendable
metal wardrobe open
and closed. A
perforated celluloid
top assures good
ventilation. The
wardrobe consists of
two elliptical halves
on tracks that can be
pulled apart or
pushed together
according to the
space needed. By
pulling on the chrome
handle at the right,
the wardrobe can be
extended to about a
third beyond its
original size (by about
two feet)

Built-in bar with steps underneath that can be pulled out to reach storage area overhead. The top of the bar and the sliding steps have a matching metal insert in the wood

The same mechanical ballet that characterized her furniture for E.1027 was still at play. A mirror can turn. Shutters, screens, and mirrors move on rails or hinges and create illusions. Nothing ever seems to be what it is. One often has the feeling that her furniture goes beyond mere objects. But with the changing function came a changing vision of the room, which Eileen choreographed by simply moving pieces around. Everything is constantly in flux: drawers slide out of cubes, chairs become stepladders. Everything creates the feeling of practicality and comfort. Everything is explored for its maximum potential. Her art in transforming even the most ordinary object is evident everywhere. Except in her early period, Eileen avoided the feeling of preciousness. After the richness of what she called the sins of her youth she increasingly looked at industrial elements—metal sheets, flexible gooseneck lamps, industrial shutters—not only for their practicality but also for their ordinariness. She always refused to be limited to a certain style or aesthetic. But in her hands the most ordinary object became extraordinary. That was her artistry.

Dining table with
metal frame and cork
top that can reverse
to zinc. This table can
be put on its side and
lowered to become an
occasional table.
The terrace
chair is made of
metal tubing and blue
stitched canvas

Right: Technical diagram showing how the table converts

Below: The table in the lower position with the zinc top. The glass and gray metal lantern is made from a commercial jar. The deck chair, in curved white metal covered in beige fabric laced to the frame, remained with Eileen to the end of her life (see page 376)

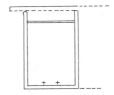

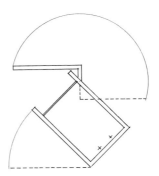

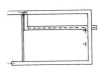

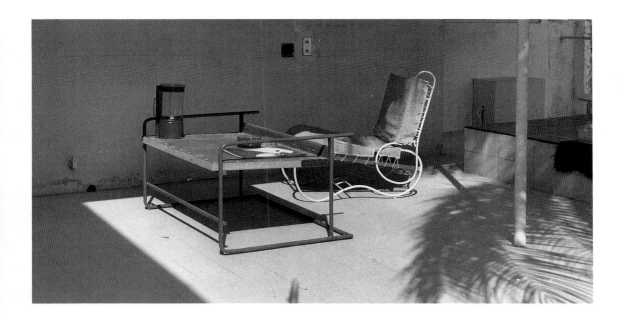

S-bend chair made of
perforated wood
painted brown and
cream. It can be
folded in half to save
space when stored

Terrace chair in
natural plywood. The
metal parts are
painted black. This chair
also can be folded up
(see model, page 46)

Opposite, far left: A versatile piece which could serve as a towel holder, steps, or a seat. It is made of wood painted white outside, black inside

Opposite, near left and bottom: Hinged wooden cube chest painted yellow on the exterior, gray inside, with glass shelves. The shelves pivot out, as in much of her earlier furniture

Right, top: The washing corner of the bedroom on a raised platform on which stand the trouser chest, a barstool, and a built-in dressing table. On the wall, a gouache by Eileen

Right, bottom: Chest on casters with a curved piano-shaped top. Modeled on a steamer trunk, it holds trousers and skirts on aluminum hangers. It is of painted wood with an aluminum and celluloid front

Above: Main bedroom
with a mosquito-net
holder above the bed.
At right, the extend-
able wardrobe and
cube chest. The
bedside table can
swing out and be
folded against the
wall underneath the
window. The head-
board holds light
switches and lights

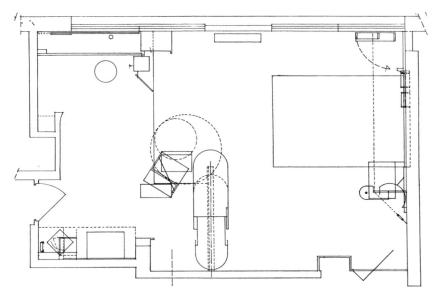

Eileen always made good use of natural light. But the way she controlled it is amazing. For her bedroom she invented an opening in the form of a disk which covered a round hole through which the light filtered. By rotating the disk, she diminished or increased the light. Thus she was able to create the effect of an eclipse of the sun by controlling the opening. The control of artificial light was no less important to her, and she achieved it in her lamps by means of special movable shades or rotating disks. She used concealed lighting in bedrooms and cupboards. Sometimes lamps were incorporated into a mirror. These various devices were often used for practical reasons, and sometimes to create a certain mood.

In her refinement she went even further than in E.1027. The reading lamp installed in the headboard could slide horizontally along, so that it was able to illuminate where one was reading. She explained in her surviving notebooks—as she often did in refining her thoughts:

> Work often with the psychology of light. Bear in mind that in our subconscious we know that light must derive from one point—sun, fire, etc. A need deeply anchored in us. To understand this explains the morose impression indirect light creates. Enlarge the light, amplify the rays which come from one point, don't encapsulate it. Interior lighting: low lamps, light the floor by light spread out 80 cm [30½ inches] from the floor or illuminate the room at 1 m to 1.50 m [39 to 59 inches] from the floor.

Eileen carefully studied the effect of color, for instance, in her "Notes on Colour and Materials":

Two lanterns

Near right: Ceiling or
table lantern in shiny
black metal with the
inside painted white
Far right: Reflecting-
glass and metal hang-
ing lantern with tube
lighting

Bottom: Guest
bedroom with a floor
lamp on a "Cubist"
foot dating from the
Monte Carlo period.
A sculpture by Eileen
is on the shelf; in the
foreground, a
convertible table

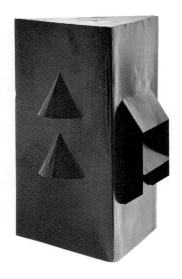
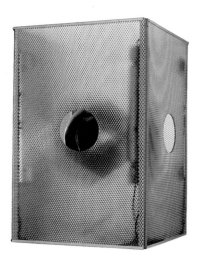

The black-tiled sandbed with a small metal table which has a built-in hotplate at the center. A lacquer tray holds flowers. The terrace chair is covered in blue stitched canvas; Eileen also made a version in brown leather

The more a colour is bright the more the form of the object has to be simple. To lift up the tone of a design scheme, use pale colours. Example: white room, with light wooden furniture, install lively coloured lamps. Blue/green.

Different solution: An interior all in the same colour, then make some break-up through colour; a niche can be very colourful . . . in another area . . . then follow this idea through to the end, generally a preponderance of *warm* colours creates a major harmony, a preponderance of cold colours a minor one.

There is something embarrassing about regional architecture which does not always suit the variety of the buildings [she observes in her notebook]. I would like to see a rigorous discipline in the application of colour, for instance, in a region of white rocks. I like to paint houses in brown and built from natural stone, they should have a square tower painted to the colour in bleu outre mer.

Castellar appears to be less playful than E.1027; it is more rigorous. Despite the many similarities, both seem to be conceived in two different tonalities. There is of course the difference of the sites: one open to the sea, the other anchored to a rock on a steep hill. E.1027 is generous with its many terraces; Castellar is restrained in more than one sense. For Castellar, Eileen again designed many pieces of furniture. These too show the difference. Those in Roquebrune were lighthearted, elegant, humorous, exquisitely made. Those in Castellar were as sophisticated and probably even more extended to their ultimate usefulness. They are rougher, the material used is less refined. Castellar is a laboratory for modular living, its furniture is prototypes (as at Roquebrune), pieces to try out certain things. They are not for keeps; they can be altered and adapted. And Eileen frequently did precisely that.

In Castellar, Eileen again displayed her ingenious and imaginative personality, which gives her two houses a modernity, even timelessness, that has not been diminished to this day. In its inner organization Castellar is more thought-out, more sophisticated than E.1027. This house was built according to her own need. It corresponds entirely to her own character. E.1027 was built for a man she loved, with the idea of a communal life. It was devoted to relaxing, playing, or entertaining. The second house is more spartan, almost more masculine. It is a house to work in.

In Eileen's two houses we have two very pure and

Right: Little wooden occasional table painted beige outside and white inside. It is on aluminum ski-like runners so that it can be easily moved to a convenient spot. The crossbars are metal

Bottom right: Occasional table originally designed for E.1027. Eileen made several versions of it with round and oval tops of different woods. This one in rosewood veneer matches the second version of the dressing table (see page 227)

Above: Occasional table of sycamore with a glass insert in the top. The chromed legs have black lacquered bands. This table is very similar to those designed for E.1027 and also could well have been designed originally for it

Around 1935 Eileen designed a series of tables with dark tubular legs. She could not possibly have had use for all these tables, so it is almost certain that some were made after the war, when she refurnished Tempe à Pailla. The table above has a red copper top. The middle table of the three with wooden tops, opposite, has a low relief design in the center. Like the barstools—none of which is exactly like any other—these tables demonstrate her remarkable inventiveness

undiluted examples of modern architecture. The line between conception, drawing, model, and final execution is short and direct. Eileen's intimate collaboration with the workmen allowed her at all stages of the building to be critical of her own design and to be flexible enough to alter it. Therefore her engagement was total and direct. The two houses were the most visible manifestation of her ideas about living. This made E.1027 and Castellar immediately accessible. And lent them a rare timelessness.

In 1934 the house in Castellar was finished; Eileen asked permission for the water to be connected. She changed the name from Le Bateau Blanc to Tempe à Pailla, after an old Provençal proverb: "Avec le temps et la paille, les figues mûrissent" ("With time and straw, the figs ripen"), making an allusion to the need for time to elapse in order for things to become mature.

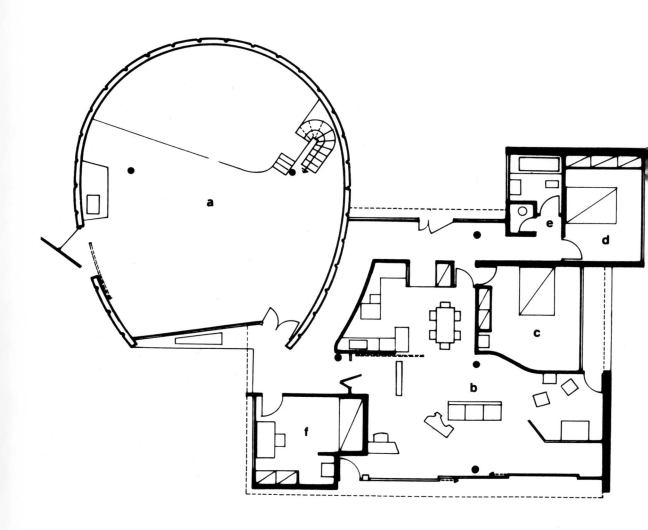

BUILDING FOR OTHERS

Tempe à Pailla was not the only project Eileen was working
on. She was making the model for a Studio for Two
Sculptors. Maybe she had it in mind for the two sculptors
Jan and Joël Martel, cofounders of UAM, for whom Mallet-
Stevens also had designed a house. It was a marvelous
building, consisting of a large oval studio with an adjoining
flat. The oversized door to the studio allowed for big pieces
of sculpture to be taken in or out. It was a vertical glass
door, hanging ingeniously on hinges, which made it possible
to either slide or swing the door. The living quarter of the
house displays Eileen's versatility and love for multipurpose
solutions. Sliding walls separate the kitchen and dining area
from the living room. Of course the guest room has its own
entrance. As can be seen in an earlier study, Eileen had
originally devised a pergola (roofed-over terrace) supported
by a sculptured column which acted as a kind of signpost at
the entrance. A second earlier drawing showed an elevation
of glass panels. This too was abandoned because of the great
heat it produced inside the studio.

She also experimented with various materials. "Today's
materials are smooth, the result of the monotony of the
machine. Try to find rugged materials—like in country
houses—some surfaces in rough wood built into smooth
walls. Sometimes put [in] pieces of protruding rough wood.
Pillars: instead of concrete, put stones, rock, granite, tree
trunks—trunks of palm trees," she noted. In one of the
models for the sculptors' house she had designed one of those
"natural pillars in the form of a trunk." Like so many of her
projects, it remained a little model, stuck on a piece of
cardboard which used to collapse and had to be glued back
together again.

In the meantime she continued to design screens. There
too she began to try out new materials. She contacted a firm
in Banolet and ordered several sheets of smoke-colored
plastic, but the color did not please her. A second order for
gray, pink, and yellow followed. After much hesitation she
produced the stunning celluloid screen which stood all her
life in her living room on the rue Bonaparte.

Studio for Two Sculptors

The project consisted of a studio area three stories high and a one-story-high living area

From top to bottom: Model of the first version, with a small pergola with a pierced roof

Elevation of the first version with the pergola but with a different entrance

Model of the first version. The large glass door is visible at center. The sloping roof was later abandoned

Elevation of the first version showing extensive use of glass

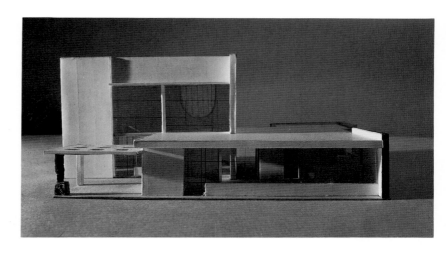

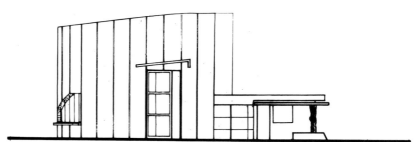

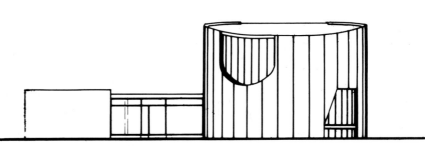

Sadly, in the same year *L'Architecture Vivante* ceased
publication. Le Corbusier wrote his last glowing article for it.
He said farewell and thanks to Badovici and his publisher,
Albert Morancé, in the name of the entire architectural
profession, for what they had done during the ten years of
the existence of the magazine now known throughout the
world. It was considered simply the essential document.
Badovici was out of a job and depressed.

Eileen tried to cheer him up and finally, in the spring of
1934, Jean and Eileen went again on a long trip. They took
a boat to Mexico. Louise kept reading about a big ship
disaster and became quite frantic. Then she got a card from
Acapulco saying that they had safely arrived. Eileen loved
Acapulco. Again she bought a big map which she would
hang on the wall. Of course Acapulco was still a small resort
with very few hotels. The owner of the hotel recommended
them to another owner in Oaxaca, which was their next stop.
On the way back they went via New York, where they saw, in
The Museum of Modern Art, the first exhibition of "Machine
Art." They also saw the newly constructed Rockefeller Center.
Eileen visited Frederick Kiesler, the Viennese architect she
had met in the early twenties when he had come to Paris to
design the international section for the theater for the Art
Deco exhibition in 1925. Kiesler, who had gone to America
in 1926, told her how difficult it was for him to establish
himself in New York. Eileen was enthralled by New York;

"the buildings look so lovely especially at night," she wrote.

When they returned, Eileen, Louise, and a stray dog named Domino moved into Tempe à Pailla. The house was not yet fully furnished. She did not feel she could take away the furniture she had designed for E.1027, so she started again, designing new pieces. Her workmen in Paris and metal workers in Menton copied the pieces, among them three Bibendum chairs and a sofa covered in moleskin. The furnishing seemed to take an eternity. From 1933 to 1939 she was still ordering two Transats, a terrace chair, six chrome dining chairs for which she had made little wooden models, a table which had zinc on one surface and reversed to cork. Many of the surviving pieces of furniture for Tempe à Pailla were made locally, by Dufour & Martin in Menton; Roattino made a lot of bamboo furniture for her. This explains why they are not of the same refined execution as the ones done for E.1027. The earlier furniture was meant to be shown in Jean Désert, and it was made by Eileen's artisans in Paris.

By the time she had finished Tempe à Pailla, the war—the second World War she would live through—forced her to move on. But on the whole those last years before World War Two were happy. For the first time in many years Eileen felt totally free of the oppressive burdens which had come with Jean Désert, the building of Roquebrune, and her association with Jean Badovici. Now she could lead her own life again. There were old friends to visit. Evelyn Wyld lived in La Bastide Caillenco, in La Roquette-sur-Siagne behind Cannes. By that time Eyre and Evelyn no longer had the shop. Evelyn continued to make carpets; Eyre continued to design lacquer furniture. At one time she had—as once upon a time, Dunand had done—"borrowed" Sugawara to lacquer a little chest, but he never finished it. Eyre de Lanux still has the piece with its beautiful unfinished surface in her apartment in New York: "the only piece left of a rich and very peculiar time."

Sometimes they would all meet in La Bastide Blanche, where Kate Weatherby still lived, going down to the deserted beach and coming back with pieces of driftwood which each of the women decorated according to her own inclination or taste. Kate had been joined by a new friend, Gert Goldsmith, known as Goldie, who also made carpets. Goldie was devoted to Kate, whom she had known from her childhood, when she and her four sisters lived on the farm of the Weatherby manor house. Eventually she had joined Kate in France. She was not very good-looking but her sunny temperament won everybody over. There was much laughter and silliness of almost girlish behavior—they played practical jokes on each other, such as serving strawberries with salt. The formidable Kate, taking herself for a water diviner, walked through the land trying to discover springs, while the others giggled behind her back. One day she was trying with her hands to hypnotize a lizard into sleep. Of course it was not like old times, but sometimes it felt like it.

The Côte d'Azur was filling up. Also the heat in the summer in Castellar was stifling, so Eileen was again drawn to Saint-Tropez. Many of her old acquaintances had settled down there. In Beauvallon, right across the Bay of Saint-Tropez, Natalie Barney and Romaine Brooks had taken a house, which was named Trait d'Union, because it consisted of two bungalows joined together by a dining room. Colette had also taken a new house. The writer Radclyffe Hall, known as John, and her friend Una Troubridge came to stay. The ladies bathed in the nude while John in ragged slacks and a ragamuffin hat looked on. But Eileen kept well out of this world. She had a horror of this showing off, but when told about it, she could not help but be amused. When Eileen wanted to relax, she escaped from the crowd to La Bastide Blanche. Eileen rented a small flat on the rue Suffren which consisted of three rooms overlooking the harbor. Every year at the end of July, Louise and Eileen closed down Castellar and moved west to Saint-Tropez. Eileen furnished the new flat completely with her furniture. There was a bed made from glass tubes and a Transat, plus several tables.

Much of the summer was spent reading, drawing, and taking photographs. Eileen went daily down to the beach to photograph shells or driftwood. Sometimes she took the objects home and created a strange kind of still life from pebbles, glass, and pieces of wire. Another time she picked up a huge piece of soft stone and began carving the head of a woman. Photography became a hobby. She searched out some buildings and industrial sites and took pictures of cranes, scaffolding, and pipes. Some of the shapes found their way into her paintings.

As she continually proved, not to do anything, to have a lazy holiday was totally alien to her. She later once talked about art as a substitute for life, but immediately corrected herself. Art could create bridges and a certain harmony in an unharmonious world, but it could never substitute for life itself. It was simply that her creative mind was always at

Kate Weatherby and
Evelyn Wyld, Eileen's
old friends, at
Evelyn's house, La
Bastide Caillenco,
near Cannes

work; she was an artist who needed to express herself
constantly.

Much of Eileen's time was spent designing. In 1936 she
took up again the elliptical form she was so fond of and
designed the Tube House—a prefabricated metal structure,
more a cell than a house, which nevertheless provided space
for a living room, bedroom, small kitchen, and a lavatory. It
stood on a base of only seven and a half by nine and a half
feet. Stone socles allowed the cabin to be fixed on the
ground. The roof was made of a thin layer of concrete. Her

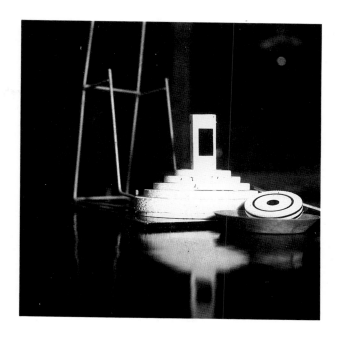

One of Eileen's
sculptures lighted and
photographed by her

Piece of driftwood
photographed against
the sea by Eileen

plans allowed for different layouts, and with the help of a
cylindrical addition, a further bedroom could be added. This
Tube House was intended for workers on site, as a shelter in
disasters, or as a holiday home. Since it had a minimum
foundation, it could be erected anywhere and could be
produced in large quantities at low cost. The combination of
the circle and the square appeared often in her designs;
Eileen had a special gift of creating a kind of magic out of
architecture by simply combining the practical with the
beautiful. The design of the elliptical house was a further
proof that she achieved a natural elegance by a built-in
sense of shape that was free of self-conscious gesture.
Unfortunately, she could not interest anybody in this
practical and beautiful idea.

Only rarely did Eileen go to Paris. In September, she and
Louise returned to Castellar. In 1936 she began working on
a project very dear to her heart: a Centre de Vacances
(Vacation Center). (Most of Eileen's notes are in French; she
spoke French fluently and preferred this language for most
of her writing.) Reading the publications of the Front
Populaire, a common movement of the Socialists, under Léon
Blum, and other left-óf-center groups, she discovered that
what she really liked to build was not individual homes but
environments from which the majority of people could profit.
"Now that paid holidays are universally recognised," she
wrote, "one thinks more and more of facilitating the holiday
so necessary to those families and persons whose means are

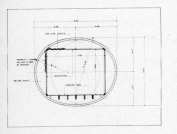

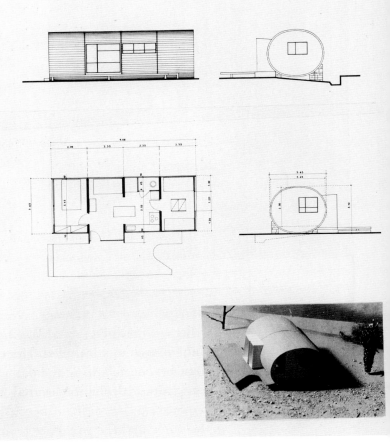

limited. It is very difficult to obtain authorisation for
camping on private grounds, and official camping places
have been established. But," she added, in her usual
practical way, "the supply of water or washing facilities is
often rudimentary."

But Eileen wanted to design a Vacation Center in a way
which would satisfy the most stringent aesthetic demands, as
well as be economical and practical.

Eileen visualized the Vacation Center as being built at
the edge of the sea. It included a restaurant-*cum*-café, which
could serve also as a cinema, an open-air theater, a special
building "for young people who are on the move," and a
special house for children. She was thinking of making the
buildings for the children and the restaurant permanent,
while the cabins to house the vacationers could easily be
erected and dismantled according to need. They could even
be transported from one place to another. There were
facilities for showers and lavatories.

Looking at her model and reading through the few notes she left, one realizes the deep social concern she developed over the years. She cared deeply and was grieved by the selfishness and gross stupidity of the world. She rejected any extravagance: "We were brought up to spend as little as possible on ourselves and as much as possible on other people." Even when she was very old, she would go by bus rather than by taxi if she could. Taking the train down to Saint-Tropez, she shared a second-class compartment with Louise; traveling in a first-class compartment she considered wasteful. She gave freely to charities, often to the exasperation of the people around her, hesitating endlessly among unmarried mothers, stray cats, or impoverished monks, finally giving to the soup kitchen.

Eileen had an inbuilt sense of justice. She always considered her own eccentric situation as privileged, and wholeheartedly rejected the notion of many of her class that most people had what they deserved. But she was no revolutionary. All she wanted was to alleviate the plight of those less fortunate. She did not want political solutions, she wanted architectural ones. Her own interest in politics never went beyond following the daily news. She had vague sympathy with the intellectuals who sided with the Left during the Spanish Civil War, without ever taking any action. She abhorred Fascism and shared the anti-German prejudices of her generation.

She also read Trotsky and Lenin and wrote down some of their thoughts. "Every regime expresses itself through its architecture," she notes from Trotsky. "The present Soviet epoch is characterised by palaces and official houses, which are the real temples of bureaucracy, houses for the Red Army, Military Clubs . . . whilst the construction of houses for the workers is miserable and terribly behind." A little later on the same page Eileen quoted: "The more the functions of power belong to the entire people, the less they become necessary."

From now on she designed only projects for the masses. Unfortunately none of them was built. Had she looked for individual clients, she might have been more successful as an architect. But she was stubborn, nearly sixty years old, and had the "*bassin* full of private clients, and all that it entails."

Le Corbusier, who often came to Roquebrune to visit Badovici, saw the project for the Vacation Center grow. When the model for it was finished, he was so excited about it that he decided to include it in his section in the International Exhibition held in Paris in 1937.

Top: Le Corbusier's Pavillon des Temps Nouveaux, designed for the International Exposition in Paris in 1937

Bottom: Interior of the Pavillon des Temps Nouveaux, showing its tentlike construction

Le Corbusier had planned a large exhibition of modern housing, but instead he was given only a little plot in an annex of the main exhibition at the Porte Maillot on the outskirts of Paris. There Le Corbusier built a tent, which he called Pavillon des Temps Nouveaux, in red, blue, green, yellow, the colors of his paintings. The inside was a construction of multicolored canvas, supported by steel pillars and stretched over fine cables. The pavilion was devoted to modern urbanism. It included Le Corbusier's plans for a futurist Paris. There was a huge project for a throughway cutting across Paris, a plan for a gigantic commercial center, and a stadium for 100,000 spectators. In the pavilion was a stand for Eileen's Centre de Vacances. It was also decided to exhibit one of Badovici's designs: an ingenious lifeboat, dating from 1934, which would inflate once it hit the water. On its bow were a letter and a number: E-7(= E. G.).

Eileen as usual was not content with the stand as it was. So Louise was sent all over town to find cork to cover the walls. They covered eight panels with the cork and a kind of mat silver material. Louise, a worker, and Eileen did all the installation themselves. The carpenter, Roattino, was brought up from Castellar to help make a finished model from the rather shaky ones Eileen had contrived from cardboard boxes and paper. Roattino spent four weeks working from morning to night. Eileen would sit next to him in her workroom and make sure that "every inch was properly done." The stand was finally finished. Above it a celluloid disk simply announced:

Centre de Vacances
Club Régional
Equipement du Logis
par
Eileen Gray

Another disk read:

Nouveau Moyen de Sauvetage
par
Jean Badovici

In the middle of the room stood Badovici's boat.

The pavilion opened July 17; Eileen did not attend. As usual, she was fussing about and angry that nothing was ready, so Louise and Roattino went alone. There was no

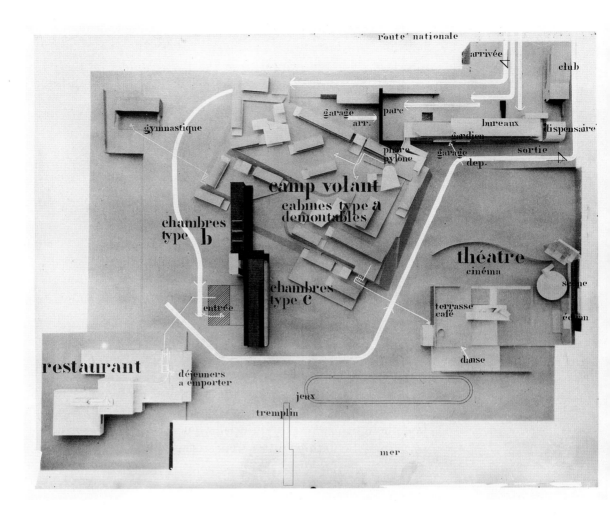

The image contains the following labels: route nationale, arrivée, club, garage arr., parc, bureaux, dispensaire, gymnastique, gardien, phare pylone, garage dep., sortie, camp volant, cabines type a démontables, chambres type b, théâtre, cinéma, scène, chambres type c, terrasse café, écran, entrée, danse, restaurant, déjeuners a emporter, jeux, tremplin, mer

Plan for the Vacation Center designed by Eileen and exhibited in the Pavillon des Temps Nouveaux

cabinet member, no public person. Le Corbusier got up and simply announced, "Nobody has turned up. I declare the pavilion open." Again, Eileen had set herself apart. Her mixture of shyness, sulkiness, and even arrogance isolated her from forming any relationships, private or professional. She could not get herself to lend her support at the official opening of an exhibition she had helped to realize and where she was asked to participate. She had not changed much since she had missed the dinner with Apollinaire.

But Le Corbusier did not seem to bear any grudge. He was preparing a pamphlet to go with the exhibition. He wrote to Badovici: "I have received the first proofs of the pavilion [catalogue]. It is not bad, there are two pages for you and two pages for E. Gray, which look very good. I hope you will be satisfied. Please pass on once more to Eileen Gray all my gratitude for her friendship. I am so happy to have spent some moments with her."

In this catalogue, *Des Canons, Des munitions? Merci! Des Logis . . . S.V.P.* (1938), Le Corbusier was no less enthusiastic about Eileen's work:

A holiday center everywhere has appeal for leisure activities. As the result of [the new law making] paid holidays [obligatory], we have seen during the summer of 1937, the country being invaded by those who benefit from it. This is a new event in the life of this country. Innkeepers make long faces because there are small purses, but other people feel that one must find new ways. One has seen happy people making contact with nature, entering monasteries, examining, studying, and opening up to a freedom which they had not known before. Here is a project which has been remarkably well thought out. It is situated on the sea, it contains a restaurant organized with the latest methods of service and distribution. . . . The movable camping site is composed of temporary cabins which can easily be erected and dismantled according to the influx of tourists. There is entertainment planned in a theater and a cinema in the open air. Theater people (what kind? new ones, amateurs maybe) will be happy to discover stages in the country able to present their manifestations full of fresh poetry.

One can understand Le Corbusier's enthusiasm. Eileen had thought of everything, even what kind of meal could be served. Anticipating future trends, she had conceived on the ground floor a self-service restaurant and a snack bar. The first floor was supposed to serve simple meals at a fixed price. On the second floor was a full-service restaurant with a dance floor. The windows opened to extend onto a vast terrace.

Her sense of detail was often touching, as in the description of the tents "to be erected by one person, light enough to be carried on a motorcycle or in a car. It had plastic disks wide enough to let the night air through, but small enough to form a barrier against stray dogs." Eileen also designed some furniture for the center, notably tables and chairs. None of it was ever executed.

Eileen's plans for the different houses were not all finished, but several earlier ideas were incorporated into her drawings. For instance, the House for an Engineer served as a model for the restaurant. The cabins are a development from the Tube House. There are sketches for different kinds of tents in various sizes. The theater was modeled on a Greek theater, with an open-air podium, adaptable for film and theater productions. The weakest point in the whole project is the large building with rooms for families. Eileen designed a pleasant but fairly conventional housing block. It

Vacation Center

Above: Model of the apartment complex and, at right, the restaurant

Right: Elevations of the building. The ground floors are supposed to house communal rooms, while the bedrooms are on the upper floors. They are of two different sizes, double and single, housed in two different wings which are linked by a central staircase and elevators

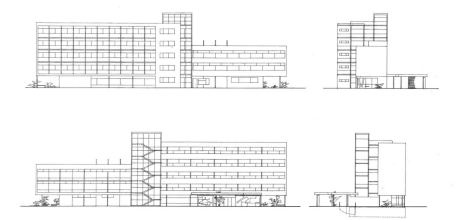

was the first time that she had designed on such a large scale, and she seemed not to have mastered it too well, although the different treatment of the two sides with their different window designs is interesting. There are some later drawings of larger buildings and even of a skyscraper Eileen experimented with.

By some coincidence, in the same exhibition, in 1937, at the Pavillon Marsan, two items were shown, described in a catalogue, *Le Décor de la Vie de 1900 à 1925*, as follows:

GREY [*sic*] Miss
1117 Paravent en laque 1913
Madame Jacques Doucet

1118 Table en laque rouge 1913
Madame Jacques Doucet

It is doubtful whether anybody noticed that the maker of these two pieces was the same Eileen Gray who showed her work in the Pavillon des Temps Nouveaux, and Eileen herself preferred not to mention it.

Le Corbusier's relationship with Eileen was ambiguous. He had a great admiration for her work, especially for the house in Roquebrune. Eileen always referred to Le Corbusier by his nickname, Corbu, which his friends and fellow architects used on account of his thick horn-rimmed glasses, which gave him the look of a raven (*corbeau*). The contact between them remained always very formal. Le Corbusier's gruff and abrupt manners had intimidated people less shy than Eileen. Had they known each other better, they might have discovered many similarities. Both were governed by high moral principles regarding mankind. Both shared a strength of purpose and a desire to submit all their doings to the creation of a more harmonious environment.

Eileen had met Charles-Edouard Jeanneret in the early twenties, shortly before he changed his name to Le Corbusier (1923). In those years he had a studio right around the corner from her own place, on the rue Jacob. At the time Eileen was beginning to be seriously interested in architecture, his book *Vers une Architecture* was published (also 1923). But Eileen had read much of his writing even earlier, since she owned a complete run of *L'Esprit Nouveau*, which Le Corbusier, Ozenfant, and Charles Dermée had begun publishing in 1919, with the words "A great epoch has begun: a spirit of construction and synthesis, led by clear conception." It had a tremendous influence on her. Le Corbusier's idea that any object he designed must be able to be mass-produced—almost as a moral obligation to mankind—had far-reaching consequences for her future designs. She admired him for his humanity and comprehension of space. It was Le Corbusier's writing, utilizing his new aesthetic language, which helped her to break with the things she had done before. It was as if she had discovered a form that was totally in accordance with her own character. At the beginning of her career, she had looked to the Art Nouveau movement, with its new kind of honesty, as a liberating force, but she soon rejected its more excessive language. She had never felt at ease, even with the more somber version, as it was practiced in England, Austria, or Germany. With the arrival of Le Corbusier she made a clear-cut decision. From now on, design and architecture had to be a distinct and practical statement.

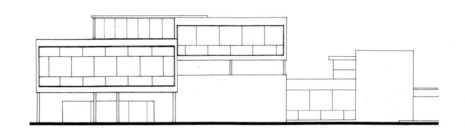

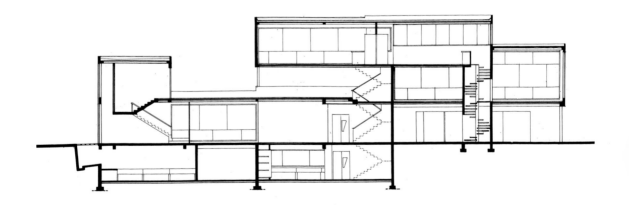

Vacation Center
Restaurant, model
and elevations. The
clear and unfussy
design of the remark-
able restaurant
complex makes it one
of Eileen's most har-
monious buildings.
She uses windows of
varying designs and
sizes to create lively
facades. Although the
building is capable of
feeding many people
simultaneously, it
creates a feeling of
privacy. The different
bodies of the building
are clearly marked,
corresponding to the
different kinds of
meals served

Cross section of the
southwest facade
(opposite, bottom)
shows the ground
floor, with a snack
bar and cafeteria; on
the next floor a
moderately priced
café; on the roof a
glassed-in formal
restaurant with a
panoramic view. The
rooftop also provided
a terrace for dancing.
In the basement were
kitchens, refrigerated
rooms, pantry, dumb-
waiters, a garage for
the manager, and a
wine cellar

Like Le Corbusier, Mies van der Rohe, and Gropius for that matter, Eileen Gray was an artist first and foremost; the functioning of a drawer or a light fixture was taken for granted.

Through Badovici, Eileen remained in contact with Le Corbusier. The two men spent much time together. They both loved good food and good stories and had a rumbustious relationship often leaning toward schoolboy pranks. Eileen had no time for such behavior. Her overrigid sense of decorum and her easily ruffled sensibility made her keep away. But Eileen closely followed Le Corbusier's career. In 1924 she visited the house that Le Corbusier and his cousin Pierre Jeanneret had built for the painter Ozenfant. Badovici wrote enthusiastically about it. In 1928, with Pierre Jeanneret, Corbu remodeled an old house at Ville d'Avray. In it he put the furniture he had designed together with Charlotte Perriand. Eileen was intrigued with the furniture, which in more than one way resembled what she was designing for E.1027. She also visited the Villa Savoye, which Le Corbusier built a year later. During the years Eileen was building the house in Roquebrune, Badovici reviewed all Le Corbusier's buildings in *L'Architecture Vivante*—the La Roche house on Doctor Blanche Square, the house in Denfert-Rochereau, the villa in Gardiens. Eileen had access to many of the plans of these houses. Without doubt they greatly influenced her.

In many cases, Eileen Gray and Le Corbusier thought along the same lines. In 1928 he had written an article about interior designs of houses in *L'Architecture Vivante*. Some of the solutions he advocated are almost the same as some of those Eileen had used in E.1027. Talking about tables, he wrote: "Shall I be hindered all my life by one large table filling my dining room? I have proposed the following wise solution: to establish a minimum table, for instance, 0.80 m × 1.20 m [30 by 47 inches]. Instead of five different tables, I have five of the same kind, but they can be placed next to each other. . . . I transport my tables easily from one place to another."

But however much Eileen admired Le Corbusier, she never blindly followed his ideas. If she was influenced by the great architectural pioneers, she never simply copied them. All her buildings were penetrated by her own sparkling spirit. Her inexperience in architecture helped her to preserve a freshness and innocence which other architects who merely copied soon lost. "L'art de l'ingénieur ne suffit pas s'il n'est pas guidé par le besoin de l'homme" ("The engineer's art is not enough unless it is guided by human needs"), she had written, rejecting Le Corbusier's idea of the house as a "machine à habiter": "Une maison n'est pas une 'machine à habiter.' Elle est la coquille de l'homme, son prolongation, son élargissement, son rayonnement spirituel. Non seulement son harmonie plastique, mais que toute son ordonnance, tout le terme de l'oeuvre, concourt à la rendre humaine dans le sens le plus profond" ("A house is not a machine to live in. It is the shell of man, his extension, his release, his spiritual emanation. Not only its visual harmony but its organization as a whole, the whole work combined together, make it human in the most profound sense").

In 1937 Eileen's relationship with Le Corbusier was amiable but distant; she saw him infrequently. She spent most of her time in Castellar, seeing Badovici from time to time for a quiet lunch.

The next year Le Corbusier and his wife, Yvonne, stayed for a couple of days with Badovici in the house at Roquebrune. Eileen had by that time moved out. Afterward Le Corbusier wrote her a letter saying how much he had missed her company and added, "I am so happy to tell you how much those few days spent in your house have made me appreciate the rare spirit which dictates all the organization

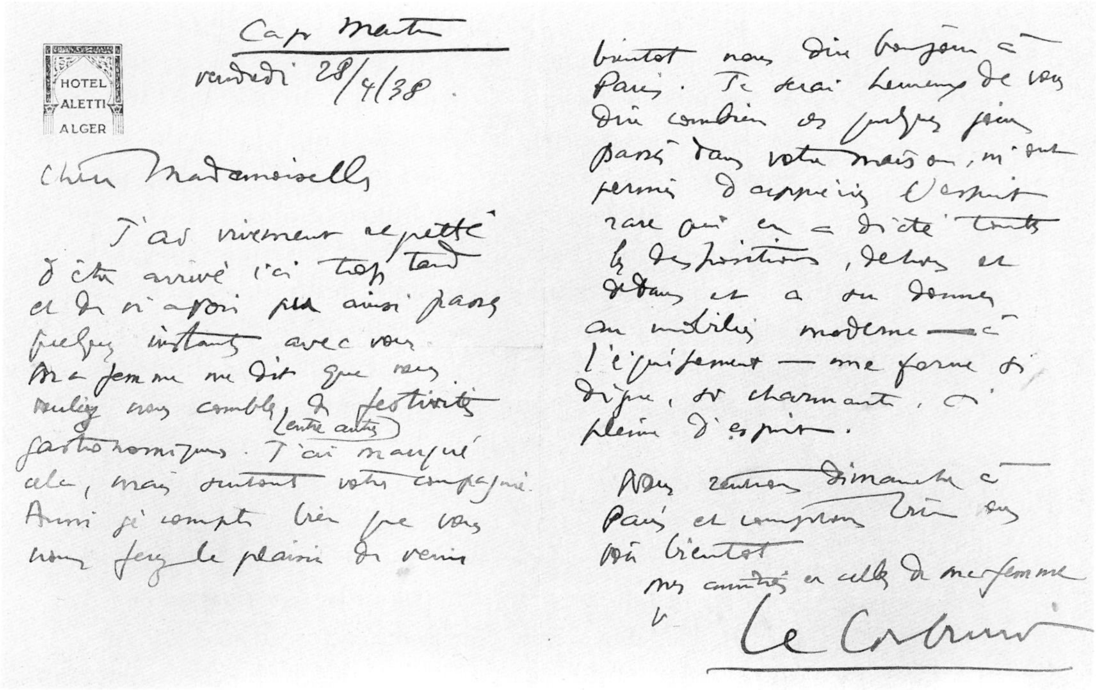
HOTEL ALETTI ALGER

Cap Martin
vendredi 28/4/38.

Chère Mademoiselle

J'ai vivement regretté d'être arrivé ici trop tard et de n'avoir pu ainsi passer quelques instants avec vous. Ma femme me dit que vous voulez nous combler de festivités (entre autres) gastronomiques. J'ai manqué cela, mais surtout votre compagnie. Aussi je compte bien que vous nous ferez le plaisir de venir bientôt nous dire bonjour à Paris. Je serai heureux de vous dire combien ces quelques jours passés dans votre maison m'ont permis d'apprécier l'esprit rare qui en a dicté toutes les dispositions, dehors et dedans et a su donner au mobilier moderne — à l'équipement — une forme si digne, si charmante, si pleine d'esprit.

Nous rentrons dimanche à Paris et comptons bien vous voir bientôt

mes amitiés et celles de ma femme

Le Corbusier

A letter from Le Corbusier to Eileen praising her architecture and interior design at E.1027

inside and outside. A rare spirit which has given the modern furniture and installations such a dignified, charming, and witty shape." This letter pleased her very much; it is one of the few she kept. Someone had actually acknowledged that it was *her* house, the house *she* had built. And this person was no less than Le Corbusier. He often returned to E.1027, especially after the war, driving his tiny apple-green Fiat up the hill to spend a few days with Badovici. But later, in 1949, he also had some criticism, as some of the letters he wrote to Badovici (now at the Fondation Le Corbusier) reveal. He particularly objected to the curved screen at the entrance, which he considered "pseudo." He advised Jean to get rid of it: "The room would be transformed and the entrance would be another thing altogether." Le Corbusier did not understand, and Badovici unfortunately did not know how to defend, Eileen's marvelous solution of creating privacy by screening off the entrance. Luckily Le Corbusier's suggestion was ignored. But their real contretemps was more serious.

In the middle thirties Le Corbusier developed a real passion for wall paintings. He began asking his friends to let him paint their walls, and in 1935 he did a mural in Badovici's house in Vézelay. Three years later he also

Frescoes painted by Le Corbusier at E.1027 (after restoration in 1977)

painted several frescoes in E.1027, without Eileen's permission—an act she deeply resented. He closed the service door in the entrance hall to paint one of his frescoes over the wall, thus removing Eileen's planned ambiguity. To cover her clear and consciously low-key house with overtly sexual, garish paintings she considered an act of vandalism. He also painted one very large fresco on the white wall behind the sofa in the living room. It dominated the entire room. There were frescoes all over the house. Eight all together (although Le Corbusier sometimes mentions nine, sometimes seven, sometimes eight). In 1979 five frescoes remained.

In Le Corbusier's book *My Work*, which was published first in 1960 in France, there is a photograph of one of the frescoes with the caption: "One of seven mural paintings in a villa at Cap Martin." In the same book he also talks about "1938–1939—eight murals (free of charge) in the Badovici and Helen [*sic*] Gray House at Cap Martin." It was rape. A fellow architect, a man she admired, had without her consent defaced her design. Le Corbusier had covered most of her walls, though sometimes respecting the neat inscriptions she had put on the outside of drawers and cupboards to mark their contents. The two witty inscriptions

**Another of Le
Corbusier's frescoes
in the living room**

"DÉFENSE DE RIRE" and "ENTREZ LENTEMENT" were
incorporated in his murals. The latter inscription he
incorporated to convey the sense of entrance by a black area
on the fresco.

During those years Eileen for the first time noticed that
her eyesight had begun to deteriorate. This caused her great
alarm. Her hands also had begun to tremble. She became
increasingly embarrassed to be seen eating in public, so she
gave up going to restaurants, preferring to take her meals at
home. There were fewer and fewer friends. From time to time
she invited Jean Badovici to Castellar, or saw Kate
Weatherby or Evelyn Wyld, but otherwise she had grown
closer to her niece, the painter Prunella Clough, in whose
rare intelligence Eileen had discovered a kindred spirit. Both
women had made their work the center of their lives. Neither

Le Corbusier, his wife, and Jean Badovici at E.1027 in front of the mural that incorporated Eileen's phrase "ENTREZ LENTEMENT"

could be pressed into any conventional mold, which gave them an unusual freedom. Into this long-lasting relationship Eileen could pour all her family instinct, her sense of protectiveness, and her desire to be protected. Prunella Clough was her only lifeline until her last day. But otherwise from now on, it would be very difficult to break the solitary pattern.

THE SECOND WORLD WAR

Eileen spent the first year of the war in Castellar. In 1940, when the Germans approached the French capital, Louise was in Paris. Eileen urged her to leave the city as soon as possible and to join her. Louise took Eileen's black Persian lamb coat and the little jewelry Eileen had and started the long trek south. There were no more trains leaving the capital and she had to hitch a ride on a truck and sleep in the open air. Eileen in the meantime was totally without news. They had agreed to meet somehow in Menton. Eileen went daily to see if there was any sign of her. Finally, one day Eileen heard a voice shouting "Mademoiselle!" It was Louise.

They were not able to stay long in Castellar. Eileen as a resident alien was not allowed to remain near the sea; all foreigners were asked to move inland. One day two gendarmes arrived and told them to vacate the house by eight o'clock the next morning. They started piling things in the little car and departed the same evening, leaving most of their possessions behind. Kate Weatherby and Evelyn Wyld also had to give up their houses. Eileen chose to go to Lourmarin, a little town north of Aix in the Vaucluse region, because her old acquaintance the architect Henri Pacon and the two Martel sculptor brothers had restored the old castle. There were already quite a number of English people living there, mostly in the only hotel. The women did not want to live in the hotel, nor did they want to mingle with the other "refugees." So Kate and Evelyn took a little house just outside Lourmarin, in a place called Lointes Bastides, and Eileen rented a house in town. It was very simple, having only two rooms with no bath and a small kitchen with a primitive stove. Louise slept in the front room, and Eileen installed herself in the back. She put a wooden plank on two trestles. This became her worktable.

While Louise as usual looked after the household, Eileen spent hours on end trying to overcome the boredom of isolation and lack of stimulation by working. Sometimes at night, when the intense summer heat receded, they would go for long walks to gather some wood for their cooking stove.

Food was scarce. "We have little to eat, even in the country, a terrible hardship, soon we hope it will end," she wrote in a letter in 1942. "No coffee, no milk, hardly any vegetables." The always inventive Louise did her best gathering salads and fruit in the fields. Kate and Evelyn kept a goat, and every day a liter of milk was delivered to Eileen's house in exchange for sugar or some eggs. Louise kept two chickens, which she put into a basket and took on her bicycle to let them run loose in the fields. At one point, Eileen managed to buy a rabbit from an old farmer. Of course, soon they were so fond of the animal that there was no question of ever eating it. Kate had also bought a rabbit, and one morning Eileen woke up to a small colony of rabbits.

At one point Eileen had considered returning to England. But her roots were too deeply embedded in France: "I would be unbearably homesick." Her letters are full of lyrical passages about the beautiful countryside, but she "felt terribly cut off from work, the only thing worthwhile to keep alive."

Somehow in the autumn of 1942 she got permission to go back for a few days to Saint-Tropez. "Life in Lourmarin is so lonely," she wrote. She considered once more going to England via Lisbon, the ordinary route being cut off by the Germans. But she soon rejected this idea. "It would be terrible to leave France." Eileen was not a moaner; she did not like seeing herself the victim of a situation. She also knew well that her plight was easy compared with many others' during those war years. But she was nearly seventy and not in good health. "Anger is perhaps the greatest inspiration in those days when the individual is separated in so many personalities. Suddenly one is all in one piece." Whipping up some anger enabled her to cope, and as so often before, she found some consolation in work. She drew and made gouaches and sculptures, using old bits and pieces, and wrote almost every day and night on architecture.

Among these drawings—none of them dated—are a number for exhibition stands, kiosks, that were probably intended for some architectural exhibition but were never used. There is a drawing for an information pavilion and a peculiar one-hundred-twenty-five-foot-high towerlike structure, not unlike a Russian Constructivist sculpture. Other sketches show a kind of bus shelter, consisting of two pillars supporting a sculptural roof.

Sometimes in the middle of a meager meal she would get

Drawings for, at top,
an information pavi-
lion and two bus
shelters

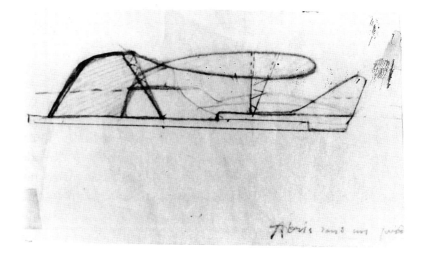

up and return to her drawing board. But it was difficult to work. She lacked reference books, libraries, and most of all some link with the outside world. From time to time Badovici came and brought the few architectural reviews that were published during the war. Occasionally Eileen and her two friends were invited to the local home of the French diplomat Couve de Murville. These were her only social contacts during almost three years. She nevertheless tried to keep up with the news and never lost her sense of irony. Answering a question about a rumor that Picasso also had been interned, she wrote: "I don't think so. I hear that he is now selling his canvasses for 200.000 frs [$4570] upwards, perhaps worse from a painting point of view than internment." At another time she wrote to England: "When one is cut off from everything one wants to do and in this chaotic phase, some sort of nonsense is necessary, even if it rarely makes one laugh, I enclose one." And she put in one of those little cartoons she loved and used to cut out from magazines.

Badovici had gone to Casablanca and sent her a ground plan of a piece of land he had bought there. Once more he wanted her to design a house for him. Eileen made some plans and a model. Unfortunately, along with other plans, they were sent to Saint-Tropez—because there was so little space in the house—where they were lost.

Eileen did not like to discuss the subject of Badovici but she said that Badovici designed only one project all by himself: "A house on the other side of the Pont de Sèvres [meaning the Right Bank]. The plans were not bad." She went to see it once and helped him to rearrange the elevations. This must have been shortly before the war. Badovici did not get on with his clients, and the project was never completely finished. Of course there were his restorations of the houses in Vézelay. She was probably also involved in this in 1925 and 1926. According to her notes, she also worked "on a project for Dakar."

She was accustomed to spend much time taking stock of her experiences. In a brown book she noted what passed in her mind. Sometimes there were thoughts of an almost utopian future. For instance, under the heading "Urbanism," she wrote: "The necessity to create in towns, special sections for all those who want to live with pure spiritual matters. For the savants, musicians, writers, in order not to expose them to the dangers of modern life," and she rather touchingly added, "not to run the risk of being run over by a truck. . . . Those people whose lives seem to happen on a different level, are always so much more vulnerable on the material side. We must create for them special places such as studios or workrooms—even collective ones—which will enable them to isolate themselves. (Maybe they could be in the open air.) Places where they can, in peace, contemplate the ideas which fill them with passion." Eileen was a romantic; the almost Platonic idea of artists whom society must look after was important to her. On the other hand, she was a realist. She knew that artists, like anybody else, need contact with society and cannot create in a cocoon, however perfectly conceived.

In a letter to her niece in London, who had had an accident, she wrote, "Artists ought not to drive at all. First of all, they are too precious, secondly, driving prevents their thoughts wandering where they should, thirdly, it puts constant tension on their eyes." Eileen certainly thought that artists are a species worth preserving.

It may be somewhat surprising that she also made some notes about a church by the sea. It would be built from the rounded pebbles washed up on the shore. The roof would be made with a cement vault in which one would set the stones. The inside walls would be lined with natural wood. Since Eileen was not a religious person in the Christian sense, the idea for the church had very little to do with any religious or Christian homage. It was an architectural solution to a given building.

In later years she was able to pray, in a sort of all-embracing way, but not to a personalized God. Of course, when anything got lost in the household, spectacles, hearing aids, or a newspaper clipping, both Louise and Eileen, accusing each other vehemently of having lost it, burst into a prayer to Saint Anthony: "Saint-Antoine, grand voleur, vieux filou, rendez-nous ce que vous avez pris, ce qui n'est pas à vous!" ("Saint Anthony, big thief, old rascal, give us back what you've taken from us and which isn't yours!") And magically, the article would turn up, followed by great laughter from the newly reconciled enemies.

On a more serious level she wrote, "I have never been able to believe like Teilhard de Chardin. I can only believe in a Universal Spirit into which one is eventually absorbed, but before, what happens?" It was the "before" that concerned her, not the "after," in which she trusted with a kind of simple faith. "Qui reviendra pour nous dire si ce que nous entoure a un sens?" ("Who, after all, returns to let us know that what surrounds us makes sense?")

When she was in her nineties, she wrote in a letter: "Something I read recently about the cell transforming itself into energy makes me wonder if there isn't a sort of Afterlife; for surely that is the transformation of material substance into something materially impalpable, which might happen to us and that would explain why a great many 'savants' seem to believe that too. Only work of some sort can help to give meaning to life even if it is really quite useless."

Elsewhere she observed, "All religion seems so medieval, and as our characters are so much dependent on our physical make-up, even if we do go on in some other dimension, we shall only be ghosts with no individuality; not that I shouldn't gladly have a change of mine."

Eileen, as always, read widely during those years, sometimes copying passages of the books into her scrapbook. It is full of quotes from Hegel, Confucius, Trotsky, H. G. Wells, Michaux, Colette, and from poems she liked. A few lines reflected her own thoughts—rather proudly marked "E. G." Did she ever think of publishing them in a book? We do not know. The few lines she left testify to a romantic disposition whose underlying quality was sincerity.

"Our days follow one another like steps in an endless staircase—" she noted down, "we mount and one day hesitate—there comes a gap, we fall through to Eternity." The poetry which is manifest in much of her design could sometimes be felt in the lyrical passages of her letters or in lines like these: "Notes de n'importe quoi: the whites of her eyes were blue like the skin of a little silverfish lit from inside."

Eileen was never a systematic reader. Having had very little formal education and a great desire to learn, she had usually read what came her way. As a young woman she had read Colette, Anatole France, the poems of Rupert Brooke, Maeterlinck, some Gide, Oscar Wilde, and Keats. Later, under the influence of the Front Populaire, she read Lenin on the economics of Communism, and Trotsky, and *The Mind and Face of Bolshevism*. She was also interested in the Far East: in her library she had books like *The Idea of Indian Art* or *Persia* or *The Awakening of the East*. She always had a great interest in philosophy. In her early years she had read Nietzsche and Schopenhauer. Later she read books like *The Introduction to the Study of Philosophy* and works by Kant, Emerson, and Herbert Spencer. She might have laughed about Aleister Crowley in her early years in Paris, but her library contained quite a few books on

Right: An African-
style mask Eileen
made from a piece of
cork she had picked
up on the beach. It
was painted in silver
with bits of wood
forming the eyes and
tinted gray all over

Below: A small ivory
sculpture in two parts
made from ivory left
over from lamps and
handles Eileen had
designed in the
twenties

psychology and the paranormal, books like *Wisdom and Destiny*, the *Secrets of Beauty*, and mystical texts such as *Mary Magdalene*.

Of course there were a great many books and magazines on art and architecture, on Marcel Breuer and on the Bauhaus, and drawings by Jean Cocteau and early books on James Ensor, Jacques Lipchitz, Francis Picabia, and Aubrey Beardsley. A number of her books dealt with Surrealism.

By the end of 1943, Kate, Evelyn, Eileen, and Louise were able to leave Lourmarin but were not yet allowed to return to Saint-Tropez. They moved to the larger town of Cavaillon, also in the Vaucluse. Louise, somehow obtaining a doctor's certificate for Eileen, who had injured her leg, saying it was contagious, and a nursing certificate for herself, managed to get everybody a single room in a hotel. At any moment they expected the Germans to advance and take this part of the country, which belonged to the so-called Free Zone. Eileen bought herself a little ivory-handled revolver, but she never even learned to load it.

In 1944 the retreating Germans blew up the port of Saint-Tropez, destroying most of the houses around it. The four women rushed there to see the damage. It was terrible: the house where Eileen had had her flat was gone. The whole place was in ruins, including the furniture and the plans she had made in Lourmarin. Louise remembers seeing Eileen's pajamas floating in the water, and while she cried, Eileen looked on dry-eyed. But she mourned for the trees: "The Germans have cut all the trees." But worse was still to come. They took the train to Menton and climbed up the steep road to the house in Castellar. It was in a terrible state; it had been totally looted. Almost all her furniture, her books, her drawings and plans had gone; Eileen wept then. She had lost not only all her personal clothes, china, and household goods, but also her rugs and furniture (including a lacquered armchair from Jean Désert and three more armchairs she had designed for Castellar). Gone were the divan, the cork-lined table, and a stunning bamboo screen framed in wood that came from an African exhibition in Paris, which Eileen dearly loved. The thieves, a mixture of looting soldiers and smugglers who crossed the nearby border, had also ripped all the built-in furniture and mirrors off the walls. Her drawings and plans had been used to light fires.

A few years before, Eileen had three places in this area;

now she had none. She returned to Paris, to the rue Bonaparte, which mercifully was intact.

This was a very low moment of her life. It was not so much the material loss that grieved her, but that her entire life's work, or so it seemed, had been destroyed. She summed up her situation: "I have saved nothing from Roquebrune. The little flat on the port was blown to bits by the Germans. There is nothing else worth keeping."

PROJET POUR UN CENTRE CULTUREL
CONCEPTION ARCHITECTURALE : EILEEN GRAY

Coupe longitudinale.

Le projet de Centre Culturel que nous présentons ici a été étudié par Eileen Gray, qui consacre une grande partie de sa vie à l'architecture et avait réalisé, avec Jean Badovici, la maison de Roquebrune que connaissent tous nos lecteurs.

Ce projet s'inscrit dans le mouvement, si nécessaire aujourd'hui, d'une recherche de décentralisation administrative et culturelle pour retenir la jeunesse en province et dans les centres ruraux.

Ce projet constitue en soi une unité architecturale comprenant, en dehors des salles de réunions, de conférences, d'expositions, une grande salle polyvalente pouvant servir pour spectacles, concerts, cinéma et dont le volume est l'élément majeur de la composition.

La salle est couverte par un toit-terrasse dont l'inclinaison suit celle de la salle. Les gradins, aménagés sur ce toit-terrasse, constituent les sièges du théâtre en plein air. On notera que des spectacles simultanés à l'extérieur et à l'intérieur peuvent être envisagés.

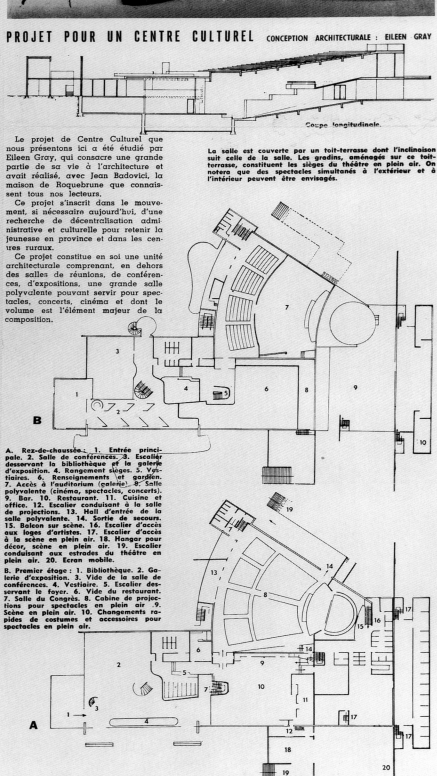

A. Rez-de-chaussée : 1. Entrée principale. 2. Salle de conférences. 3. Escalier desservant la bibliothèque et la galerie d'exposition. 4. Rangement sièges. 5. Vestiaires. 6. Renseignements et gardien. 7. Accès à l'auditorium (galerie). 8. Salle polyvalente (cinéma, spectacles, concerts). 9. Bar. 10. Restaurant. 11. Cuisine et office. 12. Escalier conduisant à la salle de projections. 13. Hall d'entrée de la salle polyvalente. 14. Sortie de secours. 15. Balcon sur scène. 16. Escalier d'accès aux loges d'artistes. 17. Escalier d'accès à la scène en plein air. 18. Hangar pour décor, scène en plein air. 19. Escalier conduisant aux estrades du théâtre en plein air. 20. Ecran mobile.

B. Premier étage : 1. Bibliothèque. 2. Galerie d'exposition. 3. Vide de la salle de conférences. 4. Vestiaire. 5. Escalier desservant le foyer. 6. Vide du restaurant. 7. Cabine du Congrès. 8. Cabine de projections pour spectacles en plein air. 9. Scène en plein air. 10. Changements rapides de costumes et accessoires pour spectacles en plein air.

STARTING ANEW

This article on the
Cultural Center which
Eileen designed in
1946—47 was
published in
*L'Architecture d'Au-
jourd'hui* in 1959.
The plans show the
lower level (A), which
has a lecture hall, an
auditorium, a bar and
restaurant, an
information booth,
checkrooms, and a
mobile screen on
which light spectacles
can be beamed. The
upper level (B)
contains a library,
exhibition gallery,
congress hall, and
equipment and
facilities for open-air
performances

Slowly normality began to set in. Paris was still hungry and
cold; there was no soap and little food. But to Eileen it
"seemed as beautiful as ever; marvellous how people manage
to dress at all at today's prices," she wrote.

She had always loved Paris. For a moment she did
contemplate living in London again. But she wrote: "I feel I
couldn't reaccustom myself to live in London again. I do
admire the big parks, the green, the comparative quiet, but
those endless little strings of houses make one feel dizzy."
No, being back in Paris meant being back home for Eileen.

Of course, at that time there was no question of going to
London, even for a visit. But she was glad that letters no
longer took three weeks. Writing to England to her sister,
she asked for a little bit of coffee—she "cannot do without
it"—and for Badovici a map of the city of London. The
coffee did not arrive, but instead a little note saying
"Exportation Prohibited," and instead of the London map, a
journal of artillery: a confusion. As usual when Eileen had
to do with some officialdom, she panicked and instead of
throwing the paper away she dutifully wrapped it up again
and returned it to London. "Hoping that no one will be
troubled. . . ."

Louise managed from time to time to get some good
meat, but mostly they had only potatoes. There were
electricity cuts and no candles to be had. At one point she
had to queue for hours to get a French residence permit.

But it was peace again and she threw herself into
anything which was on offer: magazines, exhibitions, and the
talk of the people. "It is so good sometimes to leave things
for a while and then get back to them in architecture or
painting."

Toward the end of the war Eileen was, like many
architects at that time, preoccupied with replanning the
destroyed towns. Like Le Corbusier, she spent weeks and
weeks drawing up town plans; she worked out some concrete
proposals for rebuilding the town of Maubeuge, an idea
Badovici had put to her. After the war Badovici was
appointed Adjunct Chief Architect of Reconstruction in

Maubeuge and Solesmes. There were few people who saw in the new beginning a chance to do more than repair or merely reconstruct cities as they had been in the past. Eileen often talked about the challenge that arose out of the spiritual and material devastation, and despite her advanced age she saw in the improvised forms of survival possibilities of new aims for architects and designers.

In 1946 she wrote a cheerful letter announcing that she had "begun some work on an art centre." The idea had been with her for quite a while. The first notes were made in Lourmarin. Now with some hope of building activities starting up again, she set to work on it in earnest. "One gets so totally absorbed, the days go by without one noticing it." Having experienced the "cultural desert" in the French provinces, she put down some thoughts on cultural revitalization there.

> Now that the provinces participate more and more in the diffusion of the dramatic and visual arts, and everybody can experience art, is it not the time to enlarge the horizons of those who are not able to travel to Paris? Should one not group together cultural and leisure activities, in one complex as it is done in other countries, so that everybody can make use of it? Certainly it is not the best moment to think about such superfluous things when so many people need basic shelter, but we do live and will continue to live, in times of enormous change. Times in which everything which touches human beings has to be re-thought. Human beings have eyes in the direction they walk; forwards, despite the fact that Valéry has said that they enter the world backwards. Therefore, should we never look ahead? Those who always turn backwards will never see the light. They will always live in the shadow of the past. Those who have enough strength ought to rise and make themselves heard. When one has faith one can transform the world.

These undated notes were probably made at the end of the war. They are prophetic words, spelling out very much the program of cultural decentralization and the Maisons de la Culture that André Malraux would initiate a few years later.

Using some of her ideas from the Vacation Center of 1937, she realized that a Cultural Center should not be just a place with "elitist" connotations. The more she worked on the project, the more its name changed from a "Centre Culturel" to a "Centre Culturel *et Social*"—as it became finally in her notebook. "This project aims to transform and ameliorate the social conditions of the people. The leisure hours will increase due to automatisation at work. Many

Model of the Cultural Center. The main feature is a vast cinema/theater auditorium with a sloping roof. Its steps in turn can be used as seats facing what becomes a huge open-air theater (at left). It has a large stage with an elevated round concert podium

people are now trying to find ways to help employees to spend their leisure time better. With these buildings, one hopes to help solve the problems of the monotony and solitude of those who have to live in provincial towns."

The Cultural Center was Eileen's last large project. It was designed between 1946 and 1947 but published only twelve years later in 1959 in *L'Architecture d'Aujourd'hui*. It included a conference center, a library, a restaurant, a cinema, an open-air theater, which was a refined version of her prewar theater project, and an exhibition gallery for painting and sculpture and local crafts. Two wide staircases grew out of pools with reflecting water forming huge terraces. They allowed a panoramic view over the whole Cultural Center. Eileen spent months and months on it, working daily "until her eyes gave out." The big model of the center covered her entire work table.

With her usual practical sense of detail, she thought of the food to be served in the restaurants, the problem of overcrowding, and made sure that the performers' dressing

Right: Model of the stage set Eileen designed for *L'Epopée Irlandaise* (The Irish Epic), to be performed at the Cultural Center

Opposite, top: Roof theater

Opposite, center: Pool and terraces. The different volumes, squares, and sweeping curves provide strong visual interest without distracting from the expansive roof

Opposite, bottom: Back of the building, with a huge glassed-in entrance hall. Again it is striking that the architect achieves a rhythm by using a variety of openings and visible staircases, along with the play of squares and cubes

rooms had enough light for making up. She covered pages and pages with sketches for the stage and costumes. She even made a little model of a stage set with rocks and trees for a production of *L'Epopée Irlandaise* (The Irish Epic). Even after all these years she could never completely wipe out her romantic link with Ireland.

This was Eileen's first venture into the theater world since her early set designs for the ballet. There was a period when she liked the theater and used to go to plays regularly. During her time with Damia she went of course to music halls. But the theater for her never seemed the right artifice. She always preferred films, and she never grew tired of them.

At the end of 1946 she was asked to design furniture and "equipment" for a worker's flat to be part of the International Exhibition of Reconstruction, to take place in May 1947, in Paris. After she saw the plan of the flat, "with practically no scope in materials as everything is unobtainable—I think I shall refuse." The truth was not that the lack of materials put her off, but that her eyesight was getting worse, and there was talk of a cataract operation, which worried Eileen terribly. But she went on working. Sometimes, her fingers all numb from drawing, she left her drawing board and took what she called a "5 minute breather generally looking at some 'toiles.'" After she had gone and looked at exhibitions in some of the galleries in her

Drawings of animals for a day-care center in a Workmen's Club which Eileen designed in 1947

quartier, then it was back to the maquette again. Occasionally she complained about how little really was going on in Paris: "The Salon d'Automne is a dreary affair given up mainly to retrospectives of the Salons of 1903, '04 and '05. The Palais Moko is anyway glacial and the pictures remind one of ex-votos on a tomb," she wrote in 1947.

The same year she announced that she had started planning a Workmen's Club and she was not happy with the result. She hated leaving things unfinished and was determined to complete it before she went south. She even did a set of children's drawings of animals and dances to decorate the walls of the day-care center in the club. These had the same cheerfulness and lightheartedness as her ballet drawings. They were in complete contrast to her stark and abstract paintings and gouaches, which she kept on doing to the end of her life. But the club was never built.

For a long time the rue Bonaparte had been less of a home to her than her other places. From now on it became her principal residence. In it she kept the remains of her other houses. One entered the first floor through a small entrance hall which contained only a low table and a chrome chair. On the wall hung one of her lanterns with the Christmas ball inside. There was a Persian painting of the Qatar Period and a white brick screen.

There was the large regular salon, where Eileen received her visitors. There was always impeccable order and tidiness. The white muslin curtains of the four windows on one side

Eileen in the salon of her apartment on the rue Bonaparte in Paris. The brown and red cube sofa with large cushions covered in orange canvas is a pendant to the one designed for the Mathieu-Lévy apartment on the rue de Lota. Above, a Persian painting of the Qatar period

were always drawn. A big celluloid screen made in 1931 hid the entrance. A pair of white brick screens stood on either side of the wide, comfortable sofa. Over the fireplace was an eighteenth-century mirror; the only other antique piece in the room was an armchair from the Luxembourg Palace. There was a large table made of metal, with a copper top, which came from Jean Désert. Another table consisted of a slab of lacquer simply placed on a gray wooden cube. There was the little table in sycamore and oak in the Rietveld style, which had so much pleased the Dutch in 1920. From the ceiling hung the Airplane lamp, made of wire and parchment. The floor lamp from the Monte Carlo room, a tubular armchair, a little tabouret in sycamore, plus a *pouf* in red leather completed the furnishings. On the plain parquet floor were two of her rugs. It was the total absence of any planned decoration that was striking. The pieces, dating from various parts of her life, blended well together and gave a feeling of immense comfort. "Symmetry is boring," she once said, suggesting that a window be put on one side instead of in the middle.

The far end of the salon was dominated by a large table with a black lacquer top and red lacquer underside, set on a gray wooden cube with low relief carving on each end. On its top a black Mexican jar. The table was flanked by a pair of white lacquer brick screens and stood on a beige rug with an abstract design. One of the few antique pieces was a rare and beautiful eighteenth-century chair from the royal household of the Luxembourg Palace, which Eileen had covered in simple gray canvas

In the large old-fashioned cupboards which flanked the fireplace she kept books and many souvenirs from her travels: an amber necklace, worry beads, some coins, a paper knife in jade, two fans—one in lace, the other made from ostrich feathers—several pieces in soapstone, a couple of netsuke, and some old china.

The subdued and orderly elegance of the hall and the drawing room was in complete contrast to the next room, which served as Eileen's workroom. There she sat perched on a precarious-looking barstool swinging from one side to the other. Her large oak refectory table was always covered with plans. She had stashed her architect's table away in the attic and she preferred to work on this large table. The sycamore chest she had designed for the architect Pacon now held her drawings and paintings. On top of it hung a pastel by Dunoyer de Segonzac, whom she used to see sometimes in Saint-Tropez. There were two little Japanese chests belonging to Sugawara still containing some samples of lacquer and gold leaf. On the wall Eileen used to pin up reproductions of some Cubist paintings, a couple of the funny cartoons she was so fond of, and bits of paper.

Eileen was surrounded by organized chaos. She had picked up bits and pieces of wood and metal on the beach, altered their shape, discarded them, taken them up again, and left them about. There were always unfinished models of houses she never built, and little toy models of furniture or screens made in glass or wood.

In the cheerful disorder of this room stood a stunning large lacquer screen—probably the most beautiful one she had ever made. It dated from 1928 and consisted of eight lacquer panels encrusted with silver and bronze. (It now stands in the Victoria and Albert Museum, as she had always wished that this museum should be given a piece of its choice.) From the ceiling hung the spiral lamp. The only other lamps were the precursors of her flexible-neck anglepoise lamps. She used them in all her houses, often mounted on a piece of scorched wood.

Next to the workroom was the bedroom. It was really the only room Eileen had completely changed and designed. It was similar to her bedrooms in the south of France, containing besides the bed a desk and bookshelves. Eileen, being a bad sleeper, always rose early and wrote or read in the early hours. On the bookshelves stood a little sculptured head by Sugawara, and a beautiful African wooden statue with inlaid eyes, which Eileen had mounted on a piece of brown lacquer. On the wall hung one of her drawings and a painting by her niece, Prunella Clough.

The door to the bathroom was hidden behind a perforated screen, made from big metal sheets used for sifting flour, originally designed for E.1027. The bathroom, which also served as a dressing room, was ordinary. There was a pretty set of lacquer pieces, a hand mirror, and a brush with her initials. Hidden away in the cupboards, but kept in immaculate order, were the vestiges of more frivolous times. Two evening coats by Poiret, a battery of handmade shoes, some of them in silk, some hatboxes from Schiaparelli and Madame Grès with Eileen's name on the label.

The rest of the flat consisted of Louise's room and a kitchen.

During the first years after the war, life was difficult in Paris. Louise and Eileen were often without gas or electricity because of strikes, and Eileen tried to work by candlelight. Despite the efforts of the shops to get some merchandise, there was still a grim atmosphere of misery. Eileen complained of the flood of American products that "the

Eight-panel lacquer screen with silver and bronze inlays that came from Jean Désert. It stood in Eileen's flat on the rue Bonaparte; after her death it was presented to the Victoria and Albert Museum in London

French used to do better." The general atmosphere rubbed off on her work, Eileen became feebler and more haggard every day.

Also old irritations and resentments kept surfacing. Badovici was editing the first seven volumes of Corbusier's collected works when the two quarreled in 1949, probably over the Roquebrune murals. In the April 1948 issue of *L'Architecture d'Aujourd'hui*, Le Corbusier had written: "This house which I animated with my paintings was very pretty, and it could well have existed without my talents." But he added insult to injury when he continued: "The walls chosen to receive [the] nine large paintings were the most colourless and insignificant walls. In this way the beautiful walls have remained and the indifferent ones have become interesting." It is no wonder that in Eileen's copy of this magazine this offensive passage was torn out. One of the photographs of these murals is simply described as being outside "a house in Cap Martin in 1939." There is a picture of Le Corbusier with his wife in front of the mural in the entrance. Other photographs show the murals in the living room, the staircase, and the bedroom. Not one caption mentions Eileen.

Le Corbusier made no attempt to redress the oversight. It was almost as if he wanted the world to believe that the house was not built by her. Eileen's name seemed to disappear increasingly from the literature whenever E.1027 was mentioned. Maximilien Gauthier in *Le Corbusier ou l'Architecture au Service de l'Homme* (1944) calls it "Maison Badovici." Jean Petit in *Le Corbusier Lui-Même* (1970) still speaks about the "Villa Badovici."

In 1973, Alfred Roth in *Begegnungen mit Pionieren* (Encounter with the Pioneers) mentions a "holiday home" built by Badovici. Stanislaus Moos, in *L'Architecte et Son Mythe* (1971) does the same. The name Eileen Gray does not exist. Not until 1979 does Francesco Tentori, in *Vita e Opere di Le Corbusier*, give Eileen Gray credit for the house. Needless to say, she was still called "Hélèn" Gray. And in *Casa Vogue* (no. 119, Milan, 1981) the house is proudly described as "Firmata Eileen Gray e Le Corbusier" ("signed E. G. and L. C."). Eileen's sofa has become "pezzo unico di Le Corbusier" ("unique piece by . . .").

On December 13, 1949, Badovici, obviously urged on by Eileen to complain about the old injury, wrote a letter to Le Corbusier which may have been dictated by Eileen herself:

> What a narrow prison you have built for me over a number of years, and particularly this year through your vanity. My attitude toward you on the contrary has been nothing but joy and full of happy trust—seven volumes of the heroic times of *L'Architecture Vivante*. My hut [*baraque*] served as a testing ground, embodying the most profound meaning of an attitude which formally banished paintings. It was purely functional, that was its strength for such a long time (1925).

Le Corbusier was obviously stung by the just accusation that his paintings had betrayed the pure idea expressed through E.1027. He replied, in his usual sarcastic fashion:

> You want a statement from me based on my worldwide authority to show—if I correctly understand your innermost thoughts—to

Eileen's bedroom in
the rue Bonaparte
apartment had a
headboard with a
built-in clock and light
and bell switches.
There was also a
pivoting night table

demonstrate "the quality of pure and functional architecture"
which is manifested by you in the house at Cap Martin, and has
been destroyed by my pictorial intervention. OK, you send me
some photographic documents of this manipulation of pure
functionalism.

Le Corbusier continued, poking fun at Eileen's invention of
identifying the various storage spaces with neat labels:
"PAJAMAS," "LITTLE THINGS," "SOCKS," "RAINCOATS AND
UMBRELLAS." He added: "Also send some documents on
Castellar, this U-boat of functionalism; then I will spread
this debate in front of the whole world" (letter in the
Fondation Le Corbusier). This letter, however jocular its tone,
was certainly insulting to Eileen. It contradicted all Le
Corbusier had ever said about the house.

Another view of the bedroom showing a glass and chrome writing table, a chrome armchair covered in beige canvas with a tilting back. There was also an aluminum cupboard. All these were pieces she had made for her houses or could not sell at Jean Désert

But as usual, work would see her through, and after a while in Paris, she decided to brave another look at her ravaged house in Castellar.

As a foreigner—Eileen never took French nationality despite her seventy years of residence in France—she was not entitled to any compensation for war damage. She finally got some financial settlement, but she recouped only a fraction of what she had lost. Any restoration of Castellar was impossible. There was no building material to be had. But she longed for a little place in the south. She went down to Saint-Tropez, where she found her little Morgan, which had been laid up during the war, all rusted. She managed to get it on the road and drove around searching for a place. She ventured as far as Montpellier and the region of Haute-Provence, which was much quieter than the coast. "If I could only find a ruin I would give up Menton and Saint-Tropez altogether." The feeling of leaving and starting anew was still strong within her.

Soon afterward she took a damp flat in Menton and began to repair the house in Castellar, an undertaking which

Bench with gold stripes and brown leather on African wood that was at the rue Bonaparte. It was one of three versions that she designed between 1920 and 1922 and exhibited in the Monte Carlo room

took her seven years. It was an arduous task going over old ground, filling in endless forms for the authorities. This was not the thirties; building regulations were more complicated, and she spent the cold winter of 1947 living in a "terrible hotel," while Louise stayed somewhere in a small flat in the old town of Menton. Fortunately, Roattino, her carpenter, was still around. But there were constant fights with the builder and the usual letters of complaint: "I thought the work was finished and they haven't even started yet." This was written in 1950. By 1951 she was still not living in her house.

Eileen, who could never leave things alone, began to redesign. She built some terraces, installed new shutters and a new garage door. All her furniture had to be redesigned, and workshops that were able to chrome were difficult to find. At one point she must have come to complete exasperation, because she asked Badovici to help. He wrote some stern letters to push things forward.

During the summer months, Eileen and Louise went to Saint-Tropez, where she had taken another flat at 5 place des Remparts. Sitting on the cement floor, surrounded by dead cockroaches, she drew plans for furniture. From time to time she escaped to La Bastide Blanche to visit Kate Weatherby, but traveling was not easy any more. Because of her poor eyesight she was forced to give up the car. This was terrible for her; it made her a kind of prisoner. She had loved driving from early youth; now she had to rely on others.

Finally, in 1953, when she was seventy-five, she

announced, "Castellar is finished." But she hardly lived in it. Her old love for Saint-Tropez had returned, and she was planning to build there. The excitement and charm Castellar had once spelled for her was gone. She advertised the house for sale. She found a potential buyer, a Mr. Boyd, who even made a down payment, but kept on changing his mind. Finally he pulled out.

Whenever Eileen was in Paris, she tried to keep abreast of as many things as possible. Having been starved for so long of any outside stimuli, she went to see art exhibitions and visited architectural sites around Paris. She had not lost her utter scorn for what was called "decoration" in Paris. "Modern decoration is at a complete standstill. The craze for Napoleon III and early Victorian is unabated. The prices for making modern furniture are so high it makes practical creative work impossible." After going to a show of chairs and sofas, she remarked, furious, "Some interesting things, but after 1840 a complete downfall. The most ghastly sofas and very poor modern stuff. Badly chosen. What's the matter with the world? D. H. Lawrence was right." "What's the matter with the world?" became a sort of standard joke whenever she went to see the "modern" furniture shops that mushroomed around the Saint-Germain area. She sometimes saw things she liked, but more frequently she was inclined to accept a part of a chair or technical solution and adopt the idea for her own use. "The way they fixed the legs is rather clever, but I don't think much of the upholstery," or she would just mumble "poor Rietveld." And then, "I see little creation, only destruction."

She was still as critical as always. Expecting something more mysterious, she had been disappointed in Cocteau's *Orphée*, because "Cocteau put himself too much in the foreground." A show by Bernard Buffet, a painter much in favor in society, she describes as: "Birds ninety-nine times as large or rather larger than life, plus the lady, Annabel, I suppose. I thought they were awful." Her comments on the exhibitions she saw reveal much about her own predicament as an artist. "I can see that artists want to get free of construction, lately these artists I saw seem to be denying their personality, trying to change it, upset by the general quick-change going on all round, which is probably temporary or heading for the death of paintings." She did not think much of some exhibits at the Sonnabend Gallery: "Huge life-sized peaches made of plush on grounds of imitation sponges dyed dark green. Do I sound reactionary?" she asked. "My opinion is of no importance." She was for experiment in art, admitting that in abstract art one can be very spontaneous, but she wondered if in "memorising, digesting objects or persons—as the abstract painter does—one doesn't miss the quality, the unexpected [which] reality always gives one, even in the most banal things like the branches of a tree." "Painters must come up against the same thing as architects always come up against in architecture, between the content of the plan and its visual presentation in space, which inevitably means a compromise." It was her old belief in the organic need in everything.

But an exhibition of Germaine Richier's work gave her pleasure. "Such a grasp of her métier, she always knows how to keep it subservient to what she wants to express," and she fought back at her old friend Zervos, who seemed to think that Richier was "just a disciple of Giacometti."

Eileen always had her own firm idea of art. She never followed a fashion. After having seen an exhibition of the "Jeune Peinture Anglaise," she wrote: "Colquhoun, Adler, are they really considered remarkable in England?" and she added with her usual anti-English scorn, "Standards must be different over there. Their work seems so laboured and following paths already trodden." In conversation she would politely but stoutly defend her point of view. After a Max Ernst show, she commented that there is an "abyss which seems to exist between one painting and another."

She was enthusiastic about an exhibition by Vieira da Silva and called Calder "a Miró in motion." She went to see an exhibition of Nicolas de Staël. "I was very interested though unsatisfied. The very big canvases seem not to put it over and I realised that I was moved by others only because of the brilliant colour scheme. . . . All painting is servitude—first of all because one is compelled to come down to *one* interior vision and shut out so many others. . . . During a short interval I wondered whether a new angle of vision might also result from a liberation of the present arbitrary presentation of one fixed idea, and whether that could be the cause of the stalemate one feels everywhere."

Magazines were now readily available again, and after reading through stacks of publications on modern architecture, she wrote: "Goodness, they are not terribly advanced."

She continued to follow Le Corbusier's development in detail. Seeing photographs of his monastery at La Tourette,

A junction box for multiple sockets which Eileen designed for her various homes. She used it in her last home, on the rue Bonaparte

she remarked enthusiastically, "What a vitality in that man and how much he has learned from working in India. I like the monastery better than Ronchamp where certain things, like the mass of sloping walls, seemed to be arbitrary."

In 1953 she went to see his exhibition at the Musée d'Art Moderne at the Trocadéro: "I was much impressed, this man has a genius for presentation or whatever you like to call it; the whole place, so banal generally, was changed." She loved the large photographs of Ronchamp and seemed to have made peace with Le Corbusier's colorful and expressive paintings, which were part of the exhibition.

She got deeply involved in the controversy about the architectural competition for the new opera house in Sydney and wanted to find out about Jørn Utzon, the winning architect. In 1955 she visited some New Towns in England, especially Harlow. As a good example of architecture, she cited again and again her old friends of De Stijl. "The genuine creation and revolution which was in the movement of De Stijl . . . the basis of all architecture being sincerity of the expression of its function—if there is to be enrichment—there could be invented new ways without having recourse to what was really only the leavings of the worst possible period and arose from the fear of having any space left empty."

Eileen, an inquisitive person of strong observation and sharp intellectual grasp, was longing for conversation. She turned to those few people she could open up to, often displaying a defenseless availability which softened the toughness of her determination. Sometimes she was overanxious in her unworldly way, full of enthusiasm, and then the next moment being terribly apologetic about taking up someone else's time. Her excuses were often as clumsy as her timid manifestations of sympathy.

She was a natural listener, interested in a wide range of subjects: art, politics, medicine, new inventions, and even gossip about the world of Paris. The only subject she was not interested in was Eileen Gray. She herself spoke very little and, when she spoke, used the hesitant language so often found among people who have spent much of their lives in solitude and who seldom hear themselves speak.

In her effort to overcome her shyness and inbuilt sense of failure, she had at one time copied whole pages out of a book by Dorothea Brandt called *Wake Up and Live!*, underlining phrases like "the removal of shyness," "act as if it was impossible to fail," and "recollect past failures and set free whatever group of aptitudes is for the moment required."

It is almost tragic to see that this woman had so little feeling of true achievement and that when recognition did come to her, she always looked the other way. She had lived a life with a big dream, but she had been forced to make never-ending adjustments, and whatever little confidence she had had been eroded. Although she always remained modest and unsure of herself, she never felt that her life had been wasted.

During her last years she came to deeper understanding of the many questions life had put in her way. Reading Butor, Genet, Céline, and also Jung's *Psychology of the Unconscious*, she remarked of the last: "I like the emphasis he gives to the subconscious. Not like Freud obsessed by sex, or limited by it." She began to understand why she had been so often "wounded by sex."

"The subconscious" was a term her generation was in love with. In all her dealings with art, with the outside world, with her friends and lovers, she maintained: "I am guided only by the subconscious. Anything I ever did came from it and I suppose that is why I am so inarticulate and when I see friends there is always a sort of tension, attempting to express myself and often failing. That is why, in the conscious world, difficulties seem so insurmountable and become such a worry."

Sometimes she saw Badovici, who was now living in Vézelay, "having no work at all." He was living in the old house he had shared with Le Corbusier during the war and trying to place some articles in publications. "He is leading a dog's life." Eileen's old compassion took over again, and she tried to help him with an article he prepared on the reconstruction in Maubeuge, a problem she had worked on in the lonely hours at Lourmarin. Badovici was also trying to bring out a book on her, which, alas, never happened. It would have been a formidable source of information. A few years later, when her work prompted some public interest, Eileen contemplated publishing something on Tempe à Pailla, but "it is far too late, I built it 22 years ago. The only chance would be to make some diagrams showing the difficulties which would themselves be of some interest, but I have no gift for presentation which nowadays is almost everything—and I don't see who I could ask to do it."

Incapable of being idle, she tried to design. But with her impaired sight and her trembling hands, she needed help. Her old doubts returned: "I wish I could work faster and never hesitate," she remarked.

Despite all, she continued to work. Work was for her the only way to come to terms with her life and the relentless passing of time: "As I was always working at something, my life passed without my feeling all those years accumulating."

In 1953 she had her mind fixed on the idea of "materialising prefabricated shelters"—"*abris*," as she called them—"because I cannot call them houses. I wish I could find an engineer who could help me." She had seen in *Le Figaro* pictures of horrible hovels that refugee families had to live in: "Old tents mended with paper panels, just tucked up and put together. It is unbelievable." She suggested making "bungalows like huge flattened tubes, ovoid. A tube and even an ovoid can be made in a mould and has greater resistance. No pillars, no angles, they can be made in sections and cemented on the spot. The planks for flooring can easily be placed." She looked at available shelters and decided they were all for the bourgeoisie. "One could get out something to relieve the miseries of the poor far cleaner and quicker." It was another of the many ideas that came to nothing.

Among her unfinished plans are some drawings for a small Cubist house, to be built on the hills of her beloved Bastide Blanche. "Constructed on a hill dominating the sea, this is a place for meditation." She wanted to carve out of the rocks a small platform of two hundred fifteen by two hundred forty feet, with a serpentine floor, the wall created by the natural rock and a wood sculpture. Only a little drawing survives. "With the possibility to descend to the sea," she had written in the margin. There were also drawings for an art gallery, with an intricate lighting system created by the direct access of sunlight through windows and reflecting mirrors. Other projects were various versions of houses for families with one or two children, a university complex with a dormitory and a house for a professor, a suspended house, an institute for textile design with a special exhibition hall for carpets and a school for weaving, a weekend house, and a skyscraper. These drawings and plans are not dated; some are only rough sketches. Some may go back as far as her time in Lourmarin, but most of them are probably from the postwar years. They are clear proof of how much she continued to invent right through her sixties and seventies, but none of these projects was ever realized. Few ideas ever really left the rue Bonaparte. Eileen had no friends or agents to bring her work to public attention.

In 1953, Eileen was supposed to have had an exhibition at the Pavillon Marsan, but she waited in vain to hear from the organizers—the Union des Artistes Modernes. "I guess the whole thing will collapse," Eileen wrote, and she was right. On December 20 of the same year she received a letter from UAM inviting her to attend a meeting to discuss a project for a "Cité UAM." She was still Eileen Grey (*sic*), but she was addressed as "Cher camarade." Among the other invited camarades were Badovici and Fernand Léger. For reasons only known to herself she sent her excuses.

But in 1955, René Herbst published a catalogue for the twenty-fifth anniversary of UAM which featured both E.1027 and Tempe à Pailla. This was the result of some efforts by Jean Badovici, who had written to the secretary of UAM in 1955: "I absolutely want to include some old projects, which after thirty years are still valid today. I hope they will be included in *25 Années UAM*. The house in Roquebrune, Cap Martin (1926) [*sic*], also those in Vézelay which belong in the series 'Promotions of the Avant Garde.'" When the volume was published in 1956, it included, under the heading "Interiors," three photographs of E.1027, credited to Badovici and Eileen Gray, and four photographs of Castellar for which Eileen alone received credit. Strangely, under the heading "Architecture," we find three more photographs of E.1027, this time reversing the old order, placing Eileen Gray first and Jean Badovici second. It probably was not a belated recognition of the true authorship, rather a sign of shoddy proofreading, since the dates are totally unreliable, and the location is given sometimes as Menton and sometimes as Castellar.

Despite all, the conflict between her inventiveness and her self-doubt persisted. "I have still five or six projects and I am wondering if they are worth finishing," she wrote. She was now experimenting with small tables, putting on a dark border and then, dissatisfied, scraping it off again. "A wasted day is so discouraging. If I could only find a varnish which would withstand the heat." "Sometimes in the evening I have done nothing, the day has just slipped by," she wrote angrily. Another day: "Time just flies when one gets old and much of it is just spent catching up with things." "Make something with the ribs of ebony," says another note and, "Make chair using curtain rings."

The same year Eileen undertook her last trip to her native Ireland. She was totally disappointed. The stately home of the family, Brownswood, had been sold and turned into a hospital. The Ireland she saw had nothing to do with the one she had kept sharp in her memory—despite all the anger she had always felt remembering her childhood.

She was still trying to find a buyer for Tempe à Pailla. One day a gentleman appeared at the bottom of the garden. Louise announced him as a Lord Beaver. The gentleman turned out to be Lord Beaverbrook, the Anglo-Canadian newspaper magnate, who asked to see the house. He liked it and suggested that the painter Graham Sutherland might buy it. Sutherland and his wife, Kathleen, had been looking for a house for a long time. They had often come to the south of France, sometimes staying at the home of the wealthy art collector Douglas Cooper, at Argilliers, near Pont du Gard. Sometimes they stayed at the Hôtel Voile d'Or in Cap Ferrat. Sutherland had been painting a portrait of Somerset Maugham at the Villa Mauresque and was embarking on painting Lord Beaverbrook, who had a house at Cap d'Ail.

Nothing in Eileen's life ever seemed to be without complications and so was this affair. There was a long-drawn-out exchange of letters. At one point Eileen reminded Sutherland about the agreed terms, but smoothed away any irritation immediately by her polite, almost old-fashioned, manner: "Please excuse the blue envelope, but I can find no other." This codicil says more about her than the whole correspondence. Tempe à Pailla was finally bought in 1954 by the Sutherlands for five hundred fifty thousand francs

**Still life of toilet
articles photographed
by Eileen**

Still life of toilet
articles photographed
by Eileen

(one hundred fifty-seven thousand dollars); that included
many pieces of furniture: the cupboards, the work table with
a lamp, the table which could be either a dining or coffee
table, a dressing table, a celluloid screen, a carpet, various
mirrors, beds, small tables, and a bookcase. Unfortunately,
only some of the furniture has been preserved. There is still
the wardrobe in metal, which can be extended and retracted
according to the number of clothes one has; the fireplace and
a mirror, a pivoting chest, an S-bend chair, and the chaise
longue she designed for the terrace.

The house itself was altered much. The name of the
house was changed to the conventional Villa Blanche,
echoing the name of the Sutherlands' house in England, the
White House. In 1960 the English architect Tom Wilson, son
of Peter Wilson, then chairman of Sotheby's, was asked to
enlarge the house, and the part Eileen had built was kept as
a guesthouse. Many years later Eileen was invited to tea
with the Sutherlands. A polite and not unfriendly occasion,
but of course the encounter with the house so very different
could not have been an easy one.

After she had sold the house, she wrote to her carpenter, Roattino, "I am sad to have left Menton and not to see the landscape I love so much."

In 1956 she was trying to finish "a little house with a big atelier for a sculptor," obviously still perfecting her old project. For a while she had some help from a Russian draftsman named Gabriel, but he didn't stay and she "misses" him terribly. With "bad eyes and shaky hands it is almost impossible to be accurate." She was trying to take photographs with her old camera of the little models she made and realized that this one was far too small. So she bravely started again, modeling the house twice the size. She always found it difficult to make plans and models "absolutely identical" but hoped that something would emerge in the end. Eileen destroyed many of her plans, feeling that the look of their models was not good enough to preserve them for posterity, in which she, in any case, believed only with great reservations.

THE LAST HOUSE: LOU PÉROU

The most formidable task with which Eileen challenged
herself was building another house. When she started it, she
was seventy-five, and when she finished it, she was eighty.

Before the war, in 1939, she had bought a large piece of
vineyard behind Saint-Tropez for seventy-two thousand
francs (about sixteen hundred dollars). It was in the area
which is known as Chapelle-Sainte-Anne, after the little
church which dominates the small hill. There was again "a
view"; Eileen always thought it important. To the west one
could see as far as the beach of Pampelonne and to the east
the Gulf of Saint-Tropez. There was a little building, really
a *cabanon*. But since there was no water, Eileen used the
place just for picnicking or escaping from Saint-Tropez. Now
having got rid of Castellar, she decided to arrange the
cabanon so that she and Louise could live there in the
summer.

The building consisted of only one room. But it had a
vaulted ceiling, which delighted Eileen. She separated a
small part of the rather large space to gain a bedroom for
Louise, and in 1958 added a side wing to it which housed a
small bedroom for herself, a bathroom, and her by now
statutory, small, and not very adequate kitchen. She also
built a separate garage at the bottom of the garden, cleverly
hidden from view. The roof was covered with earth, forming
a small platform from where one could watch the sun go
down. There was a small terrace at the back of the house,
shaded in summer by rush awnings.

Building this house was not easy. It took almost five
years and her energy sometimes seemed to fail her. "I am
constantly on the move, but rarely successful. The sliding
windows are not even in their place. St Tropez is not self-
supporting. Metal, wood and all accessories have to come
from Toulon or Nice." But, despite her age, she was not
easily defeated. She camped out in the half-finished house,
the rain pouring down for weeks and the roads cut off by
floods. She tried to paint the inside of the *cabanon* herself
and was furious because the colors did not mix the way she
wanted. "It has turned out Vert Veronese on one wall." She

Cabanon before
conversion

After conversion: The
house has sliding
wooden shutters on
metal tracks. At left,
Louise Dany's room

New wing with Eileen's bedroom

also painted the shutters herself. "I think I shall sell the place as soon as I can in the summer, I like doing the things, but I hate possessions," she said, as usual. In 1958 the house was finally finished and Eileen grew to like it.

It looked, from the outside, like any little country place in the area. This first impression was deceptive. The total was a remarkable and well-thought-out mixture of old and new. Eileen's conversion showed very clearly what she cared to preserve of the old *cabanon* and what she unapologetically decided to replace. Depending from which side you approached the house, each face presented a different picture. She livened the monotony of the front of the modest *cabanon* by a door with a bold abstract design in the blue glass she was so fond of. The design was very similar to the one in Badovici's house in Vézelay, done in 1930. The back of the house had two large sliding windows, echoing those of E.1027. She put a handsome traditional tile pattern around the old pigeonhole under the roof. Too frail to draw all the plans herself, she asked a local architect to make the drawings, but despite her trembling hands, she soon took over, changing and modifying his work. She was

Terrace with the S-chair from Tempe à Pailla and a commercial chair from the 1950s

View from the living room through the adjustable louvers

Window with sliding shutters; above, an entrance hole for pigeons

almost eighty, but the architect within her was still very much alive.

The inside was of the same unobtrusive simplicity. A white brick screen separated the dining and the sitting areas. There were some pine benches and a dining table, made simply from a wooden plank and four round metal legs, a sofa by the fireplace, and above it an attractive naïve painting by Eve Starr, a friend from the First World War. On the wall a piece of cork with a V-sign on it that Eileen had picked up on the beach, her contribution to Victory. There was a large blue glass bowl with flowers standing on the floor, and at night candles were put into a little blue glass to light the terrace—memorabilia which she had kept from her house in Roquebrune. On the mantelpiece stood the beginning of a sculpture in a soft stone of the head of a woman, which she had never finished. Above it, a map of Peru, the country which gave its name to the house: Lou Pérou, as it is called in Provençal. Asked why she called it that, she explained with her lovely sense of humor, " 'Lou Pérou' is slang for—what can one say?—Eldorado, but less pretentious. I didn't know what to call the place and had just

been reading a sort of manual called *Affirmez et vous obtiendrez*, so I thought I'd 'affirme.'" And she went on talking about the lovely big tortoise that lived under the bushes under the pine trees in her garden.

In her bedroom and on the terrace was furniture designed by herself. Next to the simple iron bedstead stood a chest with swinging drawers and another one to hold her trousers. Most pieces were in a rather ramshackle state, prototypes she had experimented with. Two lamp fixings and the marvelous mirror with the tilting corner hung over a small porcelain basin. On the terrace stood one version of the terrace chair from E.1027, the legs tied together with leather straps, which kept on breaking, and two chrome chairs with some faded canvas.

Nobody walking into this place could ever have guessed that the upright woman, one eye now hidden behind a clouded glass and very hard of hearing, was an architect of renown. Not that many people came. Besides Louise, her circle had now shrunk to three or four friends. It was difficult for Eileen to work and her handwriting had become so shaky that she preferred to hammer out her letters on an old typewriter. Sometimes she did some drawings or took some photographs. But it was a place which felt happy.

Many years earlier, in one of her sketchbooks, she had

Terraced garden with yuccas and a piece of the old stone wall, which Eileen preserved, and, behind, a new retaining wall

composed little "Notes sur des Jardins" (Notes on Gardens). "For a garden at an entrance where there are many stones, preferably black stones, make conical walls (dry) of about 60 cm [2 feet] high, with a very large base, like a flow of stones, preferably in a curve—and encircle, with this wall, certain parts of the garden or the terrain. Opposite such a wall and smooth lawns, flowers will take on a much more precious aspect."

Eileen never cared much for a landscaped garden. She had built a stone wall to border her terrace, which had a few oleander bushes and a flowering yucca. There was some rosemary. Louise would pluck big branches to put them in winter on the beds and into the cupboards against moths. The rest of the land was kept as a vineyard. Eileen loved her vines, and when they became too old, she had new ones planted.

Of course there was no question any longer of Eileen driving, so she sometimes walked the twenty minutes up the road from Saint-Tropez. She always was happy if someone would take her for a drive, sometimes to the beaches where she would see the displayed nudity, much of it of foreign origin.

At one time Eileen considered buying a scooter. She carefully noted down all the points she wanted to find out:

1. Price of Vespa with all accessories necessary.
2. How much tax to pay.
3. Is it too heavy for a woman to push in case of a breakdown?
4. Is it difficult to keep up?
5. Can one drive slowly on a difficult road?
6. Is it difficult to start?
7. Are there other inconveniences for an inexperienced person?
8. Can one transport a second person?
9. Does one have to pedal a lot?

The old sensible Eileen was still alive, despite the fact that she was nearly eighty. Of course the scooter was never bought.

Customarily, in July, when Saint-Tropez began to fill up and the heat became intense, Louise and Eileen closed the house and took the train from Saint-Raphaël to go to Paris, to be back in September for the vine harvest, only to return to Paris again late in October.

In August 1956 Eileen received a telephone call. Jean Badovici had died on his way to the CIAM conference. Eileen grieved deeply. Despite all the difficulties of the past, Jean Badovici and all he brought to her were a part of her life—maybe, with hindsight, the most precious part. Jean had lived with another woman for the last few years, but it was Eileen who arranged the funeral. She had seen him only shortly before, and they talked about the future of E.1027, which was really hers, but belonged legally to him. He had promised to make a will, but like so many promises before, he did not keep this one.

After Badovici's death Le Corbusier wrote an obituary, "Hommage à Jean Badovici":

Jean Badovici was extraordinarily skillful with the most refined things. He could create subtle arrangements out of nothing. His whole being was animated by the modern spirit. He made some masterpieces in Vézelay, transforming houses with clarity, taste, and with remarkable integrity toward the old. These shacks were part of himself. It is through them that I appreciated the artistic nature of Badovici.

He was furthermore a charming companion on those only too rare occasions of leisure which life had in store for those who lived there. He ran *L'Architecture Vivante* between the two wars, being interested in the work of Pierre Jeanneret and myself.

With Ellen Grey [*sic*] he built a charming house on Cap Martin, a house which sits well in the landscape, full of architectural sense.

This collaboration was certainly fruitful.

I do not know the recent work of Badovici.

One day illness overcame him; I was saddened to hear this summer that he was threatened so suddenly. And now he has passed away to the other side, leaving, I believe, a *joli souvenir* to all who knew him.

Paris, October 24, 1956
Le Corbusier

Jean Badovici's obituary in *Technique et Architecture* in November 1956 shows four illustrations of Roquebrune and refers to his flat in Paris. There is no mention of Eileen Gray. The confusion of authorship continued after her death, when the house and part of its contents were attributed to Le Corbusier, even in serious architectural magazines. In 1980, *L'Architecture d'Aujourd'hui* published four photographs of the house in Castellar, but one looks in vain for the name of the architect.

Badovici's death brought Le Corbusier again into contact with Eileen and produced the strangest affair linked with E.1027. The house was tied in more than one way to Le Corbusier's personal life. In 1950 he had acquired a small plot of land right behind Eileen's house. There he built himself a very small house, which he called La Baraque, a name he generally liked to give to houses. The little plot was bought from his friend the owner of a local bar, L'Etoile de Mer, Robert Rebutato.

Eileen never understood how the great architect could have built himself what she called "just a wooden shack." It is curious that Eileen did not understand, or chose not to understand, what Le Corbusier had intended in building this modular house, which consisted of a single room and was prefabricated in Corsica. Maybe by that time she was too angry with Le Corbusier, and she felt his presence so near was a further intrusion on her life. There he would sit and make his plans for Chandigarh and a housing complex for Cap Martin, which was never built. In 1957, Le Corbusier's wife, Yvonne, died. After sending a note extending her

La Baraque, built by
Le Corbusier for
himself in the 1950s
on land behind
E.1027

condolences, Eileen received a card with a drawing of two
joined hands saying simply, "Menton le 5 octobre à l'aube, le
souvenir d'Yvonne le Corbusier. Merci" — a card Le Corbusier
had designed for his friends.

Those who knew him said he became somber, solitary,
and mistrustful in those years. He emerged from time to
time to take a swim. He had always hoped that he could one
day purchase E.1027. Since Badovici had never made a will,
the house remained in his name, so instead of reverting to
Eileen, it went to his next of kin, his sister, a nun in
Romania. Le Corbusier was very interested in the house, and
he assumed that Badovici's sister would not want a house in

France. Not wishing to appear openly as an interested partner, he tried to persuade a close friend of his, a Swiss, Madame Schelbert, to buy the house.

Eileen would never talk about the whole affair. As usual she drew a veil. But this is how Madame Schelbert remembered it: One day she received an urgent telephone call in Zurich to come to Paris and to bring "all the money you can get hold of, and a hat!" As all the banks were closed, she borrowed money from friends but forgot about the hat, "which made Corbusier very angry." "I want you to buy a house," he said. He showed her some photographs of E.1027 and handed her the key to it. Madame Schelbert went down to Roquebrune and found the house totally overgrown. She did not much like what she saw, but thinking that it was a house designed by Le Corbusier, she gave in. An auction sale was set up in Menton. There were four prospective buyers. Madame Schelbert remembered only a man from the Bank of Paris and a man by the name of Onassis. Onassis offered the highest bid, and Le Corbusier, who had kept very much in the background during all the negotiations, disappeared with the auctioneer. When they reappeared after five minutes, the house was sold to Madame Schelbert. Onassis was furious, and berated the auctioneer, but Le Corbusier threatened to use his clout with the authorities. When Eileen heard about it, the deal had been clinched. By law she was not the rightful owner.

Le Corbusier's friend the barman Robert, opened a bar right at the entrance to the property, "a kind of watchdog," as Eileen always remembered with bitterness. Eileen tried to get some of her furniture out, but was prevented.

In fact Madame Schelbert had, according to her own account, very little interest in keeping Eileen's furniture and tried to get rid of it. But since there was no road leading to the house, no one could be found to take it away. She decided to make a bonfire. Le Corbusier luckily prevented her, saying that "she must look after the furniture as it was very special and rare." This story was told years later, after Eileen Gray's fame was reestablished, but there is no reason to doubt its authenticity. In any case, Madame Schelbert kept her promise and looked after it and kept the house until her own death very much as it must have looked when Eileen lived there.

Eileen's spirit in any case was plainly in evidence, though she would never be persuaded to see the house again. On August 26, 1965, Le Corbusier went down from the house

Fresco by Le Corbusier in E.1027, now decorated with sheer curtains and venetian blinds by a new inhabitant—much to Eileen's disgust

to the sea for a swim, never to return. He had died of a heart attack in the water; he was seventy-eight years old.

When Eileen was later shown some photographs of the house, she didn't like what she saw: "The house without any shelter to the terrace, and plastic on the roof instead of the glass. It looked smaller and lacked atmosphere."

As a sad footnote to the whole affair, the house was left to Madame Schelbert's doctor. The furniture has since been removed to Switzerland by the present owner. No attempt was made to turn this seminal house into a museum or at least to have it preserved under official protection.

In the summer of 1956, UAM organized an exhibition of Jean Badovici's work in the Pavillon Marsan. This posthumous exhibition was arranged by Badovici's last girlfriend, who put together a room that included many photographs of E.1027 labeled: "Jean Badovici with the collaboration of Eileen Gray for the furniture." Nobody bothered to check the facts. Eileen was so furious that she tore the labels off when she saw them. She complained to the president of UAM, René Herbst, "but got nowhere."

It was the last insult from an organization that she had

helped to found, and that has only rarely given her credit. At one point she had lent some of her carpets to be exhibited next to the work of Herbst; again she looked in vain for her name. Her commentary sums up what she thought of this organization, despite all the posthumous accolades: "The exhibition of J. B.'s work was—like everything the UAM does or does not do—lamentable. My offer to help was not accepted—there are pages written which are too complicated to explain in a letter." We do not know what they contained; together with most of her own letters, they were all destroyed by her own hand at the end of her life as if all this did not matter any longer. Maybe it did not, from the point of view of someone who was concerned with the business of dying. But only a few years earlier, she had written, "One must not give up and one must not destroy things. It is like losing steppingstones."

But when this auto-da-fé occurred, nobody was around to prevent her. Of course the role of Eileen Gray as the misunderstood genius has been exaggerated, often out of a sense of guilt and the desire to make amends. To leading architects, busy with their own work, often commanding large offices, she was an amateur. This was her strength, but also her tragedy.

At odds with most people whose bruised identities and ever-shifting values she despised, she had a singleminded containedness which made it impossible for her to take up the organization required by a professional architect. She was an artist, an innovator, but she totally lacked the discipline or skill to implement her ideas on a larger scale. It is impossible to visualize Eileen running an office. She was exacting, but totally inefficient. Eileen Gray realized only two houses, but however seminal they may be, in a world where whole cities were built, they are a small contribution to the history of modern architecture. Eileen never had to encounter the technical, economic, and legal complexities of the architecture of the twentieth century. She would have been the first one to admit that.

The ambivalence one feels about her was part of her extraordinary character. Of course it is endearing to think that this woman spent almost twenty-five years of her life virtually singlehandedly building and perfecting her two houses. It is also a record of disastrous professional ineptitude. Eileen was aware of that. Her criticism did not stop at her own person. In those last few years she felt that she should at least make a record of her work, that she

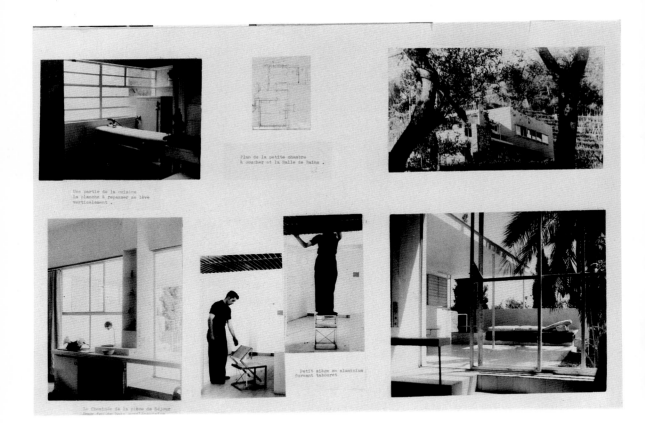

Une partie de la cuisine
la planche à repasser se lève
verticalement .

Plan de la petite chambre
à coucher et la Salle de Bains .

Le Cheminée de la pièce de Séjour

Petit siège en aluminium
formant tabouret

Two pages from
Eileen's architectural
sketchbooks featuring
Tempe à Pailla
Top left: an ironing
board in the kitchen
which folds up against
the wall; bottom: an
extra fireplace in the
living room; bottom
center: Roattino
demonstrating a
folding seat and
stepladder

should arrange and date her drawings and photographs, so
she began to compile two large scrapbooks, sticking in them
the few remaining photographs, and making little captions
for each of them. If anything, these two books prove her lack
of organization and her lack of decision—qualities vital to
the architectural profession. To talk about herself and to
make any kind of order in her past were anathema to her.
She continually changed the captions and ripped out the
photographs, so that the books, which were intended as a
record of her architectural life, remain a shambles of random
plans and photographs. Toward the end of her life, she would
go through them with students or journalists, and their
curiosity, however much a nuisance they themselves
presented, gave her some pleasure. Eileen, always brushing
aside any compliments, would say, "This is nothing—these
old things." She was totally devoid of any slavish desire to
please.

Eileen kept on designing. She was interested in new
materials, inquired about a certain kind of plastic, was
intrigued by Plexiglas. She was making some tables in it,
"but it doesn't give all I want, I will have to adopt a
humbler point of view and shall probably be reduced to

Chaise longue en bois ajouré, matelas suspendu se pliant .

ci-contre . La passerelle permet de descendre directement vers le jardin

Table en bois de sycomore et verre . Base en fer .

Top left: The folding S-chair, and some tables; top right: the bridge permitting direct access to the garden

Formica or those imitations," she moaned in a letter. She went to the World's Fair in Brussels, in 1958, swaying around in the crowd, wandering about, rather bored by what she saw. Suddenly her eye would light up, her attention caught by a little detail of a design or a new material. This was the old Eileen Gray, always fascinated by a new substance and rather bored by great concepts. Of course she went to see Le Corbusier's pavilion.

In March 1957 she made a little note of all the things still to be finished: she was trying to repair the old models which were accumulating dust and she was still organizing her scrapbook.

> Finish maquette célibataire
> finish maquette maisons tubes
> plan maisons tubes pour Centre de Vacances
> Take photos theatre interior, célibataire,
>   maisons tubes, atelier sculpteur text

and there the note ends. She was bored with her unvarying routine. Hardly a day went by without some kind of work and the drudgery of putting it into motion. She battled on with enormous energy, despite her frailness.

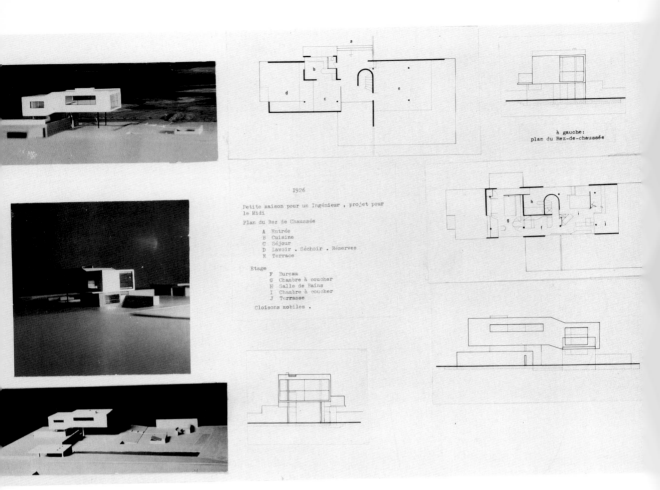

1926

Petite maison pour un Ingénieur , projet pour le Midi

Plan du Rez de Chaussée

   A Entrée
   B Cuisine
   C Séjour
   D Lavoir . Séchoir . Réserves
   E Terrace

  Etage

   F Bureau
   G Chambre à coucher
   H Salle de Bains
   I Chambre à coucher
   J Terrasse

  Cloisons mobiles .

à gauche:
plan du Rez-de-chaussée

Page of the sketch-books showing models and plans of the Small House for an Engineer

Much of her time and energy was now spent in supervising the building of the extension to Lou Pérou. Four or five times she made the tiring journey to the south battling with officialdom. All this sapped her forces. In 1958 Lou Pérou was finally finished. Except for a brief note about her Centre Culturel in *L'Architecture d'Aujourd'hui* in 1959, nobody took any notice of her. The next few years were relatively peaceful but unbelievably lonely. Eileen and Louise continued the old routine of spending the winter and the hot summer months in Paris; the rest of the time was spent in the south. There Eileen received a handful of friends on the terrace for a drink and some of the conversation this woman, so alive mentally and intellectually, was longing for.

Gradually the area was being built up, blocking even her beautiful view from the sea. The disenchantment with the Midi began.

On March 14, 1964, Kate Weatherby died. Eileen had

rushed to her sickbed. She wrote to Evelyn Wyld: "Today our dear Kate died peacefully, I suppose it was for the best, but I am all upset."

Solitude closed in around her. "Dans cette solitude qui finit par séparer un homme de lui-même" ("In this solitude which finally separates man from himself"), she mused. At times her frail body, which still housed a formidable mind, seemed to cave in. She longed to die. "Death seems to have forgotten me. It is high time that I was off." The idea that she might become a burden to her few friends was almost as terrible as the fear of losing some of her intellectual capacities. Earlier she had written: "Certains pourrissent, et d'autres s'ossifient; tous vieillissent. Seulement une grande ferveur intellectuelle triomphe de la fatigue et de la flétrissure du corps" ("Some putrify; others ossify; all age. Only a strong intellectual flame triumphs over the fatigue and the decline of the body"), quoting some lines from Gide's diary. Having a strong sense of dignity, she despised the humiliations of extreme old age. She also quoted the words of the writer Julien Green: "D'un façon générale, c'est le problème de toute vie: s'échapper. Ce que j'appelle vivre, n'est pas autre chose que la conscience que l'humanité a d'elle-même. J'ai approuvé ce sentiment à un degré si vif que notre crainte de mourir m'a paru un des plus frappants malentendus dont nous avons souffert. Il vient sans doute de cette confusion entre nous-même et notre corps. Presque toujours notre agitation est en surface, au fond de nous il y a une région de calme et du bonheur pour qui en veut" ("In general, this is the problem of all life: to escape. What I call living is nothing but humanity's consciousness of itself. I experience this feeling so strongly that our fear of dying strikes me as one of the most blatant misunderstandings under which we labor. It stems without doubt from the confusion which reigns between us and our bodies. Almost always our agitation is on the surface; deep inside there is an area of calm and happiness for those who want it"). Eileen must have been deeply touched when she read those lines for the first time.

There was still some of the fighting spirit left in her. She struggled with the electricity board to prevent them from putting up an electrical pylon on her land. "It's not for me," she wrote, "but I have to think of those who come after me."

In 1968 she had a serious intestinal operation. Lying in the small hospital room, Louise never leaving her side, she felt as if her wish "to fly away" was soon to be granted. Then, as by a miracle, she gathered her dwindling forces and, almost by sheer willpower, decided to live. She was allowed home. In a few weeks she began to design again. She was ninety years old.

She went on working through her nineties, supervising the making of a couple of chairs, and fussing over the inclination of the back. She was happy that some of her designs would now be mass-produced and "hope[d] that this can be done as cheaply as possible so that people can afford it." She thought that her little chest for slacks and skirts would be perfect to reproduce, "but I'm afraid it won't do for maxis. . . . The first one was made in cork, celluloid and polished aluminium, the one I kept for myself was never finished." She still had the original dressing table she had designed for Roquebrune but wanted the varnish redone. "If they are doing the S-chair, the rods would be better chromed or in aluminium, whatever shows less against the background."

Her health deteriorated further. As old people usually do, she had some falls, and the injuries took a long time to heal. There were weeks and weeks of insomnia, but her intellectual curiosity was undiminished. She read the conversations between Goethe and Eckermann. "Having always feared the Great," she found that Goethe contained "an awful lot of stuffing." After a conversation between Philippe Soupault and Eugène Ionesco on poetry and the theater on the radio, she was intrigued by Ionesco's idea of getting rid of tradition and starting anew. At ninety-one she went to see a production of the Argentinian theater company Groupe TSE. Invited by the leading actor, Facundo Bo, she first declined because she had "nothing to wear for theatre outings any longer." But then the old Eileen, submerged in convention, sitting attentively for two hours on the hard benches of the little theater in the Quartier Latin, found it "strange and interesting." She reread André Lhote's *Traité du Paysage*. She visited the new Fondation Maeght in Saint-Paul-de-Vence, built by her old friend Josep Lluis Sert, and spent hours examining every possible detail of the museum's building.

She also took up painting again. But as usual she was not terribly satisfied with the result. "With me there is a sharp dividing line between the conscious and the practical and the unconscious lying underneath," she had written after the war. "I cannot easily pass from one to the other. Also there is the danger of trying too many techniques and not until it becomes unconscious can one say anything worth while." But there is no doubt that Eileen in all her undertakings was an artist first and foremost, however rational her many building designs may appear. "Renouncing certain rules is only possible by inventing new ones," she once said.

RECOGNITION AT LAST

During the last few years of her life the world again took
notice of Eileen Gray. Much to her surprise, and not always
to her liking, she was suddenly newsworthy. The big sale of
the contents of the Doucet flat in 1972 had propelled her
into the forefront of the so-called Art Deco designers and
made her furniture a rare collector's item. She received the
news with incredulity, considering it totally absurd. The first
serious appreciation of her work by an architect, Joseph
Rykwert—first in *Domus* (Milan) in 1968, then in England's
Architectural Review in December 1972—gave her far
greater pleasure.

There was now a constant flow of requests from
journalists, students, and scholars. It was often difficult for
Eileen to see everybody or to cope with the increasing
correspondence. "There are so many visitors I can hardly
find time to answer all the letters," "I don't know how I can
answer all these questions," "Letters have always been a
nightmare to me," or "The damp has made the machine I
write on almost unusable" are only a few of her complaints.
"Somehow things so far back in one's life don't seem to be
part of one at all and in spite of people's kindness one finds
it hard to interest oneself. Solzhenitsyn says the same: 'I
rather try to make something new.'" But some of the interest
she now caused gave her pleasure, especially when it focused
on her work, rather than on her person. She warmed
immediately to the vivacious Joseph Rykwert and his fund of
stories, which Eileen found "so amusing." There was a young
and enthusiastic writer, Bruce Chatwin, who had visited the
house in Castellar and now wanted to write about her in
The Sunday Times. Alarmed, she replied to his request: "I
live in an old apartment with Louis XVI boiseries, no
furniture which could be photographed." Chatwin had not
yet written his marvelous book on Patagonia, but his stories
about his travels around the world fascinated her. There was
Mary Blume from *The International Herald Tribune*, whose
sensitive intelligence Eileen greatly appreciated. They all
helped to break the tedium and loneliness of her old age.
When Evelyne Schlumberger sent her the articles she wrote

on Eileen for *Connaissance des Arts*, Eileen thanked her profusely and, praising the author's gift for writing, added, "I am so grateful that you spoke not only about my failures, but also about what I planned to do, as you know what I did realise was so very small, reading it I could hardly believe it was me." Her modesty was totally genuine, almost to the point of naïveté. She expressed her joy that her chairs would be part of the permanent collection at the Victoria and Albert Museum and found it extraordinary that Roy Strong, the director of the museum, had time to write to her personally to thank her.

In 1972 she received the "Distinction of Royal Designer for Industry," an honor limited to only seventy people, which allows one to place RDI after one's name. There was no question of Eileen's making use of this privilege, and when asked for some information about herself for an official press release, she wrote, "A press release is quite unnecessary." Eileen would not go to the official ceremony but asked friends to collect the scroll. The other people who received the honor were the television and stage designer Tony Abbott and the dress designer Jean Muir. Neither of them was yet fifty years old.

There were other official honors. In 1973 the Royal Institute of the Architects of Ireland elected her an Honorary Fellow in "recognition of her outstanding contribution to the development of modern architecture and design." Eileen, too frail to attend the ceremony, wrote a letter: "I feel unworthy to receive this honour and I am so touched that at the end of my life I have been accorded this distinction, but I accept it with gratitude as a tribute from the people of Ireland and I will endeavour to justify its acceptance by future efforts." Those who knew how much of bitterness and professional insults lay behind her read this with amazement—"at the end of my life," indeed.

Maybe these official honors gave her little pleasure because when she could have used them to help establish herself as an architect and to enable her to realize a few of the plans, she had none. There was never an official body in France or England or anywhere in the world that had taken the slightest notice of her. Now there could not be enough magazines, newspapers, even television programs, all trying to step into the gap; many repeating the same meager data she chose to reveal.

Eileen did have considerable pleasure from the fact that during the last years of her life her work was at least shown

Exhibition organized
by the Scottish Arts
Council in 1979.
From left: A dining
chair, the Noncon-
formist and the
Bibendum chairs, and
a tube lamp designed
in the 1930s

in exhibitions. The first one was in 1970, in Graz and
Vienna. It showed photographs of her houses, some plans
and models. It had been arranged through a friend who was
an architect. In 1972, the Royal Institute of British
Architects also began to take notice and gave her her first
show in England. She had written to Alan Irvine, who was
responsible for the show, "I have many doubts about the
maquettes. Your colleagues will consider them both from an
architectural point of view and in their present state
unworthy to exhibit and I shall not be surprised by their
refusal." Fortunately Alan Irvine and his colleagues had a
better opinion about her models than she had. It was a
handsome show featuring photographs, architectural plans,
and some of Eileen's furniture.

Of course Eileen would not go to the opening. But she
had traveled to London, and secretly she sneaked in to have
a critical look, finding the show "interesting," well presented,
and "well done." But then her always censorious eye spotted
little defects in the cover of a chair. And it would not let her
rest. Eileen was charming and pleasant but she was not a

Another group of
chairs at the Scottish
Arts Council show,
with, at left, the
celluloid screen,
designed in 1931,
which stood in the
salon at the rue
Bonaparte; on the
wall, elevations of the
Vacation Center

person one could easily satisfy. Despite her generosity, her modesty and gentleness, she was not what one calls a "nice person."

She had also some small shows in the States—a touring exhibition, sponsored by the Architectural League of New York, which went to Princeton University, Columbia University, and Boston. To a woman who wrote to her from Los Angeles with a request for an Eileen Gray exhibition at the Feminist Studio Workshop, trying to win her for the women's cause, she replied: "I quite agree, up to now women had no legal recognition . . . but I am sorry that the building in L.A. [where her show was supposed to be] is called the *Women's* Building. For what reason? It seems to mean that women are an inferior species. Otherwise, why is this building not for everyone? Surely criticism must only be

Installation photograph of the exhibition at The Museum of Modern Art in New York, the first substantial retrospective of Eileen's work. Organized by J. Stewart Johnson, curator of design at the museum, it was mounted first at the Victoria and Albert Museum in London, in 1979, and traveled to New York in 1980. From left: The junction box, the Transat chair, a rug designed for E.1027, and an aluminum cupboard also from E.1027

based on merit, and merit implies knowledge: the perception of new angles, perhaps but not emphasising the difference between individuals." As always, her common sense prevented her from agreeing to any such scheme.

As a result of all these activities, a few pieces of furniture emerged of which Eileen had lost all trace. In 1974, Eileen herself went to search for the two Bibendum chairs which she was told were in Draguignan in the south of France. A photo and an article in the local paper produced nothing. To an American collector who told her that he had some of her lamps, she wrote: "How pleased I am after all I lost to learn that several things are preserved," and she added, "I never forget the two visits to the U.S.A. and the marvellous impression still remains."

She did not feel the same about all her pieces. When she saw again the table for Doucet with the tassels, she had only one wish: "to cut those horrors off." When a collector sent her a panel of lacquer she moaned: "I hoped never to see it again, it was just done to try and see the difficulties of trying to do people in raised lacquer and is certainly very bad. I should scrape it off if it were still mine, but what can I do; it dates from 1916."

An inquiry from a writer on the technique of lacquer almost yielded nothing. She was no longer interested in what she called "the sins of my youth." The eagerness that collectors of Eileen Gray pieces displayed amused her. The prices they paid she found absurd. It was a pity she did not live to see her E.1027 table appear in a Hennessy advertisement for "Very Special Cognac" or in a commercial for French toilet paper.

Invited to attend an important sale of her lacquer furniture, she replied, "I have no intention of going to the sale, but I study the catalogue as it will bring back memories." Sometimes she would sneak into a sale and have a look, as when the Serpent chair was for sale at Perrinet. "It was never upholstered in white. I made it for Mathieu-Lévy and the stuff was a pale beige with lines. She wanted something extravagant." Her memory had not failed her.

But it was her architecture and her latest furniture she was interested in. In 1970 when she was working on the two big scrapbooks about her work, she wrote: "It seems rather silly to have made these big portfolios giving all the importance to carpets and the early decorations that can interest no one. Whereas Tempe à Pailla and the Centre de Culture et Loisir and the Maison au Bord de la Mer plus some croquis (if I manage to finish them) might still interest students and are much more important to me."

When the American painter Frank Stella wrote to ask her if he could copy for his own use her Transat chair, she was very pleased and gladly gave her permission, because of her "admiration for him as a painter." "I am very proud that F. Stella wants a copy, I don't want any royalties." She immediately apologized for her design, "Those dreadful tags don't match, the chair was made in a great hurry in 1926 for an important client." She had made twelve, which were all sold, and she urged Frank Stella to make the armrests more curved and alter the headrest slightly, but if he preferred to have them as they were, he was perfectly "free" to do that. Fifty years after she had done a design, she could still fuss over it.

During her last years she continued to make screens, including one in red lacquer. She did not like the result at all

Eileen in her nineties
sitting in her salon in
a chair from Tempe à
Pailla. On the mantel-
piece the head by
Ossip Zadkine, the
little Greek torso,
and two candlesticks
made from Venetian
glass; above it an
eighteenth-century
mirror. The brick
screen was of black
lacquer

on account of the color. She was happier with three cork
screens, which were her last new design. She spent months
and months going to a special place in Montparnasse to
choose the right material. The irony was that when they
were finished, she had trouble selling them, finally parting
with them for the price it cost to make them. Her fame had
started, but of course, as she bitterly remarked, "It isn't
lacquer." People still were not interested in modern design.

On March 8, 1976, Eileen wrote to an architectural
student who had contacted her: "I am so glad that you too
were born in Enniscorthy. . . . You are probably going to
face the final exam. (I wish I was in London and could
prepare my congratulation.) I have heard that Brownswood
is now a hospital but the building was not the same. As a
child I loved the old Irish house but that was pulled down in
1895 or earlier and a horrible brick structure built in its
place so I went to live in France." When Eileen wrote this,
she was ninety-eight years old. The old wounds had never
healed.

EPILOGUE

I saw Eileen for the last time on Thursday, October 14, 1976. We had been to see the important exhibition "1925," at the Musée des Arts Décoratifs. This exhibition contained several pieces of Eileen's. She stood in the queue like everybody else, paid her entrance fee, and walked in with the considerable crowd. As always, her posture was impeccable; while her body was in ruins, her inner strength held the frail body upright. That day, Eileen was awkward and nervous. Since she was deaf, her voice carried above the others. Eileen was in her most censorious mood. Suddenly she called out, "There, over there, is my screen." But her joy was soon tempered by the observation that "the cupboard would have looked better if they had opened the door." Then she spotted her lamp: "It surely must have been redone." That night, having a meal in her workroom and having a few laughs about the "monstrosities of this period," she conceded that "one must be grateful to all those people who bother to unearth us and at least to preserve some of our work. Otherwise it might have been destroyed like the rest." When it was time to part, we grasped each other's hands. Then holding her bony frame, I thought how sad and arduous her life and her art had been, how frail her body and how strong her spirit.

On October 25, Eileen asked Louise to buy some wood from which Eileen wanted to make a tabletop. Louise didn't want to leave her alone in the flat, as Eileen was still feeling poorly because of the arm she had broken a couple of months before. The usual argument started. A little later Eileen tried to get up to go to her workroom. She fell and lost consciousness and was taken to the hospital. "The day I die, I don't want anybody to see me," she had said. Her wish was granted. She died at 8:30 A.M. on the morning of Sunday, October 31, 1976. At 5:30 P.M. the French radio announced her death. It was the first time her name had ever been pronounced on a radio.

The funeral was on the morning of November 5. The ashes were placed in the eastern part of the famous cemetery of Père Lachaise, in a grave numbered 17616.

Eileen Gray, age
ninety, taking a
hard look at an
example of "modern"
architecture

"Il y a un chemin vers le haut et un chemin vers le bas.
Le chemin d'en haut et le chemin d'en bas ne sont qu'une
seule et même route" ("There is a road which leads upward
and there is a road which leads downward. Both are one and
the same"). This was one of Eileen's notes.

EXHIBITIONS

Individual Exhibitions

1970   Graz and Vienna

1972   Royal Institute of British Architects, Heinz Gallery, London

1975   Exhibition organized by Architectural League of New York: traveling to Women's Building, Los Angeles; School of Architecture, Princeton University, New Jersey; School of Architecture, Columbia University, New York; City Hall, Boston

1979   Victoria and Albert Museum, London; Scottish Arts Council Gallery, Edinburgh; Museum of Modern Art, New York (1980) Monika Kinley Gallery, London

1980   "Eileen Gray and les Arts Décoratifs," Rosa Esman Gallery, New York

Group Exhibitions

1913   VIII Salon des Artistes Décorateurs, Pavillon Marsan, Paris

1922   Salon d'Automne, Paris
Exhibition of French furniture, Amsterdam

1923   XIV Salon des Artistes Décorateurs, Pavillon Marsan, Paris
Salon d'Automne, Paris

1924   XV Salon des Artistes Décorateurs, Pavillon Marsan, Paris

1930   First exhibition of Union des Artistes Modernes, Pavillon Marsan, Paris

1932   Second exhibition of Union des Artistes Modernes, Galerie Georges Petit, Paris

1933   XXIV Salon des Artistes Décorateurs, Paris

1937   Pavillon des Temps Nouveaux, Paris
"Le Décor de la Vie de 1909 à 1925," Pavillon Marsan, Paris

1956   Exhibition of Union des Artistes Modernes, Pavillon Marsan, Paris

1970   "Modern Chairs," Whitechapel Gallery, London

1976   "Cinquantenaire de l'Exposition de 1925," Musée des Arts Décoratifs, Paris

1979   "Paris-Moscou," Centre Pompidou, Paris

1984   "The Folding Image: Screens by Western Artists of the Nineteenth and Twentieth Centuries," National Gallery, Washington, D.C.

CATALOGUE RAISONNÉ

This is an attempt to catalogue all of Eileen Gray's pieces. It has been compiled from photographs and letters and from Eileen's own descriptions.

It has been extremely difficult to come to a chronology; Eileen herself was very vague about dates and never signed or dated anything—with the exception of no. 2 in this catalogue, signed at the client's request. Often pieces were left unfinished, or finished much later. Frequently pieces were altered at different times. Many were considered prototypes. Even when Eileen made the same piece several times, she often changed the design; few items are identical. We have limited the descriptions to the most essential characteristics. For more detailed descriptions, see the main text of the book. Where pieces are lost, we have adopted the descriptions by Eileen Gray herself.

Much information was gathered from the sales ledger of Jean Désert, but this information is very sketchy. In some cases, the customer was mentioned, in others not. Some items are hardly described at all. Where the customer was known, we tried (in Eileen's time) to contact them but usually failed to get any response. Most customers had died, or their addresses were no longer applicable. We have indicated the prices of the lost items in the hope that these can give some clues as to the importance of the various pieces.

We have listed only the freestanding furniture. All of Eileen's houses had numerous shelves, headboards, folding tables, etc., built in, which were an integrated part of the architecture. Information on these can be gathered from the pictures in the main part of the book. Almost all of the built-in furniture was still in existence in E.1027 when we last visited it, in 1979. Since then, the present owner has taken the freestanding

pieces to Switzerland. In Tempe à Pailla, there was still the large extendable wardrobe. The headboard remained in the rue Bonaparte bedroom. There was no built-in furniture in Lou Pérou. The studio in the rue Chateaubriand was gutted by various owners, who left only the built-in lamps. They have now been removed.

In the case of the furniture designed for E.1027, Tempe à Pailla, rue Bonaparte, and Lou Pérou, the owner was always Eileen Gray. In the case of the rue Chateaubriand, the first owner was Jean Badovici or Eileen Gray.

In 1980 the most important sale of Eileen Gray's own furniture was conducted by Sotheby's in Monte Carlo. Many of these pieces have changed hands since. All objects in private hands have been marked "Private collection." Eileen herself gave away a number of important pieces which are now in a private collection in London.

The most important exhibition since Eileen's death was that shown at the Victoria and Albert Museum in London, in 1979; at the Scottish Arts Council Gallery in Edinburgh, in 1979; and at The Museum of Modern Art in New York, in 1980. The exhibition of the Royal Institute of British Architects at the Heinz Gallery in London, in 1972, showed only a few pieces of furniture.

The most important sources of photographic material were *E.1027: Maison en Bord de Mer*, *Wendingen*, Sotheby's sale catalogue, Monaco, 1980, and Eileen Gray's own photograph archives.

There have been a number of pirated copies of Eileen Gray pieces. Only two firms have been granted the right to reproduce Eileen Gray furniture. Aram Design Ltd., London, directed by Zeff Aram, was authorized by Eileen Gray herself; the

other one, Ecart, Paris, directed by Andrée Putman, was authorized by the heirs to Eileen Gray.

Eileen left a considerable number of rug designs in various states of completion. The whole area of rugs, rug designs, and graphic works on paper is extremely complex, and not enough information is available to treat them in depth in this catalogue. A special study will have to be made to ascertain which rugs were executed.

The catalogue is arranged as follows:
Screens   1–20

Panels, Doors, and Friezes   21–31

Sofas, Divans, and Beds   32–45

Chairs, Stools, Sofas, and Benches   46–74

Tables   75–130

Bookcases, Cupboards, and Chests   131–42

Lamps   143–78

Mirrors   179–93

Miscellaneous   194–212

Abbreviations

Exhibitions

MoMA   Museum of Modern Art, New York, 1980

NG   "The Folding Image," National Gallery, Washington, D.C., 1984

RIBA   Royal Institute of British Architects, Heinz Gallery, London, 1972

SA   Salon d'Automne, Paris

SAC   Scottish Arts Council Gallery, Edinburgh, 1979

SAD   Salon des Artistes Décorateurs, Paris

V&A   Victoria and Albert Museum, London, 1979

References

Art et Décoration   Paris, 1913

MBM   *E.1027: Maison en Bord de Mer,* Paris/Winter 1929

Sotheby's   Catalogue of sale, Monte Carlo, 1980

Vogue   London, August 1917

Wendingen   Amsterdam, 1924

Provenance

E.1027   E.1027, Roquebrune

J.D.   Jean Désert; figures represent prices asked, the lower figure being the final price

L.P.   Lou Pérou, Saint-Tropez

r.B.   rue Bonaparte (Eileen Gray's flat), Paris

r.C.   rue Chateaubriand (Badovici's studio), Paris

r.L.   rue de Lota (Madame Mathieu-Lévy's flat), Paris

T.P.   Tempe à Pailla, Castellar

Auth. reprod.   Authorized reproductions in limited editions

Screens

1.
La Voie Lactée (La Nuit), 1912.
4 leaves, blue lacquer with inlaid mother-of-pearl.
Ref.: *Vogue; Wendingen.*
Prov.: Florence Gardiner.
Coll.: Location unknown.

2.
Le Destin (signed), 1913.
4 leaves, red lacquer; on one side: 3 figures in silver; on the back: abstract design in black and silver.
Exh.: V&A; MoMA; NG.
Ref.: *Vogue.*
Prov.: Doucet.
Coll.: Private collection.

3.
Block screen, 1922/25, 6 known pieces.
Black lacquer panels, central rods, 4, 5, or 6 panels wide.
Exh.: RIBA; V&A; SAC; MoMA; NG.
3.1. 7 rows high, plain panels.
Coll.: Private collection.
3.2. 7 rows high, plain panels.
Coll.: Virginia Museum of Fine Arts.
3.3. 7 rows high, relief on 4 panels.
Coll.: Private collection.
3.4. 8 rows high, relief on one side.
Prov.: r.C.
Coll.: Private collection.
3.5. 7 rows high, relief on 4 rows (finished 1971).
Coll.: V&A.
3.6. 8 rows high, 1 panel damaged.
Prov.: r.B.; Sotheby's.
Coll.: Private collection.

4.
Block screen, 1922/25, 5 known pieces.
White lacquer panels, 5 or 6 panels wide.
4.1–2. Pair, 11 rows high.
Exh.: SAD 1923.
Prov.: r.L.; Sotheby's.
Coll.: Private collection.
4.3–4. Pair, 10 rows high.
Prov.: r.B.
Coll.: Location unknown.
4.5. 7 rows high.
Prov.: L.P.; Sotheby's.
Coll.: Location unknown.

5.
Screen, 1922/25, 2 pieces.
Pair, black lacquer, 5 leaves, curved at bottom, made for J.D. to hide staircase.
Prov.: J.D.; r.B.
Coll.: Private collection.

6.
Wall screen, 1922/25.
Black lacquer with eggshell decoration, hall.
Ref.: *Wendingen.*
Prov.: r.L.
Coll.: Presumably destroyed.

7.
Screen, 1922/25.
Large important screen, 6 panels, brown lacquer with tan incisions, no visual documentation.
Prov.: J.D. stock 1930— 17,000–18,000 ff.
Coll.: Location unknown.

8.
Screen, 1922/25.
Lacquer, powdered stone (*sabi*) and silver and bronze inlay, 8 leaves.
Exh.: V&A; SAC; MoMA.
Prov.: J.D.; r.B.
Coll.: V&A, E.G. Bequest.

9.
Screen, 1922/25.
Japanese lacquer, no visual documentation.
Prov.: J.D. 1930 to Mlle. Lucy Vautrier.
Coll.: Location unknown.

10.
Screen, 1922/25.
Small, lacquer, no visual documentation.
Prov.: J.D. 1930 to Mlle. Lucy Vautrier.
Coll.: Location unknown.

11.
Screen, 1922/25.
Large, black lacquer, no visual documentation.
Prov.: J.D. 1930 to Henri Pacon.
Coll.: Could be 12 below, now at V&A.

12.
Screen, 1922/25.
Large, black and silver lacquer, geometrical design.
Prov.: J.D. stock 1930— 11,000–9,000 ff.
Coll.: V&A.

13.
Screen, 1922/25.
Small, brown lacquer, no visual documentation.
Prov.: J.D. stock 1930—
9,500–7,500 ff.
Coll.: Location unknown.

14.
Screen, 1922/25.
Black canvas, painted, probably large, no visual documentation.
Prov.: J.D. stock 1930—
7,800–5,300 ff.
Coll.: Location unknown.

15.
Screen, 1922/25.
White lacquer with mother-of-pearl inlay, no visual documentation.
Prov.: J.D. stock 1930—
10,000–6,200 ff.
Coll.: Location unknown.

16.
Screen, 1922/25.
Large, white and gold lacquer, exported to the U.S.A., no visual documentation.
Prov.: J.D. 1927.
Coll.: Location unknown.

17.
Screen, 1926/29, 3 known versions.
Perforated metal mesh, 4 leaves.
Exh.: V&A; SAC; MoMA.
17.1. Circular holes.
Prov.: r.C.
Coll.: Location unknown.
17.2. 2 leaves, rectangular holes; 2 leaves, square holes.
Prov.: r.B.; Sotheby's.
Coll.: Location unknown.
17.3. Large circular holes.
Prov.: E.1027.
Coll.: Private collection.
Auth. reprod.: Aram, London.

18.
Screen, 1930/35.
Large, metal and smoke-colored celluloid on curved base, 2 chrome handles.
Exh.: V&A; SAC; MoMA.
Prov.: r.B.; Sotheby's.
Coll.: Private collection.

19.
Cork screen, 1970, edition of 3, 2 versions.
Cork on board.

19.1. Large panels, 4 leaves.
Exh.: Monika Kinley Gallery.
Coll.: Leicester City Art Gallery.
19.2. Small panels, 4 leaves.
Coll.: Portsmouth City Art Gallery.

20.
Block screen, 1975.
Red lacquer with gold.
Prov.: r.B.
Coll.: Museum Bellerive, Zurich.

Panels, Doors, and Friezes

21.
Le Magicien de la Nuit (La Forêt Enchantée), 1912.
Blue lacquer with mother-of-pearl, depicting antique figures with lotus blossom.
Exh.: SAD 1913.
Ref.: *Art et Décoration.*
Coll.: Michel Perinet, Paris.

22.
Library panel, before 1913.
Yellow and silver lacquer.
Exh.: SAD 1913.
Ref.: *Art et Décoration.*
Coll.: Location unknown.

23.
Fireplace panel *Om Mani Padme Hum,* before 1913.
No visual documentation.
Exh.: SAD 1913.
Ref.: *Art et Décoration.*
Coll.: Location unknown.

24.
Frieze, before 1913.
Lacquer, no visual documentation.
Exh.: SAD 1913.
Ref.: *Art et Décoration.*
Coll.: Location unknown.

25.
Door panel, before 1913.
Small, blue-red lacquer, unfinished, depicting floating figure of a woman.
Ref.: *Vogue; Wendingen.*
Coll.: Private collection.

26.
Panel, before 1913.
In lacquer frame, black and red.
Prov.: Doucet.
Coll.: Private collection.

27.
Panel, 1913/15.
Black lacquer with rose, red, silver, and ivory inlay of Japanese lady in landscape; possibly not entirely E.G., probably with help of Sugawara.
Prov.: Damia.
Coll.: Private collection.

28.
Panel, 1913/15.
Brown lacquer frame, silver and red lacquer design of figure looking onto dancing couple from balcony window.
Coll.: Location unknown.

29.
Doors, 1919/22.
Lacquer doors in 3 leaves with ivory handles, abstract design for hall.
Ref.: *Feuillets d'Art,* Paris, Feb. 1922.
Prov.: r.L.
Coll.: Location unknown.

30.
Panel, 1925/30.
Red and white canvas, no visual documentation.
Prov.: J.D. stock 1930—4,000 ff.
Coll.: Location unknown.

31.
Panel. 1925/30.
Small, yellow lacquer.
Prov.: J.D. stock 1930—2,000 ff.
Coll.: Location unknown.

Sofas, Divans, and Beds*

32.
Lit Persan, 1919/20.
No visual documentation.
Prov.: J.D. stock 1930—5,500 ff.
Coll.: Location unknown.

33.
Pirogue divan (Lit-de-bateau),
1919/20, 3 versions.
Tortoiseshell-brown lacquer outside, silver inside, originally with mat gold cushions.
33.1. *Prov.*: r.L.
Coll.: Collection Frances and Sydney Lewis, Richmond, Va.
33.2. *Prov.*: J.D. stock 1930—
14,000–9,800 ff.
Coll.: Private collection.
33.3. *Coll.*: Location unknown.

*The numerous beds built in Eileen Gray's various domiciles are not included.

34.
Daybed, 1919/20, 2 versions.
34.1. Pale or white lacquer with sculptured legs and carved armrest.
Ref.: *Wendingen.*
Prov.: r.L.
Coll.: Private collection.
34.2. Red and black lacquer, solid armrest.
Prov.: J.D.
Coll.: Private collection.

35.
Daybed, 1919/22.
Orange and chestnut lacquer with silver, sculptured legs.
Ref.: *Wendingen.*
Prov.: r.L.
Coll.: Private collection.

36.
Monte Carlo bed/divan, 1922.
Black lacquer on white sculptured legs.
Exh.: SAD 1923.
Ref.: *Wendingen.*
Prov.: J.D. stock 1930—8,000–6,800 ff.
Coll.: Location unknown.

37.
Divan, 1922/25.
Scorched wood, no visual documentation.
Prov.: J.D. 1925 to Mlle. Lucy Vautrier.
Coll.: Location unknown.

38.
Sofa, 1922/25, 3 versions.
2 lacquer cubes as armrests and mattress with 4 large cushions.
38.1. White for rue de Lota.
Prov.: J.D. 1930—11,000 ff.
Coll.: Location unknown.
38.2. Red and brown for E.G.
Prov.: r.B.; Sotheby's.
Coll.: Location unknown.
Auth. reprod.: Aram, London.
38.3. Black.
Prov.: J.D. stock 1930.
Coll.: Location unknown.

39.
Divan, 1925/28.
Beige with 3 cushions, no visual documentation.
Prov.: J.D. 1930 to Comtesse de Roubillant.
Coll.: Location unknown.

40.
Divan, 1925/28.
Wooden base, mattress, 2 cushions, no visual documentation.
Prov.: J.D. 1930 to Damia (could be one of the above).
Coll.: Location unknown.

41.
Sofa, 1925/28. Black satin cover and cushions, no visual documentation.
Prov.: J.D. stock 1930—1,250 ff.
Coll.: Location unknown.

42.
Divan, 1925/28.
Scorched wood base, no visual documentation.
Prov.: J.D. stock—2,300 ff.
Coll.: Location unknown.

43.
Daybed, 1925/28.
Chromed metal with curved upholstered back, built-in table, large round bolster, quilted mattress.
Ref.: *MBM.*
Prov.: E.1027.
Coll.: Private collection.

44.
Daybed, 1925/28.
Chromed metal, quilted mattress.
Ref.: *MBM.*
Prov.: E.1027.
Coll.: Private collection.
Auth. reprod.: Aram, London.

45.
Sofabed, 1926/28.
Light wood, with built-in night table, one armrest, large cushions.
Prov.: r.C.
Coll.: Location unknown.

Chairs, Stools, Sofas, and Benches

46.
Siren armchair, before 1913.
Black lacquer with carved mermaid and seahorse.
Prov.: To Damia 1923.
Coll.: Private collection.

47.
Armchair, before 1913.
Ash and mahogany.
Exh.: SAD 1923.
Coll.: Location unknown.

48.
Armchair, 1920/22, 2 versions.
A commercial chair which E.G. transformed into:
48.1. Painted wood with cut-out holes, pale beige with stitched seat cushion.
Prov.: r.B.; Sotheby's.
Coll.: Location unknown.
48.2. Painted wood in two colors.
Exh.: SAD 1923.
Coll.: Location unknown.

49.
Serpent armchair, 1920/22.
Yellow and red dotted lacquer, original covered in pale salmon with stripes (now covered in black leather, not by E.G.), arms in form of rearing serpents.
Ref.: *Wendingen.*
Prov.: r.L.
Coll.: Collection Yves Saint Laurent.

50.
Bench, 1920/22, 3 versions.
50.1. Red and black lacquer.
Exh.: V&A; SAC; MoMA.
Coll.: Private collection.
50.2. Gold stripes with brown leather on African wood.
Prov.: r.B.; Sotheby's.
Coll.: Location unknown.
50.3. Two tones with large stripes.
Exh.: SAD 1923.
Coll.: Location unknown.

51.
Bench, 1920/22.
Red lacquer, no visual documentation.
Prov.: J.D. 1925 to Leveillé.
Coll.: Location unknown; could be one of the above.

52.
Stool, 1920/22.
Black leather on wooden base.
Exh.: SAD 1923.
Prov.: J.D. to Labourdette.
Coll.: Location unknown.

53.
Transat chair, 1925/26, edition of 12, 6 known versions (there is an authorized copy made by Max Ott for the painter Frank Stella).
Patented January 13, 1930.
53.1. Black lacquer, brown leather.
Ref.: *MBM.*
Prov.: Maharaja of Indore; Sotheby's.
Coll.: Location unknown.

53.2. Green leather.
Prov.: Kate Weatherby.
Coll.: Private collection.
53.3. Sycamore with light brown leather.
Coll.: Location unknown.
53.4—5. Black lacquer, black leather.
Ref.: MBM.
Prov.: E.1027.
Coll.: Private collection.
53.6. Black lacquer, black leather.
Exh.: RIBA; V&A; SAC; MoMA.
Prov.: Sotheby's.
Coll.: Location unknown.
Auth. reprod.: Ecart, Paris.

54.
Bibendum armchair, 1925/26, 10 pieces known.
Chromed metal, covered in white leather.
Ref.: L'Illustration, 1930.
Coll.: 5 still in private collections.
Auth. reprod.: Aram, London.
54.1. *Prov.*: r.L.
54.2. *Prov.*: E.1027.
Coll.: No longer in E.1027 in 1979.
54.3—6. *Prov.*: Mme. Tachard.
54.7—8. *Prov.*: J.D. 1930 to Pierre Meyer.
Coll.: V&A; SAC.
54.9—10. *Prov.*: J.D. 1930 to Labourdette.

55.
Armchair, 1925/26.
Chromed metal, tilting back, covered in beige.
Prov.: r.B.; Sotheby's.
Coll.: Location unknown.
Auth. reprod.: Aram, London.

56.
Nonconformist armchair, 1926/28.
Chromed metal with one armrest, beige upholstery.
Exh.: V&A; SAC.
Ref.: MBM.
Prov.: E.1027.
Coll.: Private collection.
Auth. reprod.: Aram, London.

57.
Terrace armchair, 1926/28, 5 pieces.
Collapsible, with reclining backrest, some with blue leather patches.

57.1. Heavy wood, painted gray leather cushion.
Prov.: E.1027; T.P.; Sotheby's.
Coll.: Location unknown.
57.2. Solid wood, with armrests.
Prov.: r.B.
Coll.: Private collection.
57.3. Painted in black Duco, no visual documentation.
Prov.: J.D. 1930 to Claude Lévy.
Coll.: Location unknown.
57.4—5. Pair, painted in white Duco with black oilcloth mattress, no visual documentation.
Prov.: J.D.; 1 to Mme. Schiaparelli; 1 to Mme. Regnier.
Coll.: Location of both unknown.

58.
Armchair, 1926/28.
Sycamore, no visual documentation.
Prov.: J.D. to Mme. Schiaparelli.
Coll.: Location unknown.

59.
Dining chair, 1926/28, 14 pieces.
Chromed metal with varied upholstery, later versions with slightly altered crossbars.
59.1—3. Covered in green vinyl.
Prov.: r.B.; Sotheby's.
Coll.: Location unknown.
59.4—6. Black vinyl, metal painted white.
Ref.: MBM.
Prov.: E.1027.
Coll.: Location unknown.
58.7—14. Covered in brown suede with rosewood ferrules.
Exh.: V&A; SAC; MoMA.
Coll.: Private collection.

60.
Chair, 1926/28, 2 pieces.
Pair, chromed metal with leather back and seat.
Exh.: Musée des Arts Décoratifs, Paris, 1976.
Prov.: r.B.; Sotheby's.
Coll.: Location unknown.
Auth. reprod.: Aram, London.

61.
Chair, 1926/28.
White metal with high back, round seat, crossed legs.
Prov.: E.1027.
Coll.: Private collection.

62.
Stool, 1926/28.
White metal frame, black plastic seat.
Prov.: E.1027.
Coll.: Private collection.

63.
Terrace chair, 1928/35, 2 versions.
63.1. Chromed metal. Seat originally in perforated metal, later in canvas.
Prov.: E.1027; r.B.
Coll.: Location unknown.
63.2. Seat in leather.
Prov.: T.P.
Coll.: Location unknown.

64.
Stool, 1928/35.
No visual documentation.
Prov.: J.D. stock—2,100 ff.; could be bar stool from r.B.
Coll.: Location unknown.

65.
Bar stool, 1928/35, 3 versions.
65.1. Painted metal, one central stem, seat in stitched leather.
Ref.: MBM.
Prov.: E.1027.
Coll.: Location unknown.
Auth. reprod.: Aram, London.
65.2. Metal and painted wood, seat in black vinyl, 2 stems.
Exh.: V&A; MoMA.
Prov.: T.P.; r.B.
Coll.: Location unknown.
65.3. Same with 3 stems.
Exh.: SAC.
Prov.: L.P.; r.B.; Sotheby's.
Coll.: Location unknown.

66.
S-bend armchair for terrace, 1928/35.
Perforated wood, painted brown and cream; collapsible, stitched mattress.
Exh.: Whitechapel Gallery, 1970; RIBA; V&A; MoMA.
Prov.: r.B.; Sotheby's.
Coll.: Location unknown.

67.
Armchair, 1928/35, 2 pieces.
Pair, seat and back black and white leather (Mondrian design), armrests white leather straps, wooden frame.
Prov.: Labourdette.
Coll.: Private collection.

68.
Chair/steps, 1928/35.
Aluminum, transformable into steps.
Exh.: V&A; SAC; MoMA.
Prov.: T.P.
Coll.: Location unknown.

69.
Stool/towel rack/steps, 1928/35.
Wood, the sides with pierced holes,
white outside, black inside.
Prov.: T.P.
Coll.: Location unknown.

70.
Stool, 1928/35.
Beige and white painted wood, set on
metal "skis."
Prov.: T.P.
Coll.: Location unknown.

71.
Stool, 1928/35.
Red leather on metal base, handle
concealed in the middle.
Prov.: r.B.; Sotheby's.
Coll.: Private collection.

72.
Terrace chair, 1935/38, 2 pieces.
Pair, metal painted white,
upholstered in laced beige fabric
(one cover missing), collapsible.
Exh.: V&A; SAC.
Prov.: T.P.; r.B.; Sotheby's.
Coll.: Location unknown.

73.
Terrace deck chair, 1935/38.
Unpainted plywood, collapsible with
leather straps, unfinished, original
red mattress.
Exh.: V&A; SAC.
Prov.: T.P.; L.P.; Sotheby's.
Coll.: Location unknown.

74.
Stool, after 1945.
Wood with raffia seat.
Prov.: L.P.; Sotheby's.
Coll.: Location unknown.

Tables

75.
Lotus table, before 1917.
Lacquer, green, brown, and white,
four tassels with amber balls.
Exh.: V&A; SAC.
Ref.: *L'Illustration*, 1930.
Prov.: Doucet.
Coll.: Private collection.

76.
Occasional table, before 1917.
Black lacquer, round with shelf, legs
in "African" style, red *bilboquet*
design on top not by E.G.
Exh.: V&A; SAC.
Ref.: *L'Illustration*, 1930.
Prov.: Doucet.
Coll.: Private collection.

77.
Occasional table, before 1917.
Square with sand-gray top, lacquer
with design of "white fishes in dark
pool."
Ref.: *Vogue; Wendingen.*
Coll.: Location unknown.

78.
Table, before 1917.
Blue lacquer, rectangular, design
"suggesting zodiac sign and silver
planet."
Ref.: *Vogue.*
Coll.: Location unknown.

79.
Occasional table, before 1917.
Small round, hexagonal base, brown
lacquer and powdered stone (*sabi*).
Exh.: SAD 1923.
Coll.: Private collection.

80.
Table, before 1917.
Red lacquer with 2 drawers, no visual
documentation.
Prov.: Doucet.
Coll.: Location unknown.

81.
Nénuphar table, before 1917.
Lacquer, probably simpler version of
Lotus table.
Prov.: J.D. stock 1930—
8,000–4,300 ff.
Coll.: Location unknown.

82.
Table/desk, 1919/25, 2 versions.
Black lacquer with drawers with

ivory handles (made by Inagaki).
82.1. *Exh.*: SAD 1923.
Prov.: J.D. sold 1926.
Coll.: Private collection.
82.2. *Prov.*: Labourdette.
Coll.: Private collection.

83.
Tea table, 1919/25.
Lacquer, no visual documentation.
Prov.: J.D. to Damia.
Coll.: Location unknown.

84.
Table, 1919/25.
Black or brown lacquer.
Prov.: Labourdette.
Coll.: Location unknown.

85.
De Stijl occasional table, 1919/25.
Sycamore and oak painted black and
white, "to imitate sycamore and
ebony."
Exh.: V&A; SAC; MoMA.
Prov.: r.B.; Sotheby's.
Coll.: Location unknown.

86.
Dining table, 1919/25.
Oval, lacquer, 6 legs with light
stripes.
Ref.: *Wendingen.*
Prov.: J.D.
Coll.: Location unknown.

87.
Dining table, 1919/25.
Large, brown lacquer with silver
inlay on side panels.
Ref.: *Wendingen.*
Prov.: r.L.
Coll.: Location unknown.

88.
Dressing table, 1919/25.
With drawers, no visual
documentation.
Prov.: J.D. stock 1930.
Coll.: Location unknown.

89.
Dressing table, 1919/25.
Oak and sycamore, stained black,
one front drawer and two pivoting
side drawers with ivory handles,
glass top.
Exh.: V&A; SAC; MoMA.
Ref.: *Wendingen.*
Prov.: r.B.; Sotheby's.
Coll.: Location unknown.

90.
Dressing table, 1919/25.
Oak, no visual documentation.
Prov.: J.D. stock 1930—1,400 ff.
Coll.: Location unknown.

91.
Side table, 1919/25.
Lacquer with black top with white
spots.
Prov.: r.B.
Coll.: Private collection.

92.
Dressing table, 1919/25.
No visual documentation.
Prov.: J.D. 1923 to Vicomte Charles
de Noailles.
Coll.: Location unknown.

93.
Table, 1919/25.
Large, carved wooden base, painted
gray, lacquer top red on one side,
black on other (base not necessarily
by E.G.).
Prov.: r.B.; Sotheby's.
Coll.: Location unknown.

94.
Table, 1919/25.
Small oval, 4 sculptured legs, black
lacquer top.
Ref.: *Wendingen.*
Prov.: r.L.
Coll.: Location unknown.

95.
Table, 1919/25.
Small, round, black lacquer top,
ivory feet in "Cubist" style.
Prov.: J.D.
Coll.: Location unknown.

96.
Table, 1919/25.
Oval, black and red lacquer, no visual
documentation.
Prov.: J.D. stock 1930—
8,000–4,800 ff.
Coll.: Location unknown; could be
above.

97.
Table, 1919/25.
Small, with drawers, design
unknown (certainly not lacquer).
Prov.: J.D. stock 1930—1,300 ff.
Coll.: Location unknown.

98.
Table, 1919/25.
Large black lacquer, no visual
documentation.
Prov.: Sold at J.D. 1930.
Coll.: Location unknown.

99.
Tea table, 1919/25.
Probably not lacquer, no visual
documentation.
Prov.: Sold at J.D. 1930—2,000 ff.
Coll.: Location unknown.

100.
Table, 1919/25.
Round, probably not lacquer, no
visual documentation.
Prov.: J.D. stock 1930—1,300 ff.
Coll.: Location unknown.

101.
Table, 1919/25.
Large brown lacquer, no visual
documentation.
Prov.: J.D. stock 1930.
Coll.: Location unknown.

102.
Table, 1919/25.
With two shelves, no visual
documentation.
Prov.: J.D. 1930 to Comtesse de
Roubillant.
Coll.: Location unknown.

103.
Tea table, 1919/25.
No visual documentation.
Prov.: J.D. 1930 to Madame Mathieu-
Lévy.
Coll.: Location unknown.

104.
Table, 1919/25.
Lacquer and ebony, no visual
documentation.
Prov.: J.D. 1926 to Leveillé.
Coll.: Location unknown.

105.
Tea table, 1919/25.
No visual documentation.
Prov.: J.D. 1927 to Labourdette.
Coll.: Location unknown.

106.
Desk, 1919/25.
Red lacquer, no visual
documentation.
Prov.: J.D. 1923.
Coll.: Location unknown.

107.
Desk, 1919/25.
Oak, no visual documentation.
Prov.: J.D. 1925 to Martin du Gard.
Coll.: Location unknown.

108.
Desk, 1919/25.
Lacquer, no visual documentation.
Prov.: J.D. stock 1930—
10,000–7,800 ff.
Coll.: Location unknown.

109.
Occasional table, 1925/28,
3 versions.
Small, round top.
109.1. With square metal base.
Ref.: MBM.
Prov.: E.1027.
Coll.: Location unknown.
109.2. With round wood base,
glass top.
Prov.: T.P.
Coll.: Location unknown.
109.3. With round base in wood,
wood top, base with slit, painted
brown-orange.
Prov.: r.B.; Sotheby's.
Coll.: Location unknown.

110.
Writing table, 1925/28.
Chromed metal and wood center
section lifts up to form lectern.
Ref.: MBM.
Prov.: E.1027.
Coll.: Location unknown.

111.
Component tables, 1925/28,
at least 4.
Chromed metal with wood top,
several tables to be pushed together
and interlocked to form one big table,
straight legs.
Ref.: MBM.
Prov.: E.1027.
Coll.: Private collection.
Auth. reprod.: Aram, London.

112.
Dining table, 1925/28.
Straight chromed metal legs, folding
top in wood, side flap slides out for
extension.
Ref.: MBM.
Prov.: E.1027.
Coll.: Location unknown.

113.
Dining table, 1925/28.
Straight chromed metal legs with
adjustable lamp, cork top.
Ref.: MBM.
Prov.: E.1027.
Coll.: Private collection.

114.
Tea table, 1925/28.
Chromed metal with two articulated
disks for cakes, cork top.
Ref.: MBM.
Prov.: E.1027.
Coll.: Location unknown.

115.
E.1027 occasional bedside table,
1925/28, 6 pieces.
Chromed metal, round top, several
versions with either glass or black
enamel top.
Exh.: RIBA; V&A; SAC; MoMA.
Prov.: E.1027 (3); r.C. (1); r.B. (2).
Coll.: 3 in private collections.
Auth. reprod.: Aram, London.

116.
Dressing table, 1925/28,
2 versions.
Chromed metal with wood, metal
pulls.
116.1. Leather top, 1 cupboard,
2 pivoting drawers.
Ref.: MBM.
Prov.: E.1027.
Coll.: Location unknown.
116.2. Rosewood veneer, 4 pivoting
drawers.
Exh.: V&A.
Prov.: r.B.
Coll.: Private collection.
Auth. reprod.: Aram, London.

117.
Writing table, 1925/28.
Chromed metal, wood top.
Prov.: r.B.
Coll.: Location unknown.

118.
Occasional table, 1925/28.
Chromed metal, sycamore top with
glass centerpiece, metal legs
decorated with black bands,
originally done for E.1027 but
finished only for T.P. (1935).
Exh.: V&A; SAC; MoMA.
Prov.: T.P.; Sotheby's.
Coll.: Location unknown.

119.
Side table, 1925/28.
Similar to the steel table, painted
wood, top with cut-out corners,
2 shelves.
Prov.: E.1027.
Coll.: Location unknown.

120.
Side table, 1925/28.
2 shelves with glass tops.
Prov.: E.1027.
Coll.: Private collection.

121.
Occasional table, 1925/28,
2 pieces.
Pair, small, pearwood, possibly like
the one done for E.1027, no visual
documentation.
Prov.: J.D. stock 1930—500 ff. each.
Coll.: Location unknown.

122.
"Dining for one person" table,
1925/28.
Metal structure, chromed straight
legs with built-in lamp and
extendable side, black lacquer top.
Prov.: r.C.
Coll.: Location unknown.

123.
Dining table, 1925–28.
Square chromed metal legs with
extendable part with black lacquer
top. This is similar to the one done for
E.1027 without the lamp.
Prov.: J.D.; r.B.; Sotheby's.
Coll.: Location unknown.
Auth. reprod.: Aram, London.

124.
Occasional table, 1925/28,
6 known versions.
Small, low transportable table with
top and base linked by chrome bars
and handle. Some were done in
untreated plywood, others painted,
one in rosewood veneer to match
rosewood veneer of dressing table.
Exh.: Musée des Arts Décoratifs,
Paris, 1976; V&A; SAC.
Ref.: MBM.
Auth. reprod.: Aram, London.
124.1. *Prov.*: Vézelay.
Coll.: Musée des Arts Décoratifs,
Paris.
124.2. *Prov.*: r.B.; Sotheby's.
Coll.: Private collection.

124.3. *Prov.*: E.1027.
Coll.: Private collection.
124.4. *Prov.*: T.P.
Coll.: Location unknown.
124.5. *Prov.*: L.P.
Coll.: Location unknown.
124.6. *Prov.*: r.C.
Coll.: Location unknown.

125.
Occasional table, 1930/35.
Small, low benchlike table in wood,
painted beige and off white with two
metal crossbars, sides have metal
"skis" to make the table slide.
Prov.: T.P.; r.B.; Sotheby's.
Coll.: Location unknown.

126.
Table, 1930/35.
Chromed metal base with blue
lacquer top (this table was made up
from remaining pieces).
Prov.: r.B.
Coll.: Private collection.

127.
Occasional table, 1930/35.
Prototypes, some of them redone
after World War Two, original about
1935. Thin curved metal legs with
irregular-shaped wooden tops.
127.1–2. With monograms E.G.
and J.B. incised on top and
underneath.
Prov.: T.P.; Sotheby's.
Coll.: Location unknown.
127.3. Pear-shaped top of stained
wood.
Prov.: r.B.; Sotheby's.
Coll.: Location unknown.
127.4. Copper top.
Prov.: r.B.
Coll.: Location unknown.

128.
Table, 1930/35.
To be adjusted to different heights
(dining table and coffee table), heavy
perforated metal.
Prov.: T.P.
Coll.: Location unknown.

129.
Table, 1930/35.
To be adjusted to different heights,
one side of top cork, the other zinc.
Prov.: T.P.
Coll.: Location unknown.
Auth. reprod.: Aram, London.

130.
Table, 1930/35.
Painted metal legs with pine top with geometrical decoration.
Prov.: T.P.; L.P.; Sotheby's.
Coll.: Location unknown.

Bookcases, Cupboards, and Chests

131.
Cabinet, before 1914.
Large display cabinet in red lacquer with blue lacquer interior, no visual documentation.
Prov.: Doucet.
Coll.: Location unknown.

132.
Chest, 1919/22.
Three drawers, scorched wood with round bone or ivory handles, with black lacquer top.
Exh.: SA 1922 (?).
Ref.: *Wendingen.*
Coll.: Location unknown.

133.
Bookcase, 1919/22.
Lacquered in gray and silver, three shelves.
Ref.: *Wendingen.*
Prov.: r.L.
Coll.: Private collection.

134.
Architect's cupboard, 1923/28, 2 versions.
Sycamore wood with various drawers, some pivoting, chromed handles.
134.1. *Prov.*: J.D. to Henri Pacon; Sotheby's.
Coll.: Location unknown.
134.2. *Exh.*: V&A; SAC; MoMA.
Prov.: r.B.
Coll.: Location unknown.

135.
Cupboard, 1923/28. 3 versions.
Aluminum with cork interior and glass shelves.
135.1. *Exh.*: Musée des Arts Décoratifs. Paris. 1976.
Prov.: E.1027.
Coll.: Musée des Arts Décoratifs, Paris.
135.2. *Prov.*: Vézelay.
Coll.: Location unknown.

135.3. *Prov.*: J.D. 1930 to Kate Weatherby.
Coll.: Location unknown.

136.
Chest, 1923/28.
No visual documentation.
Prov.: J.D. stock.
Coll.: Location unknown.

137.
Chest, 1923/28.
No visual documentation.
Prov.: J.D. stock to Mme. Schiaparelli.
Coll.: Location unknown.

138.
Bookcase, 1923/28.
Lacquer, no visual documentation.
Prov.: J.D. stock 1930—sold.
Coll.: Location unknown.

139.
Cupboard, 1923/28.
Probably for kitchen, painted wood, white outside, black interior, drawers, sliding doors.
Prov.: E.1027.
Coll.: Private collection.

140.
Kitchen cupboard, 1923/28, 3 versions.
Wood, painted gray, ribbed aluminum pivoting drawers, open shelves and doors.
140.1. *Prov.*: E.1027.
Coll.: Location unknown.
140.2. *Prov.*: T.P.
Coll.: Location unknown.
140.3. *Prov.*: r.B.; Sotheby's.
Coll.: Location unknown.

141.
Cube chest, 1923/28, 2 versions.
6 pivoting drawers with glass bottoms.
Exh.: V&A; SAC; MoMA.
141.1. Painted yellow with gray interior.
Prov.: T.P.
Coll.: Location unknown.
141.2. Painted white.
Prov.: L.P.; Sotheby's.
Coll.: Location unknown.
Auth. reprod.: Ecart, Paris.

142.
Mobile chest, 1923/28, 2 versions.
For trousers and skirts; wood and

clear celluloid on casters with aluminum hangers.
142.1. Curved piano-shaped top.
Prov.: T.P.
Coll.: Location unknown.
142.2. Rectangular top.
Prov.: L.P.; Sotheby's.
Coll.: Location unknown.
Auth. reprod.: Ecart, Paris.

Lamps*

143.
Floor lamp, 1919/25.
Painted metal, black lacquer, wooden base decorated with white sections, original shade missing.
Prov.: r.B.; Sotheby's.
Coll.: Location unknown.

144.
Floor lamp, 1919/25.
Copper stem, black lacquer wooden base, triangular shape, original shade missing.
Prov.: r.B.; Sotheby's.
Coll.: Location unknown.

145.
Floor lamp, 1919/25, 2 pieces.
Pair, lacquered wood, parchment lampshade in African style, one with original shade missing, base in two parts.
Prov.: r.L.
Coll.: Collection Frances and Sydney Lewis, Richmond, Va.

146.
Hanging lamp, 1919/25.
Painted lamp with red, white, and ivory shade.
Ref.: *Wendingen.*
Prov.: r.L.
Coll.: Location unknown.

147.
Hanging lamp, 1919/25.
Yellow and gray parchment shade.
Coll.: Location unknown.

148.
Ceiling lamp, 1919/25, 4 pieces.
Conical shape in parchment with decorations.
Ref.: *Wendingen.*
Prov.: 2 in r.L.; 2 in J.D.
Coll.: Location unknown.

*Dating the lamps is difficult, and it is possible that some were designed before 1914.

149.
Hanging lamp, 1919/25, 6 pieces,
3 versions.
Exh.: V&A; SAC; MoMA.
149.1—2. Pair, white lacquered
wood with ostrich egg.
Ref.: Wendingen.
Prov.: r.L.
Coll.: Location unknown.
149.3—4. The same, lacquered in
blue.
Prov.: J.D. 1923 to Levavasseur.
Coll.: Private collection.
149.5—6. The same, with lacquered
band, pierced.
Prov.: r.L.
Coll.: Private collection.

150.
Table lamp, 1919/25.
Brown wood with parchment shade,
sculptured base.
Ref.: Wendingen.
Prov.: J.D. 1927 to Canada.
Coll.: Location unknown.

151.
Table lamp, 1919/25.
Hand-carved ivory stem in two parts
with silk shade.
Prov.: r.B.; Sotheby's.
Coll.: Location unknown.

152.
Table lamp, 1919/25.
Ivory incrustations and Cubist
motifs.
Ref.: Wendingen.
Prov.: r.L.
Coll.: Location unknown.

153.
Japanese lantern, 1919/25,
3 pieces, 2 versions.
Rectangular metal structure with
glass.
153.1—2. With blue and silver glass
and silver ball (9 glass panels survive
as well).
Exh.: SAD 1923.
Coll.: Location unknown.
153.3. With white opaque glass and
silver ball.
Exh.: V&A; SAC; MoMA.
Prov.: r.B.
Coll.: Private collection.

154.
Satellite hanging lamp, 1919/25,
2 versions.
Light bulbs fitted into three cones
with disks.
154.1. *Prov.:* J.D. to Maharaja of
Indore.
Coll.: Location unknown.
154.2. *Prov.:* r.B.; Sotheby's.
Coll.: Private collection.

155.
Wall lamp, 1919/25, 2 pieces.
Pair, ivory and parchment, white and
red decoration.
Ref.: Wendingen.
Prov.: r.L.
Coll.: Location unknown.

156.
Wall lamp, 1919/25.
Pair, ebony macassar, no visual
documentation.
Prov.: J.D. stock 1930—540—340 ff.
Coll.: Location unknown.

157.
Wall lamp, 1919/25, 4 pieces.
Lacquer, gold and silver decoration,
no visual documentation.
Prov.: J.D. stock 1930—1,120 ff.
Coll.: Location unknown.

158.
Lamp, 1919/25.
Yellow parchment, no visual
documentation.
Prov.: J.D. 1923 to Damia.
Coll.: Location unknown.

159.
Lamp, 1919/25.
Parchment, no visual documentation.
Prov.: J.D. 1922 to Maison Pol.
Coll.: Location unknown.

160.
Lamp or lantern, 1919/25.
No visual documentation.
Prov.: J.D. 1923.
Coll.: Location unknown.

161.
Lamp, 1919/25.
Lacquer and sycamore, no visual
documentation.
Prov.: J.D. 1926 to Raynuard & Fils.
Coll.: Location unknown.

162.
Hall lamp, 1919/25.
Lacquer, no visual documentation.
Prov.: J.D. 1925 to Leveillé.
Coll.: Location unknown.

163.
Lamp, 1919/25.
Yellow, no visual documentation.
Prov.: J.D. 1925 to de Graffenier.
Coll.: Location unknown.

164.
Lamp, 1919/25, 2 pieces.
Pair, parchment, no visual
documentation.
Prov.: J.D. stock 1930—500 ff.
Coll.: Location unknown.

165.
Lamp, 1919/25.
Rectangular with blue glass
(probably Japanese lantern).
Prov.: J.D. 1930 to Kate Weatherby.
Coll.: Location unknown.

166.
Lamp, 1919/25.
Lacquer with ivory motif, no visual
documentation.
Prov.: J.D. stock 1930—800 ff.
Coll.: Location unknown.

167.
Lamp or lantern, 1919/25,
7 pieces.
No visual documentation (Japanese
lanterns?).
Prov.: J.D. stock 1930—700 ff. each.
Coll.: Location unknown.

168.
Lamp, 1919/25, 2 pieces.
Pair, with ivory ring, no visual
documentation.
Prov.: J.D. stock 1930—950 ff. each.
Coll.: Location unknown.

169.
Lamp, 1919/25.
Cubist design, no visual
documentation.
Prov.: J.D. stock 1930—1,600 ff.
Coll.: Location unknown.

170.
Lamp, 1919/25.
Lacquer with flowers.
Prov.: J.D. stock 1930—950 ff.
Coll.: Location unknown.

171.
Wall lamp, 1919/25, 2 pieces.
Pair, no visual documentation.
Prov.: J.D. stock 1930 to
Mme. Regnier.
Coll.: Location unknown.

172.
Staircase lamp, 1919/25, 2 pieces.
Pair, no visual documentation.
Prov.: J.D. stock 1930—1,400 ff.
Coll.: Location unknown.

173.
Lamp, 1919/25, 2 versions.
Lacquered wood with ostrich egg.
173.1. *Coll.*: Labourdette.
173.2. *Coll.*: Location unknown.

174.
Airplane hanging lamp, 1925/28,
5 versions.
Chromed metal, glass, and tube
lights, on three the original glass is
missing.
174.1. *Prov.*: r.B.
Coll.: Private collection.
174.2–5. *Exh.*: V&A; SAC; MoMA.
Prov.: Sotheby's.
Coll.: Location unknown.

175.
Bathroom wall lamp, 1925/28,
at least 6 pieces.
Pairs, chromed metal.
175.1–2. *Prov.*: E.1027.
Coll.: Location unknown.
175.3–4. *Prov.*: r.B.
Coll.: Still in r.B.
175.5–6. *Prov.*: L.P.; Sotheby's.
Coll.: Location unknown.

176.
Standing tube lamp, 1930/38.
Chromed metal base with fluorescent
tube.
Exh.: V&A; SAC; MoMA.
Prov.: r.B.
Coll.: MoMA.
Auth. reprod.: Aram, London.

177.
Terrace lantern, 1930/38.
For candle; metal painted black with
opening on two sides, painted white
inside.
Exh.: V&A; SAC; MoMA.
Prov.: T.P.; Sotheby's.
Coll.: Location unknown.

178.
Terrace lamp, 1930/38.
For candle; made of glass and gray
metal with glass ball (fishing float).
Prov.: T.P.
Coll.: Private collection.

Mirrors

179.
Hand mirror, 1919/25, 8 versions.
179.1. Lacquer with initials in ivory.
Prov.: J.D. 1927 to Labourdette.
Coll.: Location unknown.
179.2. In oak with initials.
Prov.: J.D. 1925 to Mme. Tachard.
Coll.: Location unknown.
179.3–4. Lacquer without initials.
Prov.: J.D. stock 1930.
Coll.: Location unknown.
179.5–6. In oak without initials.
Prov.: J.D. stock 1930.
Coll.: Location unknown.
179.7. Brown lacquer with initials
E.G.
Exh.: V&A; SAC; MoMA.
Prov.: r.B.
Coll.: Private collection.
179.8. No visual documentation.
Prov.: J.D. 1923 to Mme. Rouché.
Coll.: Location unknown.

180.
Dressing-table mirror, 1919/25.
Lacquer, jade, ivory, and sycamore.
Ref.: *Wendingen.*
Prov.: r.L.
Coll.: Location unknown.

181.
Wall mirror, 1919/25.
Round, red lacquer, silver leaf metal
rim frame.
Prov.: J.D. stock 1930; L.P.;
Sotheby's.
Coll.: Location unknown.

182.
Wall mirror, 1919/25.
Rectangular brown lacquer frame.
Prov.: J.D. 1930 to Henri Pacon.
Coll.: Location unknown.

183.
Wall mirror, 1919/25.
Rectangular red lacquer frame.
Prov.: J.D. to Henri Pacon.
Coll.: Location unknown.

184.
Wall mirror, 1919/25.
Rectangular, black iron frame.
Prov.: J.D. 1930 to Mme.
Schiaparelli.
Coll.: Location unknown.

185.
Wall mirror, 1919/25.
Large, lacquer, no visual
documentation.
Prov.: J.D. 1925 to Mlle. Lucy
Vautrier.
Coll.: Location unknown.

186.
Wall mirror, 1919/25.
Rectangular, brown and silver
lacquer frame with motifs.
Ref.: *Wendingen.*
Prov.: Damia (?).
Coll.: Private collection.

187.
Wall mirror, 1919/25.
Almost identical to above.
Ref.: *Wendingen.*
Prov.: Damia (?).
Coll.: Private collection.

188.
Wall mirror, 1919/25.
Red lacquer frame, no visual
documentation.
Prov.: J.D. stock 1930—
2,000–1,800 ff.
Coll.: Location unknown.

189.
Wall mirror, 1919/25.
Large, lacquer frame, no visual
documentation.
Prov.: J.D. stock 1930—3,000 ff.
Coll.: Location unknown.

190.
Wall mirror, 1919/25.
Lacquer frame, no visual
documentation.
Prov.: J.D. stock 1930—
2,000–1,600 ff.
Coll.: Location unknown.

191.
Wall mirror, 1919/25.
Long, red and silver lacquer frame.
Prov.: J.D. 1930 to Mlle. Lucy
Vautrier.
Coll.: Location unknown.

192.
Satellite mirror, 1926/28.
Chromed metal, round with
projecting shaving mirror with light
fitting.
Prov.: E.1027; Sotheby's.
Coll.: Location unknown.
Auth. reprod.: Ecart, Paris.

193.
Bathroom mirror, 1926/28,
2 pieces.
Chromed metal with pivoting
section.
Exh.: V&A; SAC; MoMA.
193.1. *Prov.*: E.1027.
Coll.: Private collection.
193.2. *Prov.*: L.P.
Coll.: Private collection.
Auth. reprod.: Aram, London.

Miscellaneous

194.
Tea trolley, circa 1925.
Designed also to keep gramophone
and bottles, painted metal and wood.
Prov.: E.1027.
Coll.: Private collection.

195.
Bowl, 1919/25.
Black lacquer.
Prov.: r.B.
Coll.: Location unknown.

196.
Tray, 1919/25, two versions.
196.1. Lacquer, black outside,
brown inside.
Prov.: r.B.; Sotheby's.
Coll.: Private collection.
196.2. Rectangular with cut-in
handles.
Prov.: r.B.; Sotheby's.
Coll.: Private collection.

197.
Plates, 1919/25, 27 pieces,
2 versions.
Small, lacquer on wood.
197.1–26. Dark brown.
Prov.: r.B.; Sotheby's.
Coll.: Private collections.
197.27. Orange with gold spots.
Exh.: V&A.
Coll.: Location unknown.

198.
Box, 1919/25.
Lacquer, gray outside, red-orange
inside, round with lid.
Prov.: r.B.; Sotheby's.
Coll.: Location unknown.

199.
Box, 1919/25.
Brown lacquer, round with lid.
Prov.: r.B.
Coll.: Private collection.

200.
Box, 1919/25.
Red and black spotted, round
with lid.
Prov.: r.B.
Coll.: Private collection.

201.
Box, 1919/25.
With stem, brown lacquer, silver
interior with lid.
Prov.: r.B.
Coll.: Private collection.

202.
Bed tray or shelf, 1919/25.
Wood, rectangular with black metal
feet, black lacquer.
Prov.: r.B.; Sotheby's.
Coll.: Location unknown.

203.
Base for sculpture, 1919/25,
2 versions.
Octagonal, in brown lacquer.
203.1. With African sculpture.
Prov.: r.B.
Coll.: Private collection.
203.2. Without sculpture.
Coll.: Location unknown.

204.
Block, 1919/25.
Lacquered for bed, no visual
documentation.
Prov.: J.D. stock 1930—800 ff.
Coll.: Location unknown.

205.
Block, 1919/25, 2 pieces.
Pair in sycamore, glass on lacquer
base.
Prov.: J.D. 1927 to Perugia.
Coll.: Location unknown.

206.
Box, 1919/25. 2 pieces.
Pair in zebra wood.
Prov.: J.D. 1930 to Damia.
Coll.: Location unknown.

207.
Junction box, 1919/25.
Movable electric switch box in
aluminum on wood base.
Exh.: V&A; MoMA.
Prov.: E.1027; L.P.; Sotheby's.
Coll.: Location unknown.

208.
Screen model, 1919/25.
Small model in black glass.
Prov.: r.B.
Coll.: Private collection.

209.
Screen model, 1919/25.
Small model in cardboard.
Prov.: r.B.
Coll.: Private collection.

210.
Screen model, 1919/25.
Small model in cardboard.
Prov.: r.B.
Coll.: Private collection.

211.
Chair model, 1919/25.
Model in cardboard for a terrace
chair.
Prov.: r.B.
Coll.: Private collection.

212.
Filing and tool cabinet, 1926/28.
Perforated metal with 9 drawers and
letters on one side.
Prov.: E.1027.
Coll.: Private collection.

BIBLIOGRAPHY

1913

Verneuil, M.-Pillard. "Le Salon de la Société des Artistes Décorateurs." *Art et Décoration* (Paris) 1913: 91.

1917

S., A. "An Artist in Lacquer." *Vogue* (London) Early August 1917: 29.

1920

"Lacquer Walls and Furniture Displace Old Gods in Paris and London." *Harper's Bazaar* (London) September 1920.

1922

"Bargain Time." *Daily Mail* (London) June 10, 1922.

Chavance, René. "Notre Enquête sur le Mobilier Moderne." *Art et Décoration* (Paris) 1922.

Gramont, Elisabeth de, Duchesse de Clermont-Tonnerre. "Les Laques d'Eileen Gray." *Feuillets d'Art* (Paris) no. 3 (1922): 147–48. Also in English, "The Laquer [*sic*] Work of Miss Eileen Gray." *The Living Arts: A Portfolio Reflecting the Literary and Artistic Taste of Our Time* (New York, London) no. 3 (March 1922): 147–48.

New York Herald June 22, 1922.

"Odd Designs at Art Studio of 'Jean Desert.'" *Chicago Tribune* June 7, 1922.

1923

"L'Art Urbain et le Mobilier au Salon d'Automne." *Art et Décoration* (Paris) 1923: 78.

"Beautiful Lacquered Furniture." *Daily Mail* (London) March 29, 1923.

Boeken, A. *Bouwkundig Weekblad* (Amsterdam) July 14, 1923. Review of XIV Salon des Artistes Décorateurs.

Chavance, René. *Beaux-Arts* (Brussels) June 1923.

———. "Le XIVe Salon des Artistes Décorateurs." *Art et Décoration* (Paris) 1923: 175.

"Eastern Influence." *Times* (London) August 5, 1923.

"Le XIVe Salon des Artistes Décorateurs." *L'Amour de l'Art* (Paris) 1923: 557.

"Le XIVe Salon des Artistes Décorateurs." *Journal* (Paris) May 10, 1923.

George, Waldemar. *Ere Nouvelle* (Paris) May 8, 1923.

Janneau, Guillaume. "Le Mouvement Moderne." *La Renaissance de l'Art Français et des Industries de Luxe* (Paris) 1923: 43.

"Le Salon des Décorateurs." *L'Intransigéant* (Paris) May 5, 1923.

V[an] R[avesteyn, Sybold]. *Bouwkundig Weekblad* (Amsterdam) July 14, 1923. Review of XIV Salon des Artistes Décorateurs.

1924

L'Architecture Vivante (Paris) 1924: 27.

Les Arts de la Maison. Paris: Editions Morancé, 1924.

Clouzot, H. "En Marge de l'Art Appliqué Moderne." *L'Amour de l'Art* (Paris) 1924: 106, 111, 124.

Janneau, Guillaume. "Introduction à l'Exposition des Arts Décoratifs: Considerations sur l'Esprit Moderne." *Art et Décoration* (Paris) 1924: 144, 152.

Mobilier et Décoration d'Intérieur. Paris: 1924, 27.

Wendingen (Amsterdam) series 6, no. 6 (1924). Entire issue devoted to Eileen Gray: "L'Art d'Eileen Gray," Jean Badovici; "Eileen Gray: Meubelen en Interieurs," Jan Wils.

1925

Badovici, Jean. *Intérieurs Français.* Paris: Editions Morancé, 1925.

Technique de Décor Intérieur. Paris: Editions Morancé, 1925.

"Un Temple de l'Art Moderne, l'Appartement de M. J. D." *Fémina* (Paris) January 1925: 29.

1926

"L'Appartement de Suzanne Talbot." *L'Architecture Vivante* (Paris) 1926.

1927

Chareau, Pierre. *Meubles.* Paris: Editions Charles Moreau, 1927.

1928

Cresswell, Howell S. "Oriental Lacquer on Modern Furniture." *Good Furniture Magazine* (London) 1928: 291–95.

Deshairs, Léon. "Une Villa Moderne à Hyères." *Art et Décoration* (Paris) 1928: 21.

1929

L'Architecture Vivante (Paris) 1929. *E.1027: Maison en Bord de Mer.* Entire issue devoted to E.1027 house. Text by E. G. and Badovici.

1930

Gray, Eileen, and Jean Badovici. "La Maison Minimum." *L'Architecture d'Aujourd'hui* (Paris) 1930: 61–62.

"Le Studio de Jacques Doucet." *L'Illustration* (Paris) May 3, 1930.

"Wohnhaus am Cap Martin, von Gray und Badovici." *Der Baumeister* (Munich) October 1930.

1931

Giedion, Sigfried. "L'Architecture Contemporaine dans les Pays Méridionaux." *Cahiers d'Arts* (Paris) 1931: 102–3.

"Une Installation de Claude Lévy." *Art et Décoration* (Paris) 1931: 83–86.

1932

Gli Elementi dell'Architettura Funzionale. Milan: 1932. Four plates by Alberto Sartoris.

1933

"Le Salon de Verre de Mme. J. Suzanne Talbot à Paris." *L'Illustration* (Paris) May 27, 1933.

1937

Le Corbusier. "Le Centre de Vacances (1936)," designed by "Eelen Gray." In *Des Canons, des Munitions...Merci! Des Logis. S.V.P.,* 96–97. Paris: C.I.A.M., 1937. Catalogue for exhibition in Pavillon des Temps Nouveaux, Paris, 1937.

Le Corbusier and Pierre Jeanneret. *Oeuvre Complète de 1910–1929.* Zurich: H. Girsberger, 1937.

"Ferienhäuser." *Moderne Bauformen* (Stuttgart) no. 8 (1937).

1939

Aloi, Roberto. *L'Arredamento Moderno* (Milan) 2nd series, 1939.

1941

Martienssen, Rex. "Mediterranean Houses." *S[outh] A[frican] Architectural Record* (Johannesburg) October 1941.

1945

Aloi, Roberto. *L'Arredamento Moderno* (Milan) 3rd series, 1945.

1947

Aloi, Roberto. *L'Arredamento Moderno* (Milan) 3rd series, 1947.

1948

L'Architecture d'Aujourd'hui (Paris) 1948. Article on Le Corbusier's frescoes at Roquebrune and Vézelay.

1949

Kennet, Lady. *Self-Portrait of an Artist.* London: 1949. The memoirs of Kathleen Bruce.

1956

Herbst, René. *25 Années de U.A.M.* Paris: Editions du Salon des Arts Ménagers, 1956.

1958

Ragon, Michael. *Le Livre de l'Architecture Moderne.* Paris: 1958.

1959

"Projet pour un Centre Culturel par Eileen Gray." *L'Architecture d'Aujourd'hui* (Paris) no. 82 (1959).

1961

Revel, Jean-François. "Jacques Doucet, Couturier et Collectionneur." *L'Oeil* (Paris) no. 84 (December 1961): 47.

1966

Brunhammer, Yvonne. *Les Années "25."* Paris: Musée des Arts Décoratifs, 1966.

Léautaud, Paul. *Journal Littéraire.* Paris: 1966. II, 141; III, 70, 75; IV, 208, 209; XIII, 270, 320.

Rykwert, Joseph. "Un Ommagio a Eileen Gray—Pioniera del Design." *Domus* (Milan) no. 468 (December 1966): 23–25.

1969

Battersby, Martin. *The Decorative Twenties.* London: Studio Vista, 1969.

Brunhammer, Yvonne. *The Nineteen Twenties Style.* London and New York: Hamlyn, 1969.

Crowley, Aleister. *The Confessions of Aleister Crowley.* London: 1969.

1970

Modern Chairs. London: Whitechapel Art Gallery, 1970.

1971

Garner, Philippe. "The Robert Walker Collection, Part I." *Connoisseur* (London) September 1971.

Rykwert, Joseph. "Eileen Gray: Two Houses and An Interior, 1926–1933." *Perspecta: The Yale Architectural Journal* (New Haven) no. 13/14 (1971): 66–73.

1972

Ancienne Collection J. Doucet Mobilier "Art Déco" Provenant du Studio Saint-James à Neuilly. Paris: Audap, Godeau, Solanet, 1972. Auction sale.

Eileen Gray, Pioneer of Design. London: Heinz Gallery, 1972. Exhibition catalogue.

Johnson, J. Stewart. "The New Antiques: Art Deco and Modernism." *Antiques* (London) no. 101 (January 1972): 230.

"Little Known Pioneer." *Building* (London) December 1972: 22, 29, 36.

"Pioneer Lady." *Architectural Review* (London) CLII (August 1972): 125.

Rykwert, Joseph. "Eileen Gray: Pioneer of Design." *Architectural Review* (London) CLII (December 1972): 357–61.

Sharp, Dennis. *A Visual History of Twentieth Century Architecture.* New York: 1972.

1973

Banham, Reyner. "Nostalgia for Style." *New Society* (London) February 1, 1973.

Brockman, Hans. "A Remarkable Pioneer." *Financial Times* (London) 1973.

Building (London) March 1973: 95. Review of RIBA exhibition.

"Eileen Gray." *Form* (London) no. 3 (1973).

"Eileen Gray." *Plan* (Dublin) January 1973.

"Eileen Gray: A Neglected Pioneer of Modern Design." *RIBA Journal* (London) LXXX (February 1973): 58–59.

"Folies pour le Style Art Déco." *Connaissance des Arts* (Paris) no. 252 (February 1973): 113.

Gardiner, Stephen. "The Magic of Eileen Gray." *Observer* (London) March 4, 1973.

Garner, Philippe. "The Lacquer Work of Eileen Gray and Jean Dunand." *Connoisseur* (London) May 1973: 2–11.

Gray, D. "The Complete Designer; The Work of Eileen Gray." *Design* (London) no. 289 (January 1973): 68–73.

"Heinz Gallery, London; Exhibit." *Apollo* (London) new series XCVII (January 1973).

"Heinz Gallery, London; Exhibit." *Burlington Magazine* (London) CXV (March 1973): 194.

Lorac-Gerbaud, Andrée. *L'Art du Laque.* Paris: 1973.

Oliver, G. "Heinz Gallery, London; Exhibit." *Connoisseur* (London) March 1973: 225.

Radford, Penny. "Design Report: A One-woman Show." *The Times* (London) February 22, 1973: 18.

"RIBA Drawings Collection, London; Exhibit." *Architectural Design* (London) no. 43 (1973): 186.

Russell, John. "Conquering the Landscape." *The Sunday Times* (London) January 28, 1973.

Schlumberger, Evelyne. "1913, Irlandaise à Paris: Premier Succès en Laque, 1973, Toujours Parisienne et une Quête d'Innovations." *Connaissance des Arts* (Paris) no. 258 (August 1973): 72–81.

"Trois Survivants des Années Folles. Eileen Gray, M. Coard, J. Dufet." *L'Estampille* (Paris) no. 40 (1973): 43–46.

Vaizey, Marina. "The Collection of Mr. and Mrs. Robert Walker, Part II." *Connoisseur* (London) April 1973: 232–34.

Walker, Dorothy. "Alphabetic Extravaganzas." *Hibernia* (London) June 8, 1973.

Wallworth, Brian. "Eileen Gray— Pioneer of Design." *Arts Review* (London) XXV, no. 4 (February 24, 1973): 102.

1974

Blume, Mary. "Eileen Gray." *International Herald Tribune* (Paris) March 11, 1974.

———. "Eileen Gray." *Réalités* (Paris) no. 281 (April 1974): 42–47.

1975

Blume, Mary. "Decorator, Architect and a Woman of Distinction." *Evening Press* (London) September 8, 1975.

Brunhammer, Yvonne. *Le Style 1925.* Paris: Baschet Editeur, 1975.

Design 1920's. Milton Keynes: Open University Press, 1975.

Eley, P. "Unflagging Gray." *Architectural Review* (London) CLVIII (June 1975): 2–3.

"Eminence Gray." *Design* (London) no. 319 (July 1975): 23.

Goldberger, Paul. "Their Vision Was Bold and Personal." *The New York Times* May 13, 1975.

Herbert, Gilbert. *Martienssen and the International Style.* Rotterdam: 1975.

Irvine, Alan. "Lady of the Rue Bonaparte." *The Sunday Times Magazine* (London) June 22, 1975: 28–40.

McCoy, Esther. "Report from Los Angeles." *Progressive Architecture* (Stamford, Conn.) LVI (July 1975): 24.

Rayon, Jean-Paul. "Eileen Gray: Un Manifeste, 1926–1929." *Architecture Mouvement Continuité* (Paris) no. 37 (November 1975): 49, 56.

Reif, Rita. "Two Who Made the Present." *The New York Times* May 13, 1975.

1976

Binchy, Maeve. "A Far from Demure Life." *Irish Times* (Dublin) February 16, 1976.

Brunhammer, Yvonne. *Cinquantenaire de l'Exposition de 1925.* Paris: Musée des Arts Décoratifs and Les Presses de la Connaissance, 1976.

"Design Review: Gray Table." *Architectural Review* (London) CLX (December 1976): 367.

Dumoulin, Marie-Claude. "Visite chez une Pionnière du Design." *Elle* (Paris) January 26, 1976: 63–65.

Grehan, Ida. "Pioneer from Enniscorthy." *Cara* (London) IX, no. 2 (April 1976): 11.

Irish Times (Dublin) November 4, 1976. Obituary.

Kay, J. H. "Who Is Eileen Gray, and Are You Sitting in One of Her Chairs?" *Ms* (New York) IV (April 1976): 80–83.

Lynch, Elisabeth. "Helen Gray, Her Life and Work." Thesis, Polytechnic of North London, 1976.

Marín de Terán, Luis. "La Visita de la Vieja Dama Eileen Gray." *Arquitecturas bis* (Barcelona) November 1976.

Murphy, Elisabeth. *Eileen Gray: A Monograph.* London: 1976.

Pusco, Renato de. *Le Corbusier Designer i Mobili del 1929.* Milan: 1976.

The Times (London) November 3, 1976: 19. Obituary.

1977

Baroni, Daniele. *I Mobili di Gerrit Rietveld.* Milan: 1977.

Connaissance des Arts (Paris) no. 299 (January 1977): 9. Obituary.

Gray, D. *Design* (London) no. 338 (February 1977): 57. Obituary.

1978

Carr, Richard. "Eileen Gray Lives." *Building Design* (London) June 30, 1978.

Gray, D. "Gray: The Production Man's Favourite 'Master.'" *Design* (London) no. 354 (June 1978): 28.

Jones, Peter Blundel. *Hans Scharoun: A Monograph.* London: 1978.

Miller, R. C. "Product Analysis: Eileen Gray's 1927 Table." *Interiors* (New York) CXXXVIII (October 1978): 104–5.

1979

Adam, Peter. "Eileen Gray." *Vogue* (Munich) August 1979: 236.

"Ahead of Her Time?" *Fulham Chronicle* (London) February 16, 1979.

Anderson, Susan Heller. "A Long Life of Versatile Activity." *The New York Times* March 29, 1979.

Baillie, Martin. "Eileen Gray's Flair and Courage." *Glasgow Herald* June 20, 1979.

Blume, Mary. "Designing Woman." *International Herald Tribune* (Paris) February 17–18, 1979.

Branzi, Andrea. "Cento Progetti da Ricordare." *Modo* (Milan) no. 25 (1979).

Darley, G. "Gray: Victoria and Albert Museum, London; Exhibit." *Connoisseur* (London) April 1979: 299.

"A Designer Far Too Little Known." *House and Garden* (London) February 1979.

"Eileen Gray." *Arts Review* (London) March 2, 1979.

"Eileen Gray." *Cosmopolitan* (London) February 1979.

Engel, A. "Gray: Victoria and Albert Museum, London; Exhibit." *Architectural Design* (London) XLIX, no. 5–6 (1979).

Feaver, William. "Apartheid for Fashionmongers." *Art News* (New York) LXXVIII (April 1979): 125. Review of Victoria and Albert Museum exhibition.

———. "The Lacquer Queen." *Observer* (London) February 4, 1979.

"Une Femme et le Design: Victoria and Albert Museum, Londres; Exposition." *Connaissance des Arts* (Paris) no. 325 (March 1979): 30.

"Gray at the V and A." *Design* (London) no. 364 (April 1979): 33.

"Gray Exhibit at MOMA, New York." *Industrial Design* (New York) XXVI (November 1979): 13.

"Gray: Victoria and Albert Museum London Exhibit." *Architects'*

Journal (London) CLXIX (January 31, 1979): 203–204, 207.

Hughes, Corin, "Shades of Gray." *Building Design* (London) February 9, 1979.

Israel, Laurent. "Les Pilotis." *Architecture Mouvement Continuité* (Paris) no. 49 (1979).

Johnson, J. Stewart. *Eileen Gray; Designer. 1879–1976.* London: Debrett's Peerage for Victoria and Albert Museum, 1979; New York: for The Museum of Modern Art, 1980. Exhibition catalogue.

Jones, R. W. "Design Liberated . . . Eileen Gray, 1879–1976: Victoria and Albert Museum, London; Exhibit." *Residential Interiors* (London) IV (March 1979): 84–85.

"Jugendstil—Art Deco." *Battenberg Antiquitäten* 1979.

Lucie-Smith, Edward. "Art Deco Saint: Eileen Gray: Victoria and Albert Museum, London Exhibit." *Art and Artists* (London) XIII (April 1979): 20–21.

———. [Review.] *Evening Standard* (London) February 1, 1979.

Mullaly, H. "Art and Design: Victoria and Albert Museum, London; Exhibit." *Apollo* (London) new series CIX (February 1979): 161–62.

Phillips, Barry. "Bold Miss Gray." *Observer* (London) February 4, 1979.

Rinn, Annette, and Paula Lakah. "Eileen Gray." Seminar paper, Technische Universität Munich, 1979.

Robertson, Bryan. "Eileen Gray." *Harpers and Queen* (London) March 1979.

Rutherford, J. "Victoria and Albert Museum, Londra: Mostra." *Casabella* (Milan) XLIII (April 1979): 3.

Shepherd, Michael. "Home Comforts." *Sunday Telegraph* (London) February 4, 1979.

Spurling, John. "In the Abstract." *New Statesman* (London) March 9, 1979.

Tentori, Francesco. *Vita e Opere di Le Corbusier.* Rome: Laterza, 1979.

"28/78 Architecture." *Domus* (Milan) March–May 1979.

"Two Extraordinary Women." *Interior Design* (London) February 1979: 19.

"Victoria and Albert Museum, London; Exhibition." *Burlington Magazine* (London) CXXI (March 1979): 189.

1980

Arwas, Victor. *Art Deco*. London: Academy; New York: Harry N. Abrams, 1980.

Barnes, H. "Architectural Digest Visits Graham Sutherland." *Architectural Digest* (Los Angeles) XXXVII (May 1980): 126–31.

Collection Eileen Gray. Monaco: Sotheby Parke Bernet, 1980. Auction sale.

Dona, C. "Il Razionalismo soft di una grande Progettista." *Modo* (Rome) no. 29 (1980).

"Eileen Gray." *International Design* (Geneva) March 1980.

K., B. "Eileen Gray." *Gazette de l'Hôtel Drouot* (Paris) October 1980.

"Eileen Gray: Surprise By Design: Museum of Modern Art, New York; Exhibit." *Art in America* (New York) LXVIII (September 1980): 88–93.

"Eileen Gray [Villa Tempe à Pailla]." *L'Architecture d'Aujourd'hui* (Paris) no. 210 (September 1980): 6–9.

Filler, Martin. "The Dark Lady of High Tech." *The New York Times Magazine* January 27, 1980.

Frampton, Kenneth. "Stellar Material." *Skyline* (Washington, D.C.) March 1980.

Gandee, C. K. "MOMA Shows the '20s Avant-Garde Work of Eileen Gray." *Architectural Record* (New York) CLXVII (March 1980): 37.

Garner, Philippe. "Möbel des 20. Jahrhunderts." *Keysersche Verlagsbuchhandlung* (Munich) 1980.

Goldberger, Paul. "Eileen Gray." *The New York Times* February 28, 1980.

"Gray—Designer: Museum of Modern Art, New York, Exhibition." *Progressive Architecture* (Stamford, Conn.) LXI (March 1980): 34.

"Gray Matter: Museum of Modern Art, New York, Exhibit." *Interiors* (New York) CXXXIX (February 1980): 11.

"Gray: Museum of Modern Art, New York, Exhibition." *Interior Design* (London) March 1980: 262–65.

Jackson, P. R. "Living." *House and Garden* (New York) March 1980: 18.

Loye, Brigitte. "Eileen Gray, un Autre Chemin pour la Modernité... Une Idée Chorégraphique." Diploma submission, Ecole Nationale Supérieure des Beaux-Arts, Paris, 1980.

Mobilier Moderniste Provenant du Palais du Maharaja d'Indore. Monaco: Sotheby Parke Bernet, 1980. Auction sale.

"Museum of Modern Art, New York; Ausstellung." *Du* (Zurich) V (1980): 90.

Nevins, Deborah F. "Maison en Bord de Mer: Eileen Gray's First Commission." *Residential Interiors* V (September–October 1980): 114–17.

Perren, Joe van der. *Architektuur en Meubels van Huib Hoste*. Ghent: Museum voor Sierkunst, 1980.

Pile, John. "Eileen Gray on Display: Museum of Modern Art, New York." *Industrial Design* (New York) XXVII (May/June 1980): 14.

Rickey, Carrie. "Shades of Gray." *The Village Voice* (New York) February 18, 1980.

Rubino, L. "Eileen Gray: una Designer Contro il 'Camping Style.'" In *Le Spose del Venti*. Verona: Bertami, 1980.

Slesin, Suzanne. "Eileen Gray: A Prophetic Designer." *The New York Times* January 24, 1980.

———. "Modernism in Milan." *International Herald Tribune* (Paris) September 27, 1980.

"Les Tapis Reviennent à la Mode." *La Maison de Marie-Claire* (Paris) April 1980.

Ten Twentieth Century Houses. London: Arts Council, 1980.

van Geest, Jan and Otakar Macel. *Stühle aus Stahl*. Cologne: 1980.

von Moos, Stanislaus. "Le Corbusier as Painter." *Oppositions* (Cambridge, Mass.) no. 19/20 (1980).

Wooster, Ann-Sargent. "Protagonisti Eileen Gray." *Casa Vogue* (Milan) no. 110 (1980).

1981

"Das Erbe der Eileen Gray." *Ambiente* (Offenburg) 1981: 163.

Kjellberg, Pierre. *Art Déco: Les Maîtres du Mobilier*. Paris: Editions de l'Amateur, 1981: 80–81.

Odoni, G. "Firmata Eileen Gray e Le Corbusier." *Casa Vogue* (Milan) no. 119 (1981).

Smithson, Alison, and Peter Smithson. *The Heroic Period of Modern Architecture*. New York: Rizzoli International, 1981.

1982

Anscombe, Isabelle. "Expatriates in Paris: Eileen Gray, Evelyn Wyld and Eyre de Lanux." *Apollo* (London) new series CXV (February 1982): 117–18.

Doelen, De. *Giuseppe Terragni 1904–1943*. Rotterdam: 1982.

Dumoulin, Marie-Claude. *Psycho-Deco, Aurore Clement*. Paris: 1982.

Exceptionnelle Vente: Art 1900–1925. Enghien: Gérard Champin and Francis Lombrail, 1982. Auction sale.

Nairn, J. "Classic Eileen Gray Furniture Designs Available for First Time in U.S." *Architectural Record* (New York) CLXX (February 1982): 128.

Putman, Andrée. Introduction to "Une Maison en Bord de Mer." *Cahier de l'Energumène* (Paris) Autumn/Winter 1982.

Rayon, Jean-Paul. "Eileen Gray, Architetto 1879–1976." *Casabella* (Milan) XLVI (May 1982): 38–45.

Rubino, L. "Eileen Gray (1879–1976), un Secolo di Totale Dedizione." In *Pierre Chareau & Bernard Bijvoet, Dalla Francia dell'Art Déco Verso un' Architettura Vera*, 148–61. Rome: 1982.

Sudjic, Deyan. "Shades of Gray." *World of Interiors* (London) June 1982.

1983

Loye, Brigitte. *Eileen Gray 1879–1976: Architecture Design*. Paris: Analeph/J. P. Viguier, 1983.

Vandenweghe, Jan. "Eileen Gray." Diss., St. Lukas Institute, Ghent, 1983.

1984

Anscombe, Isabelle. *A Woman's Touch*. London: 1984.

Chapon, François. *Mystère et Splendeurs de Jacques Doucet, 1853–1929*. Paris: J. C. Lattès, 1984.

Four Rooms. London: Arts Council, 1984. Catalogue of touring exhibition.

Reif, Rita. "Antiques View." *The New York Times* May 13, 1984.

1985

Rayon, Jean-Paul. "Eileen Gray, l'Etoile du Nord." In *De Stijl et l'Architecture en France*. Paris: Institute of French Architecture, 1985.

1986

Despont, Arlette Barré. *UAM*. Paris: Editions du Regard, 1986.

1987

Berman, Avis. "Eileen Gray: In the Vanguard of Twentieth-Century Design." *Architectural Digest* (Los Angeles) XLIV (May 1987): 62, 66, 70.

PHOTOGRAPH CREDITS